The Bahir

The Bahir

SAMUEL WEISER, INC.
York Beach, Maine

First published in 1979 by
Samuel Weiser, Inc.
Box 612
York Beach, Maine 03910

First paper edition, 1989

99 98 97 96 95 94 93
10 9 8 7 6 5 4 3

ISBN 0-87728-618-3
EB

Printed in the United States of America

The paper used in this publication meets the minimum requirements
of the American National Standard for Permanence of Paper for
Printed Library Materials Z39.48-1984.

CONTENTS

LIST OF FIGURES

LIST OF TABLES

The Bahir

Introduction

THE BAHIR is one of the oldest and most important of all classical Kabbalah texts. Until the publication of the Zohar, the Bahir was the most influential and widely quoted primary source of Kabbalistic teachings. It is quoted in virtually every major book on Kabbalah, the earliest being the Raavad's commentary on *Sefer Yetzirah*,[1] and it is cited numerous times by Rabbi Moshe ben Nachman (Ramban) in his commentary on the Torah.[2] It is also paraphrased and quoted many times in the Zohar.[3]

The name *Bahir* is derived from the first verse quoted in the text *(Job 37:21)*, "And now they do not see light, it is brilliant *(Bahir)* in the skies." It is also called the "Midrash of Rabbi Nehuniah ben HaKana," particularly by Ramban. The reason might be that Rabbi Nehuniah's name is at the very beginning of the book, but most Kabbalists actually attribute the Bahir to him and his school.[4] Some consider it the oldest Kabbalistic text ever written.[5]

Although the Bahir is a fairly small book, some 12,000 words in all, it was very highly esteemed among those who probed its mysteries. Rabbi Judah Chayit, a prominent fifteenth century Kabbalist writes, "Make this book a crown for your head." [6] Much of the text is very difficult to understand, and Rabbi Moshe Cordevero (1522–1570), head of the Safed school of Kabbalah, says, "The words of this text are bright *(Bahir)* and sparkling, but their brilliance can blind the eye." [7]

The Bahir was first published around 1176 by the Provence school of Kabbalists, and was circulated to a limited audience in manuscript form. The first printed edition appeared in Amsterdam (1651), and subsequent editions were printed in Berlin (1706), Koretz (1784), Shklav (1784) and Vilna (1883). The best edition is that recently edited by Rabbi Reuven Margolius, published in 1951 together with his commentary, *Or HaBahir* ("Light of the Bahir"). It is primarily from this edition that our translation was made.

EDITIONS OF THE BAHIR

1. Amsterdam, 1651 (together with *Mayin HaChakhmah),* 12 pp.
2. Berlin, 1706 (together with *Mayin HaChakhmah*), 4°, 13 pp.
3. Sklav, 1784, 12°, 25pp.
4. Koretz, 1784.
5. Lvov, 1800.
6. Lvov, 1830.
7. No place name, 1849 (as part of *Chamishah Chumshey Kabbalah*), 12°.
8. Lvov, 1865, 32 pp.
9. Vilna, 1883, 42 pp.
10. Vilna, 1913, 8°
11. Jerusalem, 1951 (Margolies Edition), 4°, 94 pp.

The earliest commentary on the Bahir was written in 1331 by Rabbi Meir ben Shalom Abi-Sahula, a disciple of Rabbi Shlomo ben Avraham Aderet (Rashba), and it was published anonymously under the title *Or HaGanuz* ("The Concealed Light"). Notes on the first part of the Bahir (up to **36**) were written by Rabbi Eliahu, the Gaon of Vilna (1720–1797), and these are also included in the Margolius edition. Other commentaries, existing only in manuscript, were written by Rabbis Eliahu ben Eliezer of Candia, David Chavillo, and Meir Poppers.

The Bahir was translated into Latin by Flavius Mitridates in the end of the fifteenth century, but this translation is wordy and virtually unreadable. A German translation was published in 1923 by Gerhard (Gershom) Scholem. This is the first English translation of the Bahir.

Authorship

Most Kabbalists ascribe the Bahir to Rabbi Nehuniah ben HaKana, a Talmudic sage of the first century, and the leading mystic of his generation. The reason seems to be that he is the sage who opens the text, as well as the fact that he was known to be the leader of a major mystical school that flourished in the Holy Land. Aside from this tradition, however, there would be little internal evidence in the text to support this attribution.

The attribution to Rabbi Nehuniah appears surprising for another reason; namely, because after the first paragraph, his name is never again mentioned in the text. An interesting possibility is that Rabbi Amorai, who plays an important role in the Bahir, is actually a pseudonym for Rabbi Nehuniah. Careful study indicates that this mysterious Rabbi Amorai, who is mentioned nine times in the text, is actually the source of the main teachings found in the Bahir.[8] A possible reason why this pseudonym is not used in the first paragraph is discussed in the last section of this introduction.

Rabbi Amorai is particularly intriguing, since his name is found nowhere else in classical Jewish literature. All attempts to identify him have been futile, and it is assumed by many that this is a fictitious name. More probable is the assumption that this was a pseudonym assumed by Rabbi Nehuniah. The word Amorai means "speakers," and would indicate that Rabbi Nehuniah was the primary spokesman for the group, the plural form being used as a sign of respect. The use of such a pseudonym would not be too surprising, since we find other examples of this in the Talmud. This hypothesis is also supported by the fact that the other sages of the Bahir speak of Rabbi Amorai with the greatest respect, and go to great length to explain his teachings.[9]

Although Rabbi Nehuniah be HaKana is mentioned only a few times in the Talmud, these citations leave no doubt as to the important position that he occupied. As a young man he studied in the school of Rabbi Yochanan ben Zakkai, even though he was already an ordained rabbi. In one instance, Rabbi Yochanan asked his disciples to interpret a Biblical verse, and when Rabbi Nehuniah replied, the former said that Rabbi Nehuniah's explanation was even better than his own.[10] Rabbi Nehuniah was a native of Ammaus,[11] and apparently was wealthy enough to have servants, who stood up to protect his honor on one occasion.[12] He lived to a very old age, and when asked the reason, replied that it was because he never gained from another's downfall, never took a grudge to bed, and always took a relaxed attitude with respect to money.[13]

Precise interpretation of the Torah was a prime quest of Rabbi Nehuniah, and it was he who taught Rabbi Ishmael (ben Elisha) how to properly interpret every word.[14] It was from this tradition that Rabbi Ishmael was later to expound his famed Thirteen Principles for interpreting the Torah.[15] Rabbi Nehuniah's opinion regarding Jewish Law is also cited a number of times in the Talmud,[16] and an early Midrash quotes him regarding the power of repentance.[17]

So careful was Rabbi Nehuniah in his teachings, that, as the Mishnah records, each day before he would begin his studies, he would pray that he not be in error.[18] His favorite saying was, "Whoever accepts the yoke of the Torah is relieved of the yokes of government and livelihood." [19]

Another picture of Rabbi Nehuniah, not found in the Talmud, is brought out in the *Hekhalot Rabatai,* written by his disciple, Rabbi Ishmael. This is the same Rabbi Ishmael who served as High Priest just before the destruction of the Temple, and one of his transcendental visions is described in the Talmud.[20] In the *Hekhalot,* Rabbi Ishmael describes how Rabbi Nehuniah taught him about the heavenly chambers and the names of the angels who guarded their gates.[21]

A clear picture emerges of Rabbi Nehuniah as a master of the mystical arts and teacher of his entire generation. In one place, the *Hekhalot* describes how he taught the correct method for projecting oneself into the supernal universes. Sitting before him as disciples were the luminaries of his time: Rabbi Shimon be Gamaliel, Eliezer the Great, Akiba, Yonatan ben Uziel, and many others.[22] When there was a decree to kill the sages, it was Rabbi Nehuniah who ascended to heaven to ascertain the reason.[23]

Besides the Bahir, also attributed to Rabbi Nehuniah is the prayer *Anna BaKoach.* The initial letters of the words in the prayer spell out the 42 letter Name of God, which is discussed at length in mystical literature.[24]

Sages of the Bahir

Although the Bahir had its origins in Rabbi Nehuniah's teachings, considerable portions are directly attributed to other sages. Rabbi Nehuniah taught the mysteries of Kabbalah to many sages of his generation, and it must be assumed that this school preserved his teachings after his death. It is to this school that we must attribute the main text of the Bahir.

A number of sages mentioned in the Bahir are also well known from the Talmud. As would be expected, they would be the ones who were engaged in the mystical arts, much of which they would have learned from Rabbi Nehuniah's teachings. Thus, Rabbi Akiba is quoted three times in the Bahir (**19, 32, 186**), and the Talmud states that he was the one sage who entered Paradise and emerged unharmed.[25]

Rabbi Eliezer the Great is also quoted (**104**), and he is also known for his mystical experiences.[26] His chief work, *Pirkey DeRabbi Eliezer* ("Chapters of Rabbi Eliezer"), also exhibits considerable influence from the Bahir. As we know from the *Hekhalot,* both of them learned the mystic arts from Rabbi Nehuniah.[27]

The most prominent sage of the Bahir, mentioned more often than any other, is Rabbi Rahumai, whose name appears thirteen times in the text. No mention of Rabbi Rahumai is found in the Talmud or Midrash, but in the Zohar we find that he knew Rabbi Pinchas ben Yair, father-in-law of the Zohar's author, Rabbi Shimon bar Yochai. It is told that he was with Rabbi Pinchas near the Kinneret on the day that Rabbi Shimon emerged from the cave where the Zohar was revealed to him.[28] It is also related that he spent a week in Ono, a suburb of Jerusalem, together with an otherwise unidentified Rabbi Kisma ben Geira.[29] From the Bahir itself there is evidence that it was Rabbi Rahumai who led the school after Rabbi Nehuniah's death.

Also prominent in the text is Rabbi Berachia, mentioned seven times in all. Also not mentioned in the Talmud, he is quoted in *Pirkey DeRabbi Eliezer* as well as in the Zoharic literature.[30] In the Bahir, it is he who defines a number of difficult terms from *Sefer Yetzirah* (**106**), and explains the meaning of the World to Come (**160**). From the context of one statement (**97**), it appears that he was a disciple of Rabbi Rahumai. This together was the fact that he is the second one mentioned in the Bahir, lend support to the theory that it was Rabbi Berachia who led the Kabbalistic school after Rabbi Rahumai. His prominent mention may also be due to the fact

that it was under his influence that the initial draft of the
Bahir was composed.

A certain Rabbi Yochanan is also prominent in the Bahir,
mentioned six times in all. Although not directly identifiable
with any Talmudic sage, this name is found a number of times
in *Pirkey DeRabbi Eliezer*.[31] One interesting possibility is that
he might be Rabbi Yochanan ben Dahabai, who is cited as a
disciple of Rabbi Nehuniah in the mystic arts.[32] That this
Rabbi Yochanan was a mystic is obvious, since in the Talmud
he relates four things taught to him by the angels.[33]

Another sage whom we can attempt to identify is Rabbi
Levitas ben Tavros.[34] He is of particular importance, since in
one place it appears that Rabbi Rahumai responds to his teachings (23). He might be identified with Rabbi Levitas of Javneh,
mentioned in the Mishnah and in *Pirkey DeRabbi Eliezer*.[35]
Assuming that he moved, he might also be identical with Rabbi
Levitas of Ono, mentioned in the Zohar.[36] The fact that he lived
in Ono is significant, since, as mentioned above, Rabbi
Rahumai is known to have visited there. This allows us to
hypothesize that Ono may have been a center of Kabbalistic
activity, and further research into this is indicated. There is
also a possibility that Rabbi Levitas originally lived in Em-
maus together with Rabbi Nehuniah.[37]

This mystical school was active during the entire Talmudic period, as evidenced from numerous accounts in the
literature. Among the last ones to openly make use of these
mystical arts were Rabba and Rav Zeira, who flourished in
Babylon in the fourth century. The Talmud reports how they
performed miraculous cures, and used the Kabbalah to create
living creatures.[38]

One of these accounts is related in the Bahir (196), and is
the second to last major theme in the text. Since Rabba and Rav
Zeira were leaders of this school, and since they are the most
recent sages mentioned in the Bahir, it can be assumed that it
was around their time that the final redaction of the text was
made. It is for this reason that there exists a tradition that the
Bahir was written by Amaraim, the later sages of the
Talmud.[39]

Publication

With the closing of the Talmudic period, the circle of Kabbalists diminished, and at times may have consisted of not more than a few dozen individuals. So closely knit was this group, that outsiders often did not even know of its existence. While it was important to maintain the tradition of the Kabbalah, it was equally important that it not fall into the wrong hands.

During some periods, leadership of this school was under the religious leaders of the generation, while at others, it may have included individuals whose names have been completely lost to history. It is known that such individuals as Natronai Gaon (794–861) and Hai Gaon (939–1038) had knowledge of these mysteries.[40] There is also evidence that Sherira Gaon (906–1006) had access to many of these teachings.[41] While these individuals were leaders of the Jewish community as a whole, they were also active in the circle of Kabbalah.

Central to much of this activity was the Bahir. Just how wide a circle had access to the text during this period is not known, but the number could not have been large. Manuscripts may have existed, but these remained in the hands of the group's leaders, with all others receiving the tradition orally. Members of the group were bound by an oath not to reveal its mysteries to outsiders, and the community at large was totally unaware of its existence.

For this reason, it is not surprising that such prominent scholars as Saadia Gaon (882–942) and Maimonides (1135–1204) never saw the Bahir, or that in his extensive commentary on *Sefer Yetzirah,* Rabbi Yehudah ben Barzillai of Barcelona (1035–1105) does not make any mention of it. The text was the private domain of a small secret society, and those outside the circle were not meant to even know that it existed.[42] Thus, in one of the earliest published Kabbalistic texts, Rabbi Avraham ben David (Raavad) states, "All these things and their mysteries were transmitted only from one mouth to the next." [43]

This is not surprising, since the mysteries of the Kabbalah were not meant to be transmitted to everybody. Much of this mystery is alluded to in the opening chapters of Ezekiel, and the Kabbalah in general is often called the "workings of the Chariot," a term also used in the Bahir.[44] As a matter of law, the sages state that these mysteries "cannot even be taught to a single individual, unless he is wise enough to understand with his own knowledge." [45] Even in such a case, the complete tradition was only given over to the head of the group, and then he would limit its instruction to those whom he saw fit. Only individuals possessing the highest qualities of scholarship and piety would be admitted to the circle of initiates.[46]

Another important relevant injunction was, "Things transmitted by mouth may not be written down." [47] As a result of this, even mundane teachings involving the Oral Law were not put into writing during the earliest Talmudic period. Although each master might keep personal notes, these were called "concealed documents," and were not even made available to his closest disciples.[48] If this was true of mundane matters, it was certainly true of the Kabbalah, which was considered to contain the "secrets of the Torah." If any texts existed, they were most carefully guarded.

Tradition has it that the Bahir was kept by a small school of Kabbalists in the Holy Land. During this period, parts of it were paraphrased in another Kabbalistic text known as *Raza Rabba* ("Great Mystery"), which as a whole has been lost, but is quoted by some eastern writers of the tenth century.[49] From there, the center of activity moved to Germany and Italy, bringing the Bahir with it.

By the year 1100 some of the Bahir's teachings were known to a small group in Spain, and its influence can be seen in the writings of Rabbi Avraham bar Chiyah, particularly in his *Megilat HaMegillah* ("Scroll of Scrolls"). Soon after this, the main Kabbalistic school moved to France, particularly to Provence. This city became an important center of Kabbalah, and it was here that the decision was made to publish the Bahir.[50]

The earliest known members of this school were Isaac Nazir and Yaakov Nazir of Lunel. The title "Nazir" indicated that they did not engage in any worldly activity, but were supported by the community so that they could devote their entire life to Torah and worship. It was in such a contemplative life that the teachings of Kabbalah could flourish.[51]

Also important in this group were Rabbi David ben Isaac, and Rabbi Avraham ben Isaac of Narbonne, author of the *Eshkol*. Son of the former and son-in-law of the latter was Rabbi Avraham ben David (Raavad) of Posqueres (1120–1198), author of a gloss on Maimonides' Code. A master of the mystic arts, he received the tradition from his father and father-in-law, and later became head of the school. In his legal commentaries, he writes that his school was subject to divine inspiration and the revelation of mysteries.[52]

It was Raavad's son, known as Isaac the Blind, who inherited the leadership of the Kabbalistic school and brought it to Provence.[53] Even though he was blind, he was reputed to be able to look into a person's soul and see his thoughts.[54] In his commentary on the Torah, Rabbi Bachya ben Asher (1276–1340) calls him the "father of Kabbalah."[55]

There was a tradition that revelation of a sort would return in 1216, and this was even known to Maimonides from his ancestors.[56] Like the entry into the Holy Land, this would require forty years of preparation, and part of this preparation was the dissemination of the Kabbalah. It was in this spirit that the Bahir was first published around 1176.

Since the Bahir was restricted to a small closed group for several hundred years, there has been considerable confusion among historians regarding its transmission and publication. Oral traditions and secret societies do not lend themselves to historical research, and jealously guarded manuscripts do not find their way into libraries. The only viable data regarding the Bahir comes from traditions preserved over the centuries, and, as many modern historians and anthropologists have discovered, these traditions are usually reliable and accurate.

The tradition was passed on from Isaac the Blind to his disciples Ezra and Azriel, and from them, to Rabbi Moshe ben Nachman (Nachmanides), known as the Ramban (1194–1270). Through his commentary on the Torah, where he frequently quotes the Bahir, he popularized many of its teachings to the Jewish world at large.

Until the Zohar was published around 1295, the Bahir remained the most important classical Kabbalah text. There are many places where the Zohar expands upon concepts found in the Bahir, and careful study reveals an important similarity of content in both works. This is not surprising, since the author of the Zohar, Rabbi Shimon bar Yochai, was doubtlessly familiar with Rabbi Nehuniah's teachings. Even before his special revelation in the cave, Rabbi Shimon must have been initiated into the mystical tradition, and a possible link may have been his father-in-law, Rabbi Pinchas ben Yair, whom, as

mentioned above, was close to Rabbi Rahumai. An interesting
point is the fact that the names of both the Bahir and the Zohar
have the connotation of light and brilliance.[57]

Structure

Although a cursory examination does not reveal any apparent
order in the Bahir, careful examination uncovers a definite
structure. The text can be roughly divided into five parts.

1. The first verses of creation (**1-16**).
2. The alphabet (**27-44**).
3. The Seven Voices and Sefirot (**45-123**).
4. The Ten Sefirot (**123-193**).
5. Mysteries of the soul (**194-200**).

The text begins with a statement by Rabbi Nehuniah. In
rapid order, Rabbis Berachia, Rahumai and Amorai enter the
discussion, explaining the concept of a "filling" *(Maley)*, which
is probably an allusion to *(Isaiah 6:3)*, "The whole earth is
filled *(Maley)* with His glory" (**2-7**). In particular, *Bet,* the
initial letter of the Torah, receives considerable attention.

The second part deals with the first eight letters of the
Hebrew Alphabet, from *Alef* to *Chet*. The fact that the discussion terminates before reaching the letter *Tet* may be ac-
counted for by a late statement that it does not pertain to the
Sefirot (**124**). Also discussed at the end of this section are a
number of vowel points and cancellations signs (**40-44**). The
concept of creation is also woven into this section, but it clearly
plays a secondary role.

The third section begins with a discussion of the seven
voices heard at Sinai, and asking the relation between the
seven voices and Ten Commandments, begins a discussion of
the Sefirot. The Sefirot are used to explain the anthropomorphisms appearing in the Bible (**82**), and this is expanded upon in
the next section.

Important subsections of this part include explanations of
the fifty-fifth chapter of Isaiah (**51-56**) and the third chapter of
Habakkuk (**68-81**). A number of concepts from the *Sefer Yetzirah* are introduced and explained (**63, 106**)[58] and this leads to
a discussion of the various mystical names of God (**106-112**).
Especially important is the number thirty-two, which corresponds to the paths of Wisdom, the numerical value of *Lev* or
heart (**63**), and the number of strings in the *Tzitzit* (**92**). It is in

relation to this number that all these concepts are introduced.

The fourth section contains the primary discussion of the Sefirot found in the Bahir. It is introduced with a discussion of the Priestly Blessing, where the ten fingers are said to allude to the Ten Sefirot, a concept also found in the *Sefer Yetzirah*. The word Sefirah is defined, being that which expresses *(Saper)* God's power and glory (**125**). The Sefirot are then listed and defined, one by one in order.

Within the context of the Sefirot, there are subsections on the Israelites' sojourn in Elim (**161-167**), and the commandment concerning the *Lulav* (**172-178**). The section concludes with a discussion of the relationship between the Sefirot and the spheres (**179ff**), with a brief introduction to reincarnation (**183**), also in relation to the Sefirot.

The fifth and final section deals with the soul, beginning with a discourse on reincarnation and its relationship to divine justice (**194**). The idea of the soul is also discussed in the context of creating life through the mystic arts, and this being the account of Rabba and Rav Zeira mentioned earlier (**196**). Finally, the concept of masculine and feminine souls is introduced, beginning with an analysis of Tamar (**197**), and concluding with an explanation of why Eve was the one who was tempted. The concludes the text.

Teachings

Although the Bahir is the primary text of Kabbalah, it does not use this term, prefering the Mishnaic term, *Maaseh Merkavah,* which literally means "Workings of the Chariot," in allusion to Ezekiel's vision. It states that delving into these mysteries is as acceptable as prayer (**68**), but warns that it is impossible to do so without falling into error (**150**).

The Talmud states that the Kabbalah should only be taught through hints and allusions, and this is the course followed by the author of the Bahir. One who merely reads it as a book will find that large portions make little if any sense. It is not a subject for casual perusing, but for serious and concentrated study, and it was accepted among Kabbalists that the major texts were written so that they could only be understood when analyzed as an integrated whole.[59] We are warned that one who reads the Kabbalah literally and shallowly is almost certain to misunderstand it.[60]

The proper way to study any Kabbalistic text is to take it

as a whole, using every part to explain every other one. The
student must find threads of ideas running through the text,
and follow them back and forth, until the full meaning is
ascertained. In a small text like the Bahir, this is relatively
straightforward, and our index should be helpful. In larger
texts such as the Zohar, this methodology assumes even greater importance, and without it, much of the writings of the Ari
will appear like little more than gibberish.

One of the most important concepts revealed in the Bahir
is that of the Ten Sefirot, and with the exception of three, their
names are also introduced. Careful analysis of these discussion
yields much of what will be found in later Kabbalistic works, as
well as their relation to anthropomorphisms and the reason for
commandments.

Particularly interesting is the order in which the Sefirot
are given. The last seven of these correspond to the seven days
of the week, and are derived from the verse *(1 Chronicles
29:11)*, "Yours O God are the Greatness, the Strength, the
Beauty, the Victory and the Splendor, All (Foundation) that is
in heaven and earth, Yours O God is the Kingdom." This is the
order followed by most Kabbalistic texts.

In the Bahir, however, the order of the last four is reversed.
The last four Sefirot are then Kingship (*Aravot,* 7), Foundation
(8), Victory (9), and Splendor (10). The reason given for this is
that Kingship must be in the middle of the seven, and since it
corresponds to the Sabbath, it is also fitting that it be the
seventh Sefirah (**153, 157**). Similarly, since Foundation corresponds to the sign of circumcision, it is fitting that it be
eighth, since circumcision is performed on the eighth day (**168**).

With the exception of Beauty, Splendor and Kingship, all
the Sefirot are given their standard names. Beauty is called the
Throne of Glory (**146**), while Kingship is called *Aravot* (**153**).
Splendor is simply called the second Victory (**170**). In a number
of places, Foundation is also called the Righteous One (**102,
180**), the Life of Worlds (**180ff**), and "All" (**22, 78**).

Another important concept that is revealed is that of reincarnation or *Gilgul*. It is interesting to note that this idea is
first introduced in the name of Rabbi Akiba (**121, 155**) This
concept is used to explain the problem of apparent injustice and
why even innocent children suffer and are born maimed. The
fact that Saadia Gaon rejects reincarnation is aimple proof that

he did not have access to the secret teachings of the Kabbalah.[61] This concept is further developed in the Zohar, and in even greater detail in the *Sefer Gilgulim* and other writings of the Ari's school.

Other subjects included in the Bahir include an interpretation of the letters of the Hebrew alphabet, fifteen of which are mentioned. Such commandments as *Tefillin, Tzitzit, Lulav* and *Etrog,* as well as "sending the mother bird" are discussed, usually in the context of the Sefirot or other previously introduced concepts. A number of ideas found in the *Sefer Yetzirah,* such as the Thirty-two Paths of Wisdom (**63**), the twelve diagonal boundaries (**95**), as well as the "Axis, Sphere and Heart" (**106**) are discussed. In general, numbers play a highly significant role in the Bahir.

Two unusual terms are found in the Bahir, both of which apparently refer to angels or angelic forces. One is *Tzurah,* which literally means "form" [62] while the other is *Komah,* which can be translated as "structure" (**8, 166**). In Kabbalistic literature, these are more familiar in their Aramaic form, the former being *Diukna,* and the latter, *Partzuf.* Other terms used for angels are Directors *(Manhigim)* and Functionaries *(Pekidim).*

Another important revelation is the various names of God, the most mystical being found in **112**. The Name containing twelve letters, mentioned in the Talmud,[63] is also discussed (**107, 111**). This is also true of the Name consisting of seventy-two combinations, which is also derived (**94, 107, 110**). This name is mentioned in early Talmudic sources,[64] and its derivation is discussed as early as 1100 by both Rashi (1040–1105) and the *Midrash Lekach Tov (Pesikta Zutrata).*[65]

Tzimtzum

One of the important concepts introduced in the Bahir is that of Tzimtzum, the self-constriction of God's Light. This involves one of the most important philosophical concepts of the Kabbalah, as well as one which has been a source of confusion to many scholars.

The clearest statement of the Tzimtzum can be found in the writings of Rabbi Isaac Luria (1534–1572), known as the Ari, who headed the Safed school of Kabbalah. As described in

Etz Chaim ("Tree of Life"), the process was as follows:[66]

> Before all things were created . . . the Supernal Light was simple, and it filled all existence. There was no empty space. . . .
>
> When His simple Will decided to create all universes . . . He constricted the Light to the sides . . . leaving a vacated space. . . . This space was perfectly round. . . .
>
> After this constriction took place . . . there was a place in which all things could be created. . . . He then drew a single straight thread from the Infinite Light . . . and brought it into that vacated space. . . . It was through that line that the Infinite Light was brought down below. . . .

In its literal sense, the concept of Tzimtzum is straightforward. God first "withdrew" His Light, forming a vacated space, in which all creation would take place. In order for His creative power to be in that space, He drew into it a "thread" of His Light. It was through this thread" that all creation took place.

Fig. 1. The Vacated Space resulting from the Tzimtzum, showing the thin Thread of Light reaching toward its center

Virtually all the later Kabbalists warn that the Tzimtzum is not to be taken literally, since it is impossible to apply any spatial concept to God. Rather, this is speaking in a conceptual sense, since if God filled every perfection, man would have no reason to exist. God therefore constricted His infinite perfection, allowing a "place" for man's free will and accomplishment.[67]

Another important point stressed by many Kabbalists is the fact that the Tzimtzum did not take place in God's essence, but in His Light. This Light was the first thing brought into being, representing God's power of creation, this itself having been brought into existence for the purpose of creating the universe.[68]

Many historians erroneously conclude that the Tzimtzum originated in the teachings of the Ari. Actually, however, it is a much older teaching, and a clear reference to it is found in the Zohar. Consider the following passage:[69]

> At the head of the King's authority
> He carved out of the supernal luminescence
> a Lamp of Darkness.
> And there emerged out of the Hidden of Hidden —
> the Mystery of the Infinite —
> an unformed line, imbedded in a ring . . .
> measured with a thread. . . .

According to most Kabbalists, this is a direct reference to the Tzimtzum.[70]

A close look at 25 in the Bahir will also reveal a clear allusion to the Tzimtzum. Rabbi Berachiah says that the Light was like a "beautiful object" for which the King had no place. It is explicitly stated that this light had existed earlier, but that there was no place in which to put it. Only after a "place" was provided could the light be revealed. The reference is clearly to the "thread" of Light mentioned in the *Etz Chaim,* which brought forth all creation. This is also the "unformed line embedded in a ring," mentioned in the Zohar.

The reason for the Tzimtzum stems from a basic paradox. God must be in the world, yet, if He does not restrict Himself from it, all creation would be overwhelmed by His Essence. Both the paradox and its resolution are clearly alluded to in the Bahir **54**.

There is, however, a more difficult paradox involved in the
Tzimtzum. Since God removed His Light from the vacated
space, it must be empty of His Essence. Still, God must also fill
this space, since "there is no place empty of Him." [71] This is a
most basic paradox, and it is closely related to the dichotomy of
God's imminence and transcendence.[72]

The main point brought out by this paradox is the fact that
this space is only "dark" and "vacated" with respect to us. The
"Lamp of Darkness" mentioned in the Zohar is "darkness" to
us, but with relation to God, it too is a "lamp." With respect to
God, it is actually light, since for Him it is as if the Tzimtzum
never took place.[73] The reason for the Tzimtzum was so that
creation could take place, and this is required for us, but not for
God. Close study indicates that this is is precisely the question
and answer found in the opening statement of the Bahir.

It is particularly interesting to note that it is precisely
with this apparent paradox that Rabbi Nehuniah opens the
Bahir. The main point of the theoretical Kabbalah is to resolve
the paradox of how an absolutely transcendental God can interact with His creation.[74] The structure of the Sefirot and
similar concepts are what form the bridge between God and the
universe. Lest it be thought that this implies any change in
God Himself, Rabbi Nehuniah clearly states that the darkness
of the vacated space is actually light with respect to God. The
creation of the vacated space, as well as all worlds, spiritual
and physical, that exist in it, did not in any way change or
diminish God's Light.

Such an introduction is reminiscent of a similar warning
found at the beginning of the *Idra Rabba,* one of the most
mysterious portions of the Zohar, and one containing much
anthropomorphic symbolism. At the very beginning of this
section, Rabbi Shimon quotes the verse *(Deuteronomy 26:15),*
"Cursed is the man who makes any image . . . and puts it in a
hidden place." [75] In the context in which it is used here, the
"hidden place" refers to the highest supernal universes. Even
though anthropomorphisms may be used in describing the
Sefirot and other Kabbalistic concepts, they are in no way
meant to be taken literally.

Rabbi Nehuniah is giving a very similar warning at the beginning of the Bahir. Do not think that the Sefirot are lights coming to fill any darkness with respect to God, since for Him all is Light. In order to avoid error, Rabbi Nehuniah's name appears here without disguise — this principle is so important that it must be backed by the full prestige of the master himself.

The Bahir

1. Rabbi Nehuniah ben HaKana said:

One verse *(Job 37:21)* states, "And now they do not see light, it is brilliant *(Bahir)* in the skies . . . [round about God in terrible majesty]."

Another verse, however, *(Psalm 18:12)*, states, "He made darkness His hiding place." It is also written *(Psalm 97:2)*, "Cloud and gloom surround Him." This is an apparent contradiction.

A third verse comes and reconciles the two. It is written *(Psalm 139:12)*, "Even darkness is not dark to You. Night shines like day — light and darkness are the same."

2. Rabbi Berachiah said:

It is written *(Genesis 1:2)*, "The earth was Chaos *(Tohu)* and Desolation *(Bohu)*.

What is the meaning of the word "was" in this verse? This indicates that the Chaos existed previously [and already *was*].

What is Chaos *(Tohu)*? Something that confounds *(Taha)* people.

What is Desolation *(Bohu)*? It is something that has substance. This is the reason that it is called *Bohu*, that is, *Bo Hu* — "it is in it."

3. Why does the Torah begin with the letter *Bet?* In order that it begin with a blessing *(Berachah)*.

How do we know that the Torah is called a blessing?

Because it is written *(Deuteronomy 33:23)*, "The filling is God's blessing possessing the Sea and the South."

The Sea is nothing other than the Torah, as it is written *(Job 11:9)*, "It is wider than the sea."

What is the meaning of the verse, "The filling is God's blessing?" This means that wherever we find the letter *Bet* it indicates a blessing.[1]

It is thus written *(Genesis 1:1)*, "In the beginning *(BeReshit)* [God created the heaven and the earth." *BeReshit* is *Bet Reshit.*]

The word "beginning" *(Reshit)* is nothing other than Wisdom. It is thus written *(Psalm 111:10)*, "The beginning is wisdom, the fear of God."

Wisdom is a blessing. It is thus written, "And God blessed Solomon." [2] It is furthermore written *(I Kings 5:26)*, "And God gave Wisdom to Solomon."

This resembles a king who marries his daughter to his son. He gives her to him at the wedding and says to him, "Do with her as you desire."

4. How do we know that the word *Berachah* [usually translated as blessing] comes from the word *Baruch* [meaning blessed]? Perhaps it comes from the word *Berech* [meaning knee].

It is written *(Isaiah 44:23)*, "For to Me shall every knee bend." [*Berachah* can therefore mean] the Place to which every knee bends.

What example does this resemble? People want to see the king, but do not know where to find his house *(Bayit)*. First they ask "Where is the king's house?" Only then can they ask, "Where is the king?"

It is thus written, "For to Me shall every knee bend" — even the highest — "every tongue shall swear."

5. Rabbi Rahumai sat and expounded:

What is the meaning of the verse *(Deuteronomy 33:23)*, "The filling is God's blessing, possessing the Sea and the South"?

This means that wherever we find the letter *Bet* it is blessed.

This is the Filling referred to in the verse, "The filling is God's blessing." ·

From there it nourishes those who need it. It was from this Filling that God sought advice.

What example does this resemble? A king wanted to build his palace among great cliffs. He mined into the bedrock and uncovered a great spring of living water. The king then said, "Since I have flowing water, I will plant a garden. Then I will delight in it, and so will all the world."

It is therefore written *(Proverbs 8:30)*, "I was with Him as a craftsman, I was His delight for a day, a day, frolicking before him at every time."

The Torah is saying, "For two thousand years I was in the bosom of the Blessed Holy One as His delight."

The verse therefore says, "a day, a day." Each day of the Blessed Holy One is a thousand years, as it is written *(Psalm 90:4)*, "A thousand years in Your eyes is as but yesterday when it is passed."

From then on, it is at times, as the verse states, "[frolicking before Him] at every time."

The rest is for the world. It is thus written *(Isaiah 48:9)*, "I will [breathe out] My praise through My nose for you."

What is the meaning of "My praise"? As it is written *(Psalm 145:2)*, "A *praise* of David, I will raise You high [my God, O King, and I will bless Your name for the world and forever]."

Why is this a praise? Because I will "raise You high."

And what is this elevation? Because "I will bless Your name for the world and forever."

6. What is a blessing?

It can be explained with an example. A king planted trees in his garden. It may rain and water them, and the ground may be wet and provide them with moisture, but still, he must water them from the spring.

It is thus written *(Psalm 111:10)*, "The beginning is Wisdom, the fear of God, good intelligence to all who do them [His praise endures forever]."

You may think that it lacks something. It is therefore written, "His *praise* endures forever."

7. Rabbi Amorai sat and expounded:

What is the meaning of the verse *(Deuteronomy 33:23)*,

"The filling is God's blessing, possessing the Sea and the South?"

Moses was saying, "If you follow my decrees, you will inherit both this world and the next."

The World to Come is likened to the sea, as it is written *(Job 11:9)*, "It is wider than the sea."

The present world is referred to as the South. It is thus written *(Joshua 15:19)*, [Give me a blessing] for you have set me in the land of the south, [therefore give me springs of water]." The Targum translates this, "behold the earth is the south."

8. Why did God add the letter *Heh* to Abraham's name, rather than any other letter? [3]

This was so that all parts of man's body should be worthy of life in the World to Come, which is likened to the sea.

To the extent that we can express it, the Structure was completed in Abraham. [Regarding this Structure] it is written *(Genesis 9:6)*, "For in the form of God, He made the man."

The numerical value of Abraham is 248, the number of parts in man's body.

9. What is the meaning of *(Deuteronomy 33:23)*, "[The filling is God's blessing, the Sea and the South] he shall inherit it *(YiRaShaH)*?" It would have been sufficient if the verse said, "inherit *(RaSh)* [the Sea and the South]."

But this comes to teach us that God must also be included. The word *YiRaShaH* thus contains the letters *RaSh YH* [meaning, "inherit God].

What does this resemble? A king had two treasuries, and he hid one away. After many days he said to his son, "Take what is in these two treasuries." The son replied, "Perhaps you are not giving me all that you have hidden away." The king said, "Take everything."

It is thus written, "the Sea and the South, he shall inherit it." Inherit God *(YH RaSh)* — everything will be given to you if you only keep My ways.

10. Rabbi Bun said:

What is the meaning of the verse *(Proverbs 8:23)*, "I was set up from eternity *(Me-Olam)*, from a head, before the earth?"

What is the meaning of "from eternity *(Me-Olam)?*" This means that it must be concealed *(He-elam)* from the world.

It is thus written *(Ecclesiastes 3:11)*, "He has also placed the world *(Ha-Olam)* in their hearts [that they should not find out the work that God has done from the beginning to the end]." Do not read *Ha-Olam* (the world), but *He-elam* (concealment).

The Torah said, "I was first, so that I might be the head of the world." It is thus written, "I was set up from eternity, from a head."

You may think that the earth was before it. It is therefore written, "before the earth."

It is thus written *(Genesis 1:1)*, "In the beginning created God the heaven and the earth."

What is the meaning of "created"? He created everything that was needed for all things. And then God. Only after that is it written "the heaven and the earth."

11. What is the meaning of the verse *(Ecclesiastes 7:14)*, "Also one opposite the other was made by God."

He created Desolation *(Bohu)* and placed it in Peace, and He created Chaos *(Tohu)* and placed it in Evil.

Desolation is in Peace, as it is written *(Job 25:2)*, "He makes peace in His high places."

This teaches us that Michael, the prince to God's right, is water and hail, while Gabriel, the prince to God's left, is fire. The two are reconciled by the Prince of Peace. This is the meaning of the verse, "He makes peace in His high places."

12. How do we know that Chaos is in Evil? It is written *(Isaiah 45:7)*, "He makes peace and creates evil."

How does this come out? Evil is from Chaos, while Peace is from Desolation.

He thus created Chaos and placed it in Evil, [as it is written "He makes peace and creates evil." He created Desolation and placed it in Peace, as it is written, "He makes peace in His high places."]

13. Rabbi Bun also sat and expounded:

What is the meaning of the verse *(Isaiah 45:7)*, "He forms light and creates darkness?"

Light has substance. Therefore, the term "formation" is used with regard to it. Darkness has no substance, and therefore, with regard to it, the term "creation" is used. It is similarly written *(Amos 4:12)*, He forms mountains and creates the wind."

Another explanation is this:

Light was actually brought into existence, as it is written *(Genesis 1:3)*, "And God said, let there be light." Something cannot be brought into existence unless it is made. The term "formation" is therefore used.

In the case of darkness, however, there was no making, only separation and setting aside. It is for this reason that the term "created" *(Bara)* is used. It has the same sense as in the expression, "That person became well *(hi-Bria)*."

14. Why is the letter *Bet* closed on all sides and open in the front? This teaches us that it is the House *(Bayit)* of the world. God is the place of the world, and the world is not His place.

Do not read *Bet,* but *Bayit* (house).

It is thus written *(Proverbs 24:3)*, "With wisdom the *house* is built, with understanding it is established, [and with knowledge are its chambers filled]."

Fig. 2. The letter *Bet,* showing how it has a tail in back (right) and is open to the front. (#14, 15)

15. What does the *Bet* resemble? It is like a man, formed by God with wisdom. He is closed on all sides, but open in front.

The *Alef*, however, is open from behind.

This teaches us that the tail of the *Bet* is open from behind. If not for this, man could not exist.

Likewise, if not for the *Bet* on the tail of the *Alef*, the world could not exist.

Fig. 3. The *Alef*, showing the *Bet* on its tail. (#15)

16. Rabbi Rahumai said:

Illumination preceded the world, since it is written *(Psalm 97:2)*, "Cloud and gloom surround Him." It is thus written *(Genesis 1:3)*, "And God said, 'let there be light,' and there was light."

They said to Him, "Before the creation of Israel your son, will you then make him a crown?" He replied yes.

What does this resemble? A king yearned for a son. One day he found a beautiful, precious crown, and he said, "This is fitting for my son's head."

They said to him, "Are you then certain that your son will be worthy of this crown?"

He replied, "Be still. This is what arises in thought."

It is thus written *(2 Samuel 14:14)*, He thinks thoughts [that none should be cast away]."

17. Rabbi Amorai sat and expounded:

Why is the letter *Alef* at the beginning? Because it was before everything, even the Torah.

18. Why does *Bet* follow it? Because it was first.

Why does it have a tail? To point to the place from which it came.

Some say, from there the world is sustained.

19. Why is *Gimel* third?

It has three parts, teaching us that it bestows *(gomel)* kindness.

But did Rabbi Akiba not say that *Gimel* has three parts because it bestows, grows, and sustains. It is thus written *(Genesis 21:8)*, "The lad grew and was bestowed."

He said: He says the same as I do. He grew and bestowed kindness to his neighbors and to those entrusted to him.

20. And why is there a tail at the bottom of the *Gimel*?

He said: The *Gimel* has a head on top, and is like a pipe. Just like a pipe, the *Gimel* draws from above through its head, and disperses through its tail. This is the *Gimel*.

21. Rabbi Yochanan said:

The angels were created on the second day. It is therefore written *(Psalm 104:3)*, "He rafters His upper chambers with water [He makes the clouds His chariot, He walks on the wings of the wind]." It is then written *(Psalm 104:4)*, "He makes the winds His angels, His ministers from flaming fire." [4]

[Rabbi Haninah said: The angels were created on the fifth day, as it is written *(Genesis 1:20)*, "And flying things shall fly upon the firmament of heaven." Regarding the angels it is written *(Isaiah 6:2)*, "With two wings did they *fly*."]

Rabbi Levatas ben Tavrus said: All agree, even Rabbi Yochanan, that the water already existed [on the first day]. But it was on the second day that "He raftered His upper chambers with water." [At that time He also created] the one who "makes the clouds his chariot," and the one who "walks on the wings of the wind." But His messengers were not created until the fifth day.

22. All agree that none were created on the first day. It should therefore not be said that Michael drew out the heaven at the south, and Gabriel drew it out at the north, while God arranged things in the middle.

It is thus written *(Isaiah 44:24),* "I am God, I make all, I stretch out the heavens alone, the earth is spread out before Me." [Even though we read the verse "from Me" *(May-iti),* it can also be read] *Mi iti* — "Who was with Me?"

I am the One who planted this tree in order that all the world should delight in it. And in it, I spread All.[5]

I called it All because all depend on it, all emanate from it, and all need it. To it they look, for it they wait, and from it, souls fly in joy.

Alone was I when I made it. Let no angel rise above it and say, "I was before you."

I was also alone when I spread out My earth, in which I planted and rooted this tree. I made them rejoice together, and I rejoiced in them.

"Who was with Me?" To whom have I revealed this mystery?

23. Rabbi Rahumai said: From your words we could conclude that the needs of this world were created before the heavens.

He answered yes.

What does this resemble? A king wanted to plant a tree in his garden. He searched the entire garden to find a spring flowing with water that would nourish the tree, but could not find any. He then said, "I will dig for water, and will bring forth a spring to nourish the tree." He dug and opened a well, flowing with living water. He then planted the tree, and it stood, giving forth fruit. It was successfully rooted, since it was always watered from the well.

24. Rabbi Yanai said: The earth was created first, as it is written *(Genesis 2:4),* "[On the day that God made] earth and heaven."

They said to him: Is it not written *(Genesis 1:1),* "[In the beginning God created] the heaven and the earth"?

He replied: What is this like? A king bought a beautiful object, but since it was not complete, he did not give it a name. He said, "I will complete it, I will prepare its pedestal and attachment, and then I will give it a name."

It is thus written *(Psalm 102:26)*, "From eternity You founded the earth" — and then, "the heavens are the work of Your hands." [6]

It is furthermore written *(Psalm 104:2)*, "He covered Himself with light like a garment, He spread out the heaven like a curtain, He rafters His upper chambers with water." It is then written *(Psalm 104:4)*, "He makes the winds His angels, His ministers of flaming fire." Finally, it is written *(Psalm 104:5)*, "He founded the earth on its pedestals, that it not be removed for the world and forever."

When He made its pedestal, He strengthened it. It is therefore written, "that it not be moved."

What is its name? [7] "And Forever" *(VoEd)* is its name. And [the name of] its pedestal is "World" *(Olam)*. It is therefore written, "for the World And Forever."

25. Rabbi Berachiah said:

What is the meaning of the verse *(Genesis 1:3)*, And God said, 'Let there be light,' and there was light"? Why does the verse not say, "And it was so"? [8]

What is this like? A king had a beautiful object. He put it away until he had a place for it, and then he put it there.

It is therefore written, "Let there be light, and there was light." This indicates that it already existed.

26. Rabbi Amorai said: What is the meaning of the verse *(Exodus 15:3)*, "God is a man *(Ish)* of war"?

Mar Rahumai said to him: Great master, do not ask about something that is so simple. Listen to me and I will advise you.

He said to him: What is this like? A king had a number of beautiful dwellings, and he gave each one a name. One was better than the other. He said, "I will give my son this dwelling whose name is *Alef*. This one whose name is *Yud* is also good, as is this one whose name is *Shin*." [9] What did he do then? He gathered all three together, and out of them he made a single name and a single house.

He said: How long will you continue to conceal your meaning?

The other replied: My son, *Alef* is the head. *Yud* is second to it. *Shin* includes all the world.

Why does *Shin* include all the world? Because with it one writes an answer *(T'shuvah)*.

27. The students asked him: What is the letter *Dalet*?

He replied: What is this like? Ten kings were in a certain place. All of them were wealthy, but one was not quite as wealthy as the others. Even though he is still very wealthy, he is poor *(Dal)* in relation to the others.

28. They said to him: What is the letter *Heh*?

He grew angry and said: Did I not teach you not to ask about a later thing and then about an earlier thing?

They said: But *Heh* comes after [*Dalet*].

He replied: The order should be *Gimel Heh*. Why is it *Gimel Dalet*? Because it must be *Dalet Heh*.

And why is the order *Gimel Dalet*?

He said to them: *Gimel* is in the place of *Dalet*, on its head it is in the place of *Heh*. *Dalet* with its tail is in place of the *Heh*.[10]

Fig. 4. How the *Gimel* transforms into a *Dalet*, and then into a *Heh*. (#28)

29. What is the letter *Vav*?

He said: There is an upper *Heh* and a lower *Heh*.[11]

30. They said to him: But what is *Vav*?

He said: The world was sealed with six directions.[12]
They said: Is not *Vav* a single letter?
He replied: It is written *(Psalm 104:2)*, "He wraps Himself in light as a garment, [he spreads out the heavens like a curtain]."

31. Rabbi Amorai asked: Where is the Garden of Eden?
He replied: It is on earth.

32. Rabbi Ishmael expounded to Rabbi Akiba:
What is the meaning of the verse *(Genesis 1:1)*, "[In the beginning God created] *(et)* the heaven and *(et)* the earth"? [Why is the word *et* added in both places?]
If the word *et* (an untranslated preposition that connects a transitive verb to its predicate noun) were absent, we would think that "heaven" and "earth" were gods. [For we could have read the verse, "In the beginning, God, the heaven and the earth created . . ." taking all three nouns as subjects of the sentence.]
He replied: By the Divine Service! You may have reached out for the true meaning, but you have not sorted out, and therefore you speak in this manner. But [in the case of "heaven"] the word *et* comes to include the sun, moon, stars and constellations, while [in the case of "earth"] it comes to add trees, plants, and the Garden of Eden.[13]

33. They said to him: It is written *(Lamentations 2:1)*, "He threw the beauty of Israel from heaven to the earth." From here we see that it fell.[14]
He replied: If you have read, you did not review, and if you reviewed, you did not go over it a third time. What does this resemble? A king had a beautiful crown on his head and a beautiful cloak on his shoulders. When he heard evil tidings, he cast the crown from his head and the cloak from his shoulders.

34. They asked him: Why is the letter *Chet* open? And why is its vowel point a small *Patach*? [15]
He said: Because all directions *(Ruach-ot)* are closed, except for the North, which is opened for good and for evil.[16]
They said: How can you say that it is for good? Is it not written *(Ezekiel 1:4)*, "And behold, a stormy wind coming from the north, a great cloud and burning fire." Fire is nothing other

than fierce anger, as it is written *(Leviticus 10:2),* "And fire went out from before God, and it consumed them and killed them."

He said: There is no difficulty. One case is speaking of when Israel does the will of God, while the other is speaking of when they do not do His will. When Israel does not do His will, then the fire comes close [to destroy and punish]. But when they do God's will, then the Attribute of Mercy encompasses and surrounds it, as it is written *(Micah 7:18),* "He lifts up sin and passes over rebellion."

35. What is this like? A king wanted to punish and whip his slaves. One of his governors stood up and asked the reason for this punishment. When the king described the offense, the governor said, "Your slaves never did such a thing. I will be their bondsman until you investigate it more thoroughly." In the meantime, the king's anger was calmed.

36. His students asked: Why is the letter *Dalet* thick on the side? [17]

He replied: Because of the *Segol* which is in the small *Patach*. [18]

It is thus written *(Psalm 24:7),* "The openings *(pitchey)* of the World." There He placed a *Patach* above and a *Segol* below. It is for this reason that it is thick.

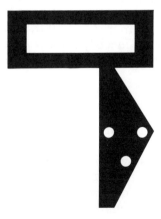

Fig. 5. The *Dalet* with a *Patach* on top, and three dots representing the *Segol* on the side. (#36)

37. What is the *Patach*? It is an opening *(Petach)*.

What is meant by an opening? This is the direction of north, which is open to all the world. It is the gate from which good and evil emerge.

And what is good?

He mocked them and said: Did I not tell you that it is a small *Patach* (opening)?

They said: We have forgotten, teach us again.

He reviewed it and said: What is this like? A king had a throne. Sometimes he carried it on his arm, and sometimes on his head.[19]

They asked why, and he replied: Because it is beautiful and it is a pity to sit on it.

They asked: Where did he place it on his head?

He replied: In the open *Mem*.[20] It is thus written *(Psalm 85:12)*, "Truth sprouts up from the earth, and righteousness looks down from heaven."

38. Rabbi Amorai sat and expounded:

What is the meaning of the verse *(Psalm 87:2)*, "God loves the gates of Zion more than all the dwellings of Jacob."

"The gates of Zion" are the "openings of the World." [21]

A gate is nothing other than an opening. We thus say, "Open for us the gates of mercy." [22]

God said: I love the "gates of Zion" when they are open. Why? Because they are on the side of evil. But when Israel does good before God and are worthy that good be opened for them, then God loves them — "more than all the dwellings of Jacob."

["The dwellings of Jacob"] are all peace, as it is written *(Genesis 25:27)*, "Jacob was a simple man, dwelling in tents."

39. This is like two men, one who is inclined to do evil and does good, and the other who is inclined to do good and does evil.

Who is more praiseworthy? The one who is inclined to do evil and does good, for he may do good again.

It is therefore written *(Psalm 87:2)*, "God loves the gates of Zion more than all the dwellings of Jacob." These [dwellings] are all peace, as it is written *(Genesis 25:27)*, "Jacob was a simple man, dwelling in tents."

40. His students asked: What is *Cholem*? [23]

He replied: It is the soul — and its name is *Cholem*.[24]

If you listen to it, your body will be vigorous *(Chalam)* in the Ultimate Future. But if you rebel against it, there will be sickness *(Choleh)* on your head, and diseases *(Cholim)* on its head.

41. They also said: Every dream *(Chalom)* is in the *Cholem*.

Every white precious stone is in the *Cholem*. It is thus written [with regard to the High Priest's breastplate] *(Exodus 28:19)*, "[And in the third row ...] a white stone *(aChLaMah)*." [25]

42. He said to them: Come and hear the fine points regarding the vowel points found in the Torah of Moses.

He sat and expounded: *Chirek* hates evildoers and punishes them. Its side includes jealousy, hatred and competition.

It is thus written *(Psalm 37:12)*, "He gnashes *(Chorek)* his teeth at them." Do not read *chorek* (gnashes), but *rochek (repels)*.

Repel *(rachek)* these traits from yourself, and repel yourself from evil. Good will then certainly attach itself to you.

43. *Chirek*. Do not read *ChiRiK* but *KeRaCh* (Ice). Whatever the Chirek touches becomes ice. It is thus written *(Exodus 34:7)*,"and cleanses."

44. What is the indication that *Chirek* has the connotation of burning? [26]

This is because it is fire that burns all fire. It is thus written *(1 Kings 18:38)*, "And God's fire fell, and it consumed the burnt offering, the wood, the stones, the dust, and evaporated the water that was in the trench."

45. He said:

What is the meaning of the verse *(Exodus 20:15)*, "And all the people saw the voices."

These are the voices regarding which King David spoke.

It is thus written *(Psalm 29:3)*, "The voice of God is upon the waters, the God of glory thunders." [This is the first voice.]

[The second voice is] *(Psalm 29:4)*, "The voice of God comes in strength." Regarding this it is written *(Isaiah 10:13)*, "By the *strength* of my hand have I done it." It is likewise written *(Isaiah 48:13)*, "Also *My hand* has founded the earth."

[The third voice is] *(Psalm 29:4)*, "The voice of God is with majesty." It is also written *(Psalm 111:3)*, "Splendor and majesty are His works, His righteousness stands forever."

[The fourth voice is] *(Psalm 29:5)*, "God's voice breaks the cedars." This is the bow that breaks the cypress and cedar trees.

[The fifth voice is] *(Psalm 29:7)*, "God's voice draws out flames of fire." This is what makes peace between water and fire. It draws out the power of the fire and prevents it from evaporating the water. It also prevents [the water] from extinguishing it.

[The sixth voice is] *(Psalm 29:8)*, "God's voice shakes the desert." It is thus written *(Psalm 18:51)*, "He does kindness to his Messiah, to David and his descendents until eternity" — more than [when Israel was] in the desert.

[The seventh voice is] *(Psalm 29:9)*, "God's voice makes hinds to calf, strips the forests bare, and in His Temple, all say Glory." It is thus written *(Song of Songs 2:7)*, "I bind you with an oath, O daughters of Jerusalem, with the hosts, or with the *hinds* of the field."

This teaches us that the Torah was given with seven voices. In each of them the Master of the universe revealed Himself to them, and they saw Him. It is thus written, "And all the people saw the voices."

46. One verse states *(2 Samuel 22:10)*, "He bent the heavens and came down, with gloom under His feet." Another verse says *(Exodus 19:20)*, "And God came down on Mount Sinai, to the top of the mountain."

Still another verse, however, *(Exodus 20:22)* states, "From heaven I spoke to you."

How is this reconciled? His "great fire" was on earth, and this was one voice. The other voices were in heaven.

It is thus written *(Deuteronomy 4:36)*, "From the heavens He let you hear His voice, that He might instruct you. And on the earth He showed you His great fire, and His words you heard from the fire."

Which [fire] was that? It was the "great [fire" that was on the earth.]

From where did the speech emanate? From this fire, as it is written, "and His words you heard from the fire."

47. What is the meaning of the verse *(Deuteronomy 4:12)*, "You saw no form, only a voice"?

This was explained when Moses said to Israel *(Deuteronomy 4:15)*, "You did not see an entire image." You saw an image, but not an "entire image."

What is this like? A king stands before his servants wrapped in a white robe.[27] Even though he is far away, they can still hear his voice. This is true even though they cannot see his throat when he speaks. In a similar manner, they saw an image, but not an "entire image."

It is therefore written, "You saw no form, only a voice." It is also written *(Deuteronomy 4:12)*, "A voice of words you heard."

48. One verse *(Exodus 20:15)*, states, "and all the people saw the voices." Another verse, however, *(Deuteronomy 4:12)*, states, "The voice of words you heard." How can [the two be reconciled]?

At first they saw the voices. What did they see? The seven voices mentioned by David. But in the end they heard the word that emanated from them all.

But we have learned that there were ten.[28]

Our sages taught that they were all said with a single word.[29]

But we have said that there were seven.

There were seven voices. Regarding three of them it is written *(Deuteronomy 4:12)*, "The voice of words you heard, but you saw no form, only a voice." This teaches us that they were all said with a single word.

This is so that Israel should not make a mistake and say, "Others helped him. It might have been one of the angels. But His voice alone could not be so powerful." It was for this reason that he came back and included them [in a single word].

49. Another explanation:

It was so that the world should not say that since there were ten sayings for ten kings, it might be that He could not speak for them all through one. He therefore said *(Exodus 20:2)*, "I am [the Lord your God]," which included all ten.

What are the ten kings? They are the seven voices and three sayings *(Amarim)*.

What are the sayings? [They are the ones alluded to in the verse] *(Deuteronomy 26:18)*, "God has said for you today."

What are the three? [Two are mentioned in the verse] *(Proverbs 4:7)*, "The beginning is Wisdom: Acquire Wisdom, with all your acquisition, acquire Understanding."

It is thus written *(Job 32:8)*, "The soul of Shadai gives them Understanding." The soul of Shadai is what gives them Understanding.

What is the third one?

As the old man said to the child, "What is hidden from you, do not seek, and what is concealed from you, do not probe. Where you have authority, seek to understand, but you have nothing to do with mysteries." [30]

50. We have learned *(Proverbs 25:2)*, "The glory of God is to hide a word."

What is "a word"? That of which it is written *(Psalm 119:160)*, "The Beginning of Your word is truth."

[It is also written] *(Proverbs 25:2)*, "The glory of kings is to probe a word."

What is this "word"? That of which it is writen *(Proverbs 25:11)*, "A word spoken in its proper place *(Aphen-av)*," Do not read "its proper place" *(Aphen-av)*, but "its wheel" *(Ophen'av)*. [31]

51. The students asked Rabbe Berachia, "Let us discuss these words with you," but he would not give them permission. Once, however, he did give them permission, but he did so to test them, to see if they would now pay good attention.

One day he tested them and said, "Let me hear your wisdom."

They began and said:

"In the beginning" is one.

[Two is] *(Isaiah 57:16)*, "The spirit that enwraps itself is from Me, and I have made souls."

[Three is] *(Psalm 65:10)*, "The divisions of God are filled with water."

What are these "divisions?" You taught us, our master, that God took the waters of creation and separated them, placing half in the skies and half in the ocean. This is the meaning of "the divisions of God are filled with water."

Through them, man studies the Torah.

Rabbi Chama thus taught: Because of the merit of deeds of kindness, a person can study the Torah. It is thus writtten *(Isaiah 55:1),* "Ho, let all who are thirsty come for water, let him without silver come, stock up and eat." Go to Him, and He will do kindness with you, and you will "stock up and eat."

52. "Let him without silver come," can also be explained in another way. Let him come to God, for He has silver. It is thus written *(Haggai 2:8),* "Mine is the silver, and Mine is the gold."

What is the meaning of the verse, "Mine is the silver, and Mine is the gold?"

What is this like? A king had two treasuries, one of silver, and one of gold. He placed tha of silver to his right, and that of gold to his left. He said [of the silver], "This should be ready, and easy to take out."

He keeps his words calm. He is attached to the poor and directs them calmly. It is thus written *(Exodus 15:6),* "Your right hand, O God, is mighty in power."

If he rejoices in his portion, then all is well. If not, then *(Exodus 15:6),* "Your right hand, O God, crumbles the enemy."

He said to them: This is referring to the gold. It is thus written, "Mine is the silver, and Mine is the gold."

53. Why is [gold] called *ZaHaV?* Because it includes three attributes, [alluded to in its three letters, *Zayin, Heh, Bet*].

[The first attribute is] Male, *(Zachar).* This is the *Zayin.*

[The second is] the Soul. This is the *Heh.* [The numerical value of *Heh* is five, alluding to] the five names of the soul: *Nefesh, Ruach, Neshamah, Chayah, Yechidah.*[32]

What is the purpose of the *Heh?* It is a throne for the *Zayin.* It is thus written *Ecclesiastes 5:7),* "For one above the other watches."

The *Bet* is its sustenance. It is thus written *(Genesis 1:1),* "In *(Bet)* the beginning [God] created . . ."

54. What is its function here?

What is this like? A king once had a daughter who was good, pleasant, beautiful and perfect. He married her to a royal prince, and clothed, crowned and bejeweled her, giving her much money.

Is it possible for the king to ever leave his daughter? You will agree that it is not. Is it possible for him to be with her constantly? You will also agree that it is not. What can he then do? He can place a window between the two, and whenever the father needs the daughter, or the daughter needs the father, they can come together through the window.

It is thus written *(Psalm 45:14)*, "All glorious is the king's daughter inside, her garment is interwoven with *gold.*"

55. What is the *Bet* at the end? [As it is written] *(Proverbs 24.3)*, "With wisdom will the house *(Bayit)* be built." [33]

The verse does not say "was built," but "will be built." In the future God will build and decorate it, thousands of times more than it was.

It is as we have said: Why does the Torah begin with a *Bet*? As it is written *(Proverbs 8:30)*, "I was with Him as a craftsman, I was His delight for a day, a day, [frolicking before Him at every time]." These are the two thousand years, which are the "beginning." [34]

Two? But the scripture says seven, as it is written *(Isaiah 30:26)*, "The light of the moon shall be like the light of the sun, and the light of the sun shall be sevenfold [like the light of the seven days]." And we said, "Just like the sun was for seven, so the moon was for seven."

[He replied,] "I said thousands."

56. They said to him: Up until now there are five. What comes next? [35]

He replied: First I will explain gold. What is gold? We learn that it is where justice emanates. If you bend your words to the right or left, you will be punished.

57. What is the meaning of the verse *(Isaiah 30:26)*, "The light of the moon shall be like the light of the sun, and the light of the sun shall be sevenfold, like the light of the seven days."

The verse does not say "seven days," but "*the* seven days."

These are the days regarding which it is written *(Exodus 31:17)*, "For six days God made [the heaven and the earth],"

As you said, God made six beautiful vessels. What are they? "The heaven and the earth."

Are they not seven? Yes, as it is written *(Ibid.)* "And on the seventh day, He rested and souled."

What is the meaning of "souled?" This teaches us that the Sabbath sustains all souls. It is therefore written that it "souled."

58. Another explanation:

This teaches us that it is from there that souls fly forth. It is thus written, "and He souled."

This continues for a thousand generations. It is thus written *(Psalm 105:8)*, "The word that He commanded until a thousand generations." [36]

Immediately after this it says, "[the covenant] that He cut with Abraham."

What is the meaning of "cut"? He cut a covenant between the ten fingers of his hands and the ten toes of his feet.[37]

Abraham was ashamed. God then said to him *(Genesis 17:4,* "And I, behold My covenant is with you," and with it, "you will be the father of many nations."

59. Why is heaven called *Shamayim?*

This teaches that God kneaded fire and water, and combined them together. From this He made the "beginning of His word." It is thus written *(Psalm 119:160)*, "The beginning of Your word is truth." [38]

It is therefore called *Shamayim — Sham Mayim* (there is water) — *Esh Mayim* (fire water).

He said to them: This is the meaning of the verse *(Job 25:2)*, "He makes peace in His heights." He placed peace and love between them. May He also place peace and love among us.

60. We also say *(Psalm 119:164)*, "seven times each day I praised You for Your righteous judgment."

They asked him, "What are they?"

He replied, "You do not look at it carefully. Be precise, and you will find them."

61. They asked him, "What is the letter *Tzadi*?
He said: *Tzadi* is a *Nun* and a *Yud*. Its mate is also a *Nun*
and a *Yud*.[39]

It is thus written *(Proverbs 10:25)*, "The righteous
(Tzadik) is the foundation of the world."

Fig. 6. The *Tzadi*, showing how it is constructed from a *Nun* and a *Yud*.

62. They asked him: What is the meaning of the verse
[with regard to Balak and Balaam] *(Numbers 23:14)*, And he
took him to the field of the seers."

What is the "field of the seers"? As it is written *(Song of
Songs 7:12)*, "Come my beloved, let us go out to the field."

Do not read *Sadeh* (the field), but *Sidah* (carriage).

What is this carriage? He said, "The Heart of the Blessed
Holy One."

His heart said to the Blessed Holy One, "Come my beloved,
let us go out to the carriage to stroll. It will not constantly sit in
one place."

63.   What is his heart?
He said: If so, Ben Zoma is outside, and you are with

him.[40]

The heart *(Lev)* [in numerical value] is thirty-two. These are concealed, and with them the world was created.

What are these 32?

He said: These are the 32 Paths.[41]

This is like a king who was in the innermost of many chambers. The number of such chambers was 32, and to each one there was a path. Should the king then bring everyone to his chamber through these paths? You will agree that he should not. Should he reveal his jewels, his tapestries, his hidden and concealed secrets? You will again agree that he should not. What then does he do? He touches the Daughter, and includes all the paths in her and in her garments.

One who wants to go inside should gaze there.[42]

He married her to a king, and also gave her to him as a gift. Because of his love for her, he sometimes calls her "my sister," since they are both from one place. Sometimes he calls her his daughter, since she is actually his daughter. And sometimes he calls her "my mother."

64. Furthermore, if there is no wisdom, then there is no justice.

It is thus written *(I Kings 5:26),* "And God gave wisdom to Solomon." He then judged the case [of the two mothers and the infant] correctly, and it is then written *(I Kings 3:28),* "And all Israel heard of the judgment that the king had judged, and they feared the king, for they saw that the wisdom of God was in him to do judgment."

65. And what wisdom did God give to Solomon?

Solomon had God's name. We have thus said that whenever Solomon is mentioned in the *Song of Songs,* it is a holy name, except in one case.[43]

God said to him, "Since your name is like the name of My Glory, I will let you marry my daughter."

But she is married!

Let us say that He gave her to him as a gift. It is thus written *(I Kings 5:26),* "And God gave wisdom to Solomon."

Here, however, it is not explained. Where then is it explained? When the scripture states *(I Kings 3:28),* "For they

saw that the wisdom of God was in him to do judgment." We
then see that the wisdom that God gave him was such that he
could "do judgment."

What is the meaning of "to do judgment?" As long as a
person does judgment, God's wisdom is inside him. This is what
helps him and draws him near. If not, it repels him, and not
only that, but it also punishes him. It is thus written *(Leviticus
26:28)*, "I will chastise you, also I."

66. And Rabbi Rahumai said: What is the meaning of the
verse *(Leviticus 26:28)*, "[I will chastise you,] also I"?

God said, "I will chastise you."

The Congregation of Israel said, "Do not think that I will
seek mercy for you, but I will chastise you. Not only will I
render judgment, but I will also chastise you." [44]

67. What is the meaning of *(Leviticus 26:28)*, "[I will
chastise you, also I], seven for your sins"?

The Congregation of Israel said: "I will chastise you, also
I" — and also those regarding which it is written *(Psalm
119:164)*, "Seven each day I praised You." [45]

They joined her and replied: Also us seven. Even though
among us is the one who reverses itself, the one who oversees
good and merit, we too will reverse ourselves and chastise.
Why? Because of your sins.

But if you return to Me, then I will return to you. It is thus
written *(Malachi 3:7)*, "Return to Me, and I will return to you."

The scripture does not say, "I will bring you back to Me."
Instead it says, "I will return to you" — with you. We will all
seek mercy from the King.

What does the King say? [He says] *(Jeremiah 3:22)*, "Return you backsliding children, I will heal your backslidings."
[He also says] *(Ezekiel 18:30)*, "Return and bring back."

What is the meaning of the verse, "Return and bring
back"? Come back and ask those Seven to return with you. The
scripture therefore says, "and bring back " — those regarding
which it is written, "seven for your sin."

68. The disciples asked Rabbi Rahumai: What is the
meaning of the verse *(Habakkuk 3:1)*, "A prayer of Habakkuk
the prophet, for errors." A prayer? It should be called a praise
[since it speaks of God's greatness].

But whoever turns his heart from worldly affairs and delves in the Works of the Chariot[46] is accepted before God as if he prayed all day. It is therefore called "a prayer."

What is the meaning of "for errors"? As it is written [regarding wisdom] *(Proverbs 5:19),* "With its love you shall always err." [47]

Regarding what is this speaking? The Works of the Chariot, as it is written *(Habakkuk, 3:2),* "O God, I heard a report of You and I feared."

69. What is the meaning of, "I heard a report of You and I feared, [O God, bring to life Your works in the midst of the years]"?

Why does the verse say "I feared" after "I heard a report of You," and not after "in the midst of the years"?

But it was "from the report of You" that "I feared."

What is the "report of You"? It is the place where they listen to reports.

Why does the verse say "I heard" and not "I understood"? [The word "heard" has the connotation of understanding] as we find *(Deuteronomy 38:49),* "A nation whose language you do not hear."

70. Why did he say "I feared"? Because the ear looks like the letter *Alef.*

The *Alef* is the first of all letters. Besides this, the *Alef* causes all the letters to endure.

The *Alef* looks like the brain.

When you mention the *Alef* you open your mouth. The same is true of thought, when you extend your thoughts to the Infinite and the Boundless.

From *Alef* emanate all letters. Do we not see that it is first?

It is thus written *(Micah 2:13),* "God *(YHVH)* is at their head." We have a rule that every Name that is written *Yud Heh Vav Heh* is specific to the Blessed Holy One and is sanctified with holiness.

What is the meaningness of "with holiness"? This is the Holy Palace.[48]

Where is the Holy Palace? We would say that it is in thought and in the *Alef.*

This is the meaning of the verse, "I heard a report of You and I feared."

71. Habakkuk therefore said: I know that my prayer is accepted with delight. I also delighted when I came to that place where I understood "a report of You and I feared." Therefore, "Bring to life your works in the midst of the years" — through Your unity.

What is this like? A king who was talented, hidden and concealed went into his house and commanded that no one seek him. One who does seek is therefore afraid, lest the king find out that he has violated the king's order. [Habakkuk] therefore said, "I feared, O God, bring to life Your works in the midst of the years."

This is what Habakkuk said: Because Your name is in You, and in You is Your name, "bring to life Your works in the midst of the years." Thus will it be forever.

72. Another explanation of "Bring to life Your works in the midst of years":

What is this like? A king had a beautiful pearl, and it was the treasure of his kingdom. When he is happy, he embraces it, kisses it, places it on his head, and loves it.

Habakkuk said: Even though Kings are with You, the beloved pearl is in Your world.[49] Therefore, "Bring to life Your works in the midst of years."

What is the meaning of "years"? It is written *(Genesis 1:3)*, "And God said, 'Let there be light.' " Light is nothing other than day, as it is written *(Genesis 1:16)*, "The great light to rule the day, and the small light to rule the night."

Years are made from days.

It is thus written, "Bring to life Your works in the midst of years" — in the midst of that pearl that gives rise to years.

73. But it is written *(Isaiah 43:5)*, "[Fear not, for I am with you,] I will bring your seed from the east." The sun rises in the east, and you say that the pearl is day.

[He replied:] I am only speaking with regard to the verse *(Genesis 1:5)*, "And it was evening and it was morning, day." Regarding this it is written *(Genesis 2:4)*, "In the day that God made earth and heaven."

74. And it is written *(Psalm 18:12)*, "He made darkness His hiding place round about, His *Succah* the darkness of waters, thick clouds of the skies *(Shechakim)*." [50]

He said: Regarding this it is written *(Isaiah 45:8)*, "The skies *(Shechakim)* pour down righteousness."

This righteousness *(Tzedek)* is the Attribute of Judgment for the world. It is thus written *(Deuteronomy 16:20)*, "Righteousness, righteousness, shall you pursue."

Immediately after this, it is written, "that you may life and occupy the land." If you judge yourself, then you will live. If not, then it will judge you, and it will be fulfilled, even against your will.

75. Why does the Torah say "righteousness, righteousness" twice?

He said: Because the scripture continues *(Psalm 18:13)*, "At the glow opposite Him." [51]

The first "righteousness" is literal righteousness *(Tzedek)*. This is the Divine Presence. It is thus written *(Isaiah 1:21)*, "Righteousness dwells in it."

What is the second "righteousness"? This is the righteousness that frightens the righteous.

Is this righteousness charity *(Tzadakah)* or not?

He said that it is not.

Why? Because it is written *(Isaiah 59:17)*, "He put on righteousness like a coat of mail, and [a helmet of salvation on His head]."

His head is nothing other than Truth. It is thus written *(Psalm 119:160)*, "The head of Your word is truth."

Truth is nothing other than peace. It is thus written [that King Hezekiah said] *(Isaiah 39:8)*, "There shall be peace and truth in my days."

Is it possible for a man to say this? But this is what Hezekiah said: The attribute that You gave to David my ancestor is half of my days, and peace and truth are half of my days. It is for this reason that he mentioned "my days."

He mentioned both "peace and truth" and "in my days," since it is all one. It is thus written *(Genesis 1:5)*, "And it was evening, and it was morning, one day."

[The day reconciles morning and evening, and is therefore peace.] Just as the day is peace, so he chose peace. It is therefore written *(II Kings 20:19)*, "Peace and truth shall be in my days."

This shall be through the attribute that You gave to David. Regarding this, it is written *(Psalm 89:37)*, "His throne shall be like the sun before Me."

76. What is the meaning of the verse *(Habakkuk 3:2)*, "In the midst of years make it known"?

He said: I know that You are the holy God, as it is written *(Exodus 15:11)*, "Who is like You, mighty in holiness?" Holiness is in You and You are in holiness.[52] Nevertheless, "in the midst of years make it known."

What is the meaning of "make it known"? [This means] that You should have mercy. It is thus written *(Exodus 2:25)*, "And God saw the children of Israel, and God knew."

What is the meaning of, "and God knew"?

What is this like? A king had a beautiful wife, and had children from her. He loved them and raised them, but they went out to bad ways. He then hated both them and their mother.

The mother went to them and said, "My children! Why do you do this? Why do you make your father hate both you and me?" [She spoke to them in this manner] until they had remorse and did the will of their father.

When the king saw this, he loved them as much as he did in the beginning. He then also remembered their mother. This is the meaning of the verse, "And God saw . . . And God knew."

This is also the meaning of the verse, "In the midst of years make it known."

77. What is the meaning of the verse *(Habakkuk 3:2)*, "In anger, you shall remember love *(rachem)*"?

He said: When Your children sin before You and You are angry at them, "remember love."

What is the meaning of "remember love"? That regarding which it is written *(Psalm 18:2)*, "I love *(rachem)* You O God, my strength."

And You have him this attribute, which is the Divine Presence of Israel.[53] He recalled his son whom he inherited, and whom You gave to him. It is thus written *(I Kings 5:26)*, "And God gave wisdom to Solomon."

And You should remember their father Abraham, as it is written *(Isaiah 41:8)*, "The seed of Abraham My friend" — "In the midst of years make it known."

78. Where do we see that Abraham had a daughter? It is written *(Genesis 24:1)*, "And God blessed Abraham with all *(BaKol)*." [54]

It is also written *(Isaiah 43:7)*, *"All* that is called by My name, for My glory I created it, I formed it, also I made it."
Was this blessing his daughter, or was it not?
Yes, it was his daughter.
What is this like? A king had a slave who was complete and perfect before him. The king tested the slave in many ways, but the slave withstood all temptation.
The King said, "What will I give that slave? What should I do for him? I can do nothing but command my older brother to advise him, watch over him and honor him." [55] The slave thus went to the older brother and learned his attributes. The brother loved him very much, and called him his friend. It is thus written *(Isaiah 41:8)*, "The seed of Abraham My friend."
He said, "What will I give him? What can I do for him? Behold I have made a beautiful vessel, and in it are beautiful jewels. There is nothing like it in the treasuries of kings.[56] I will give it to him, and he will be worthy in his place."
This is the meaning of the verse, "And God blessed Abraham with all."

79. Another explanation:
[It is written] *(Habakkuk 3:2)*, "I heard a report of You and I feared." [This means] "I understood what was reported about You and I feared." [57]
What did he understand? He understood God's thought. Even [human] thought has no end, for man can think, and descend to the end of the world.
The ear also has no end and is not satiated. It is thus written *(Ecclesiastes 1:8)*, "The ear is not satiated from hearing."
Why is this so? Because the ear is in the shape of an *Alef*.[58] *Alef* is the root of the Ten Commandments.[59] Therefore, the ear is not satiated from hearing."

80. What is the meaning of the letter *Zayin* in the word *OZeN* (ear)?
We have said that everything that the Blessed Holy One brought into His world has a name emanating from its concept. It is thus written *(Genesis 2:19)*, "All that the man called each living soul, that was its name." This teaches us that each thing's body was thus.
And how do we know that each thing's name is its body?

It is written *(Proverbs 10:7)*, "The memory of the righteous shall be a blessing, and the name of the wicked shall rot." What actually rots, their name or their body? [One must agree that it is their body.] Here too, [each thing's name refers to] its body.

81. What is an example of this?

Take the word for root — *ShoReSh (Shin Resh Shin)*.

The letter *Shin* looks like the roots of a tree.[60]

[*Resh* is bent, since] the root of every tree is bent.

And what is the function of the final *Shin*? This teaches us that if you take a branch and plant it, it will root again.

What is the function of the *Zayin* [in *OZeN* — ear]?

[Its numerical value is seven] corresponding to the seven days of the week. This teaches us that each day has its own power.

And what is its function [in the word *OZeN*]?

This teaches us that just like there is infinite wisdom in the ear, so is there power in all parts of the body.

82. What are the seven parts of man's body?

It is written *(Genesis 9:6)*, "In the form of God, He made man." It is also written *(Genesis 1:27)*, "In the form of God He made him" — counting all his limbs and parts.

But we have said: What does the letter *Vav* resemble? It is alluded to in the verse *(Psalm 104:5)*, "He spreads out light like a garment." For *Vav* is nothing other than the six directions.[61]

He replied: The covenant of circumcision and man's mate are considered as one.[62]

His two hands then make three, his head and body, five, and his two legs make seven.[63]

Paralleling these are their powers in heaven. It is thus written *(Ecclesiastes 7:14)*, "Also one opposite the other has God made."

These are the days [of the week, as it is written] *(Exodus 31:17)*, "Because six days God made the heaven and the earth." The scripture does not say "in six days," but rather, "six days." This teaches us that each day [of the week] has its own specific power.

83. What is the significance of the *Nun* [in the word *OZeN*]?

This teaches us that the brain is the main part of the spinal cord. It constantly draws from there, and if not for the spinal cord, the brain could not endure. And without the brain, the body could not endure.

The entire body exists only in order to provide for the needs of the brain. And if the body did not endure, then the brain would also not endure.

The spinal cord is the channel from the brain to the entire body. It is represented by the bent *Nun*.[64]

But [in the word *OZeN*] the *Nun* is a straight one.

The straight *Nun* is the one that is always at the end of a word. This teaches us that the straight *Nun* includes both the bent one and the straight one.

But the bent *Nun* is the Foundation. This teaches us that the straight *Nun* includes both male and female.

84. The open *Mem*. What is the open *Mem?*
It includes both male and female.
What is the closed *Mem?*
It is made like a belly from above.

But Rabbi Rahumai said that the belly is like the letter *Tet*.[65]

He said that it is like a *Tet* on the inside, while I say that it is like a *Mem* on the outside.

85. What is a *Mem?*
Do not read *Mem,* but *Mayim* (water). Just like water is wet, so is the belly always wet.

Why does the open *Mem* include both male and female, while the closed *Mem* is male?

This teaches us that the *Mem* is primarily male. The opening was then added to it for the sake of the female.

Just like the male cannot give birth, so the closed *Mem* cannot give birth. And just like the female has an opening with which to give birth, so can the open *Mem* give birth. The Mem is therefore open and closed.

86. Why should the *Mem* have two forms, open and closed?
Because we said: Do not read *Mem,* but *Mayim* (water).

The woman is cold, and therefore must be warmed by the male.

Why should the *Nun* have two forms, bent and straight?
Because it is written *(Psalm 72:17),* "Before the sun shall

his name reign *(ya-Nun)*." [This is] from two *Nuns,* the bent *Nun* and the straight *Nun,* and it must be through male and female.

87. It is written *(Ecclesiastes 1:8),* "The ear is not satiated from hearing." It is also written *(Ecclesiastes 1:8),* "The eye is not satiated from seeing." This teaches us that both draw from thought.

What is thought?

It is a king that is needed by all things that were created in the world, both above and below.

88. What is the meaning of the expression, "It rose in thought"? [66] Why do we not say that "it descended [in thought]"?

Indeed, we have said, "One who gazes into the vision of the Chariot first descends and then ascends." [67]

We use the expression [of descent] there because we say, "One who gazes into the vision *(Tzafiyat)* of the Chariot." The Aramaic translation of "vision" *(Tzafiyat)* is *Sechuta* [meaning a covering, and alluding to the fact that one is looking down from above].[68] It is also written *(Isaiah 21:8),* "And he called as a lion: 'Upon the watchtower *(MiTzPeh),* O God.' " [69]

Here, however, we are speaking of thought, [and therefore only speak of ascent]. For thought does not include any vision, and has no ending whatsoever. And anything that has no end or limit does not have any descent.

People therefore say, "Someone descended to the limit of his friend's knowledge." One can arrive at the limit of a person's knowledge, but not at the limit of his thought.

89. Rabbi Amorai sat and expounded:

What is the meaning of the *Segol*? [70] Its name is *Segulah* (treasure). It comes after the *Zarka.*

What is the meaning of *Zarka*?

It is like its name — something that is thrown *(ni-Zrak).* It is like something that is thrown, and after it comes *(Ecclesiastes 2:8),* "the treasures of kings and lands."

90. What is the reason that it is called *Zarka*?

It is written *(Ezekiel 3:12),* "Blessed is the glory of God from His place." This indicates that no being knows His place.

We recite [God's] name over the Crown, and it goes to the head of the Owner.[71] It is thus written [regarding God] *(Genesis 14:19),* "Owner of heaven and earth."

When it goes, it is like it is thrown *(Zarka).* Following it is treasure *(Segulah).* It is at the head of all letters.[72]

91. Why is [this accent] at the end of a word, and not at the beginning?

This teaches us that this Crown rises higher and higher.

It is included and crowned, as it is written *(Psalm 118:22),* "The stone that the builders rejected has become the head cornerstone." It ascends to the place from which it was graven, as it is written *(Genesis 49:24),* "From there is the Shepherd, the Stone of Israel." [73]

92. He also said:

What is the reason that we place blue wool in the *Tzitzit?*[74] And why are there 32 [threads]?[75]

What is this like? A king had a beautiful garden, and in it were 32 paths. He placed a watchman over them to show that all these paths belong to him alone. [The king] said to him, "Watch them, and walk upon them every day. As long as you walk these paths, you will have peace."

What did the watchman do? He appointed other watchmen [as his assistants to watch] over them. He said, "If I remain alone on these paths, it is impossible for me, a single watchman, to maintain them all. Besides that, people may say that I am the king." The watchman therefore placed his assistants over all the paths. These are the 32 paths.[76]

93. What is the reason for the blue?

The watchman said, "Perhaps those assistant watchmen will say that the garden belongs to us." He therefore gave them a sign, and told them, "See this. It is the sign of the king, indicating that the garden belongs to him. He is the one who made these paths, and they are not mine. This is his seal."

What is this like? A king and his daughter had slaves, and they wanted to travel abroad. But [the slaves] were afraid, being in terror of the king. He therefore gave them his sign. They were also afraid of the daughter, and she [also] gave them a sign.[77] They said, "From now on, with these two signs, 'God will watch you from all evil, He will safeguard your soul.' " [78]

94. Rabbi Amorai sat and expounded:

What is the meaning of the verse *(I Kings 8:27)*, "Behold the heaven and the heaven of heaven cannot contain You"?

This teaches us that the Blessed Holy One has 72 names.[79]

All of them were placed in the Tribes [of Israel]. It is thus written *(Exodus 28:10)*, "Six of their names on one stone, and the names of the other six on the other stone, according to their generations."

It is also written *(Joshua 4:9)*, "He raised up twelve stones." Just like the first are *(Exodus 28:12)*, "stones of memorial," so these are *(Joshua 4:7)*, "stones of memorial."

[There are therefore] 12 stones [each containing six names] making a total of 72. These parallel the 72 names of the Blessed Holy One.

Why do they begin with twelve? This teaches us that God has twelve Directors. Each of these has six Powers [making a total of 72].

What are they? They are the 72 languages.[80]

95. The Blessed Holy One has a single Tree, and it has twelve diagonal boundaries:[81]

> The northeast boundary, the southeast boundary;
> The upper east boundary, the lower east boundary;
>
> The southwest boundary, the northwest boundary;
> The upper west boundary, the lower west boundary;
>
> The upper south boundary, the lower south boundary;
> The upper north boundary, the lower north boundary;
>
> The continually spread forever and ever;
> They are the "arms of the world." [82]

On the inside of them is the Tree. Paralleling these diagonals there are twelve Functionaries. Inside the Sphere[83] there are also twelve Functionaries.

Including the diagonals themselves, this makes a total of 36 Functionaries.

Each of these has another. It is thus written *(Ecclesiastes 5:7),* "For one above another watches." [This makes a total of 72.]

It therefore comes out that the east has nine, the west has nine, the north has nine, and the south has nine.

These are twelve, twelve, twelve, and they are the Functionaries in the Axis, the Sphere, and the Heart.[84]

Their total is 36. The power of each of these 36 is in every other one.

Even though there are twelve in each of the three, they are all attached to each other. Therefore, all 36 Powers are in the first one, which is the Axis. And if you seek them in the Sphere, you will find the very same ones. And if you seek them in the Heart, you will again find the very same ones.

Each one therefore has 36. All of them do not have more than 36 Forms.

All of them complete the Heart [which has a numerical value of 32].[85] Four are then left over.

Add 32 to 32 and the sum is 64. These are the 64 Forms.

How do we know that 32 must be added to 32? Because it is written *(Ecclesiastes 5:7),* "For one above another watches, [and there are higher ones above them]."

We thus have 64, eight less than the 72 names of the Blessed Holy One. These are alluded to in the verse, "there are higher ones above them," and they are the seven days of the week.

But one is still missing. This is referred to in the next verse *(Ecclesiastes 5:8),* "The advantage of the land in everything is the King."

What is this "advantage"? This is the place from which the earth was graven. It is an advantage over what existed previously.

And what is this advantage? Everything in the world that people see is taken from its radiance. Then it is an advantage.

96. What is the earth from which the heavens were graven?

It is the Throne of the Blessed Holy One. It is the Precious Stone and the Sea of Wisdom.

This parallels the blue in the Tzitzit.

Rabbi Meir thus said:[86] Why is blue chosen above all other colors [for the Tzitzit]? Because blue resembles the sea, the sea resembles the sky, and the sky resembles the Throne of Glory. It is thus written *(Exodus 24:10)*, "They saw the God of Israel, and under His feet was like a pavement of sapphire, like the essence of heaven in clarity." It is furthermore written *(Ezekiel 1:26)*, "As the likeness of a sapphire stone was the appearance of a Throne."

97. Rabbi Berachiah sat and expounded:

What is the meaning of the verse *(Exodus 25:2)*, "And they shall take for Me a lifted offering *(Terumah)*"? It means, "Lift Me up with your prayers."

And whom? Those whose "hearts make them willing." These are the ones who are willing to draw themselves away from this world.

Honor him, for it is in him that I rejoice, since he knows My name. From him it is fitting to take My lifted offering, as it is written *(Exodus 25:2)*, "from each man whose heart makes him willing, you shall take My lifted offering." From he who makes himself willing.

Rabbi Rahumai said: [This refers to] the righteous and pious in Israel who raise Me over all the world through their merit. From them the Heart is sustained, and the Heart sustains them.

98. And all the Holy Forms oversee all the nations. But Israel is holy, taking the Tree itself and its Heart.

The Heart is the beauty *(hadar)* of the fruit of the body. Similarly, Israel takes *(Leviticus 23:40)*, "the fruit of a beautiful *(hadar)* tree." [87]

The date palm is surrounded by its branches all around it and has its sprout *(Lulav)* in the center. Similarly, Israel takes the body of this Tree which is its Heart.

And paralleling the body is the spinal cord, which is the main part of the body.[88]

What is the *Lulav*? [It can be written] *Lo Lev* — "it has a heart." The heart is also given over to it.

And what is this Heart? It is the 32 hidden paths of wisdom that are hidden in it.[89]

In each of their paths there is also a Form watching over it.

It is thus written *(Genesis 3:24),* "To watch the way of the Tree of Life."

99. What are these Forms? They are that regarding which it is written *(Genesis 3:24),* "And He placed the Cherubim to the east of the Garden of Eden, and the flame of a sword revolving, to guard the way of the Tree of Life."

What is the meaning of, "He placed to the east *(kedem)* of the Garden of Eden"? He placed it in those paths that preceded *(kadmu)* the place that was called the Garden of Eden. It was also before the Cherubim, as it is written, "the Cherubim." It was furthermore before the flame, as it is written, "the flame of a sword revolving."

Is it then before [the flame]? Heaven is called *Shamayim,* indicating that fire and water existed before it.[90] It is written *(Genesis 1:6),* "Let there be a firmament in the midst of the waters, and let it be a division between water and water." It is then written *(Genesis 1:8),* "And God called the firmament heaven *(Shamayim)."*

How do we know that the heaven is fire? It is written *(Deuteronomy 4:24),* "For the Lord your God is a consuming fire, a jealous God."

100. And how do we know that "Heaven" refers to the Blessed Holy One?

It is written *(I Kings 8:36),* "And you, O Heaven, shall hear." Was Solomon then praying to heaven that it should hear their prayers? But [we must say that he was praying] to the One whose name is Heaven.

It is thus written *(I Kings 8:27),* "Behold the heaven and the heaven of heaven cannot contain You." This is the name of the Blessed Holy One.[91]

You therefore have fire. How can you then say that it was before?

But we must say that their Power existed before the Forms of that place. Only then did these Holy Forms come into existence.

What is their Power? It is that regarding which it is written *(I Samuel 2:2),* "There is none holy like God, there is none other than You, and there is no Former like our God."

101. Rabbi Berachiah sat and expounded:

What is the *Lulav* that we discussed? It is 36 *(Lu)* given over to 32 *(Lav)*.[92]

And how?

He replied: There are three Princes, the Axis, the Sphere and the Heart.[93] Each one is twelve, and the three therefore constitute a sum of 36, through which the world is sustained. It is thus written *(Proverbs 10:25)*, "And Righteous is the foundation of the world." [94]

102. We learned: There is a single pillar extending from heaven to earth, and its name is Righteous *(Tzadik)*.[95]

[This pillar] is named after the righteous. When there are righteous people in the world, then it becomes strong, and when there are not, it becomes weak.

It supports the entire world, as it is written, "And Righteous is the foundation of the world." If it becomes weak, then the world cannot endure.

Therefore, even if there is only one righteous person in the world, it is he who supports the world. It is therefore written, "And a righteous one is the foundation of the world."

You should therefore take My lifted offering from him first. Then *(Exodus 25:3)*, "And this is the lifted offering that you should take from them" — from the rest. What is it? "Gold, silver and copper."

103. Another explanation:

It is written *(Exodus 25:2)*, "and they shall take for Me *(Li)* a lifted offering." [*Li* (for Me) can also be read, "for the *Yud*."] They shall take the *Yud*, which is the tenth, as a lifted offering to make it holy.[96]

How do we know that the tenth is holy? Because it is written *(Leviticus 27:32)*, "The tenth shall be holy to God."

What is holy? That regarding which it is written *(Ezekiel 44:30)*, "The *beginning* of all the first fruits . . . and every lifted offering of every thing."

It is furthermore written *(Psalm 111:10)*, "The *beginning* of wisdom is the fear of God." Do not read "is the fear" but "and the fear." [The verse will then read, "The beginning is wisdom and the fear of God.][97]

104. The disciples asked Rabbi Eliezer: Our master, what is the meaning of the verse *(Exodus 13:2),* "Sanctify to Me every first-born"? Does the Blessed Holy One then have a first-born?

He replied: "Sanctify to Me *(Li)* every first-born" refers to nothing other than the second level of holiness.[98]

It is the name that is given to Israel, as it is written *(Exodus 7:22),* "My son, My first-born, Israel."

To the extent that we can express it, He was with them [in Egypt] in the time of their oppression. It is therefore written *(Exodus 4:27),* "Send forth My son and he will serve Me." [Here, only "My son" is mentioned,] and not "My first-born."

Rabbi Rahumai said:

What is the meaning of the verse *(Deuteronomy 22:7),* "You shall surely send away the mother, and the children you shall take for yourself"? [99] Why does it not say, "You shall surely send away the father"?

But the scripture says, "you shall surely send away the mother" in honor of the one who is called the Mother of the World. It is thus written *(Proverbs 2:3),* "For you shall call Understanding a Mother." [100]

105. And what is the meaning of, "and the children you shall take for yourself"?

Rabbi Rahumai said: These are the children that she raised. And who are they? They are the seven days of creation, and the seven days of *Succot.*[101]

Are the seven [days of *Succot*] then not the same as the seven days of the week?

The difference is that [the days of *Succot*] are more holy. Regarding them it is written *(Leviticus 23:37),* "holy convocations."

But then, why not [also include the seven weeks before] Shavuot, since this is also called *(Leviticus 23:21),* "a holy convocation."

He replied: Yes, but this is one and the other is two. It is thus written *(Exodus 12:16),* "The first day shall be a holy convocation, and the seventh day shall be a holy convocation." [102]

He said:

Why is Shavuot one [day]?

Because the Torah was given to Israel on that day. And when the Torah was created in the beginning, the Blessed Holy One ruled His world alone with it. It is thus written *(Psalm 111:10)*, "The beginning is wisdom, the fear of God." [God] said [to it], "This being so, your holiness shall be yours by yourself."

And what is Succot?

He replied: The letter *Bet* [which has the connotation of a house *(Bayit)*]. It is thus written *(Proverbs 24:3)*, "With wisdom a house is built." 103

And how do we know that *Succot* has the connotation of a house? As it is written *(Genesis 33:17)*, "And Jacob traveled to Succot. He built himself a house, and for his livestock he built *Succot* (huts). Therefore, he named the place Succot."

106. Rabbi Berachiah sat and expounded:

What is the Axis *(Teli)*? 104

This is the likeness that is before the Blessed Holy One. It is thus written *(Song of Songs 5:11)*, "His locks are curled *(Taltalim)*." 105

What is the Sphere? This is the Womb.106

What is the Heart? It is that regarding which it is written *(Deuteronomy 4:11)*, "unto the heart of heaven." In it are included the 32 mystical paths of Wisdom.107

107. What is the meaning of the verse *(Numbers 6:24–26)*, "May God *(YHVH)* bless you and watch you. May God *(YHVH)* make His face shine on you and be gracious to you. May God *(YHVH)* lift His face to you and give you peace." 108

This is the explicit Name of the Blessed Holy One. It is the Name containing twelve letters, as it is written, *YHVH YHVH YHVH.*109

This teaches us that God's names consist of three troops. Each troop resembles the other, and each one's name is like [the other's] named. All of them are sealed with *Yud Heh Vav Heh.*

And how?

The [four letters] *Yud Heh Vav Heh* can be permuted 24 different ways, forming one troop. This is, "May God *(YHVH)* bless you . . ."

In a similar manner, the second one, "May God *(YHVH)* make His face shine . . ." These are 24 names of the Blessed Holy One.

In a similar manner, the third one, "May God *(YHVH)* lift His face. . . ." These are 24 names of the Blessed Holy One.

This teaches us that each army, with its leaders and officers, has 24. Multiply 24 by three and you have the 72 names of the Blessed Holy One.

These are the 72 names derived from the verses *(Exodus 14:19-21)*, "And traveled . . . And came . . . And stretched. . . ." [110]

108. And who are the Officers? We learned that there are three.

Strength *(Gevurah)* is the Officer of all the Holy Forms to the left of the Blessed Holy One. He is Gabriel.

The Officer of all the Holy Forms to His right is Michael.

In the middle is Truth. This is Uriel, the Officer of all the Holy Forms [in the center]. [111]

Each Officer is over 24 Forms. But there is no reckoning of his troops, as it is written *(Job 25:3)*, "Is there a number to His troops?"

But if so, then there are 72 plus 72 [making a total of 144] [112]

He said: This is not the case. For when Israel brings a sacrifice before their Father in heaven, they are united together. This is the unification of our God.

109. Why is a sacrifice called a *Karban* [which means "bringing close"]?

Because it brings the Forms of the Holy Powers close. It is thus written *(Ezekiel 37:17)*, "And you shall join one of them to the other, making one stick, and they shall become one in your hands."

And why is [the sacrifice] called a "pleasant fragrance"?

Fragrance is only in the nose. The sense of smell is through breath, and this is nowhere but in the nose. [113]

"Pleasant" *(nicho'ach)* means nothing other than "descending." It is thus written *(Leviticus 9:22)*, "And he descended," and the Targum translates this as *VeNachit* [having the same root as *nicho'ach*].

The fragrance-spirit descends and unifies itself with those Holy Forms, bringing itself close through the sacrifice. It is for this reason that [a sacrifice] is called a *Karban.*

110. There is a name that is derived from the three verses *(Exodus 14:19-21),* "And traveled ... And came ... And stretched. ..." [114]

The letters of the first verse, "And traveled ..." are arranged in this name in the order that they are in the verse.

The letters of the second verse, "And came ..." are arranged in the name in reverse order.

The letters of the third passage, "And stretched ..." are arranged in the name in the same order as they occur in the verse, just like the case of the first verse.

Each one of these verses has 72 letters.

Therefore, each of the names that is derived from these three sentences, "And traveled ... And came ... And stretched ..." contains three letters.

These are the 72 names. They emanate and divide themselves into three sections, 24 to each section.

Over each of these sections is a higher Officer.

Each section has four directions to watch, east, west, north and south. They are therefore distributed, six to each direction. The four directions then have a total of 24 Forms. [This is true of the first section] as well as the second and the third.

All of them are sealed with *YHVH,* God of Israel, the living God, Shadai, high and exalted, who dwells in eternity on high, whose Name is holy, *YHVH.* Blessed be the name of the glory of His kingdom forever and ever. [115]

111. Rabbi Ahilai sat and expounded:

What is the meaning of the verse, "God *(YHVH)* is King, God *(YHVH)* was King, God *(YHVH)* will be King forever and ever."? [116]

This is the Explicit Name *(Shem HaMePoresh),* for which permission was given that it be permuted and spoken. It is thus written [regarding the above mentioned Priestly Blessing] *(Numbers 6:27),* "And they shall place My name upon the children of Israel, and I will bless them."

This refers to the Name containing twelve letters. It is the name used in the Priestly Blessing, "May God bless you ..." It contains three names [each having four letters] making a total of twelve.

Its vowel points are *Yapha'al Y'pha'oel Yiph'ol.*[117]

If one safeguards it and mentions it in holiness, then all his prayers are heard. And not only that, but he is loved on high and below, and immediately answered and helped.

This is the Explicit Name that was written on Aaron's forehead.[118]

The Explicit Name containing 72 letters and the Explicit Name containing twelve letters were given over by the Blessed Holy One to [the angel] Mesamariah, who stands before the Curtain. He gave it to Elijah on Mount Carmel, and with them he ascended and did not taste death.[119]

112. These are the Explicit Holy Exalted Names. There are twelve Names, one for each of the twelve tribes of Israel: [120]

> AH-TzYTzaH-RON
> AKhLYThaH-RON
> ShMaKTha-RON
> DMUShaH-RON
> Ve-TzaPhTzaPhYTh-RON
> HURMY-RON
> BRaChYaH-RON
> EReSh GaDRa-AON
> BaSAVaH MoNA-HON
> ChaZHaVaYaH
> HaVaHaYRY HAH
> Ve-HaRAYTh-HON

All of them are included in the Heart of heaven.[121]

They include male and female. They are given over to the Axis, the Sphere and the Heart, and they are the wellsprings of Wisdom.

113. Rabbi Rahumai sat and expounded:

What are the twelve tribes of Israel?

But this teaches us that the Blessed Holy One has twelve rods [on high. The word *Shevet* is the same for both "tribe" and "rod."]

What are they?

What is this like? A king had a beautiful fountain. All his

brothers had no water other than this fountain, and could not endure thirst. What did he do? He made twelve pipes for the fountain, and named them after his brothers' children.

He then said to them, "If the sons are as good as their fathers, they will be worthy, and I will let water flow through the pipes. The fathers will then drink all they wish, and so will the sons. But if the sons are not worthy and do not do what is right in my eyes, then regarding this, these pipes will stand. I will give them water only on the condition that they give none to their children, since they do not obey my will."

114. What meaning of the word *Shevet* [which has the connotation of both a tribe and a rod]?

It is something simple and not square.

What is the reason?

Because it is impossible to have one square inside another square. A circle inside a square can move. A square inside a square cannot move.

115. What are the things that are circular?

They are the vowel points in the Torah of Moses, for these are all round. They are to the letters like the soul, which lives in the body of man.

It is impossible for [man] to come [into this world] unless [the soul] endures within him. It is impossible for him to speak anything, great or small, without it.[122]

In a similar manner, it is impossible to speak a word, great or small, without the vowel points.

116. Every vowel point is round, and every letter is square.

The vowel points are the life of the letters, and through them, the letters endure.

These vowel points come through the pipes to the letters through the fragrance of a sacrifice, which immediately descends. It is therefore called "A descending (pleasant) fragrance to God" — indicating that it descends to God.[123]

This is the meaning of the verse *(Deuteronomy 6:4)*, "Hear O Israel, the Lord is our God, the Lord is One." [124]

117. Rabbi Yochanan said:

What is the meaning of the verse *(Exodus 15:3)*, "God is a

man *(Ish)* of war, God *(YHVH)* is His name"? [125]

Man *(Ish)* indicates a sign. The Targum thus renders, "God is a man of war," as "God is the Master of victory in war."

What is this Master?

Alef is the first, the Holy Palace.[126]

Do we then say that the Palace is holy? Instead we say, "the Palace of the Holy One."

118. *Yud* is the Ten Sayings with which the world was created.[127]

What are they? They are the Torah of Truth, which includes all worlds.

What is the *Shin?*

He said: It is the root of the tree. The letter *Shin* is like the root of a tree.[128]

119. What is this tree that you mentioned?

He said: It represents the Powers of the Blessed Holy One, one above the other.

Just like a tree brings forth fruit through water, so the Blessed Holy One increases the Powers of the Tree through water.

What is the water of the Blessed Holy One?

It is wisdom. It is the souls of the righteous. They fly from the fountain to the great pipe, ascend and attach themselves to the Tree.

Through what do they fly?

Through Israel. When they are good and righteous, the Divine Presence dwells among them. Their deeds then rest in the bosom of the Blessed Holy One, and He makes them fruitful and multiplies them.

120. How do we know that the Divine Presence is called *Tzedek* (Righteous)?

It is written *(Deuteronomy 33:26),* "He who rides in the heavens is your help, and His majesty is in the skies *(Shechakim)."* It is also written *(Isaiah 45:8),* "The skies *(Shechakim)* run with Righteousness *(Tzedek)."* [129]

Tzedek is the Divine Presence, as it is written *(Isaiah 1:21),* "Righteousness *(Tzedek)* dwells in it." [130]

Righteousness was given to David, as it is written *(Psalm 146.10),* "May God reign forever, your God O Zion, for generation to generation." It is also written *(I Chronicles 11:1)*, "Zion is the city of David."

121. What is the meaning of "generation to generation"?

Rabbi Papias said: "A generation goes and a generation comes *(Ecclesiastes 1:4)*."

Rabbi Akiba said: "The generation came" — it already came.[131]

122. What is this like? A king had slaves, and he dressed them with garments of silk and satin according to his ability. The relationship broke down, and he cast them out, repelled them, and took his garments away from them. They then went on their own way.

The king took the garments, and washed them well until there was not a single spot on them. He placed them with his storekeepers, bought other slaves, and dressed them with the same garments. He did not know whether or not the slaves were good, but they were [at least] worthy of garments that he already had and which had been previously worn.

[The verse continues] *(Ecclesiastes 1:4)*, "But the earth stands forever." This is the same as *(Ecclesiastes 12:6)*, "The dust returns to the earth as it was, but the spirit returns to God who gave it."

123. Rabbi Amorai said:

What is the meaning of the verse *(Leviticus 9:22)*, "And Aaron raised up his hands to bless the people, and he blessed them and he descended [from making the sin offering, the burnt offering, and the peace offerings]."

Did he not already descend? But he descended "from making the sin offering, the burnt offering, and the peace offerings," and then "Aaron raised up his hands to bless the people."

What is the meaning of this raising [of hands]?

It was because he had offered a sacrifice and brought them before their Father in heaven, as we have said.[132] Those who offer sacrifice must elevate them, [and those who] unify them [must] unify them among these.

And what are they? The people, as it is written "to the people." [This means] ? "for the sake of the people."

124. Why are the hands lifted when they are blessed in this manner?

It is because the hands have ten fingers, alluding to the Ten *Sefirot* with which heaven and earth were sealed.[133]

These parallel the Ten Commandments.

In these Ten are included the 613 Commandments. If you count the letters in the Ten Commandments, you will find that there are 613 letters.[134]

They contain all 22 letters except *Tet,* which is missing in them.

What is the reason for this? This teaches us that *Tet* is the belly — and it is not included among the Sefirot.[134a]

125. Why are they called *Sephirot*?

Because it is written *(Psalm 19:2),* "The heavens declare *(me-SaPRim)* the glory of God." [135]

126. And what are they?

They are three. Among them are three troops and three dominions.

The first dominion is light. Light is the life of water.

The second dominion includes the holy Chayot, the Ophanim, the wheels of the Chariot, and all the troops of the Blessed Holy One. They bless, exalt, glorify, praise and sanctify the mighty King with the *Kedushah.*[136] Arranged in the mystery of the great *Kedushah* is the fearsome and terrible King. And they crown Him with three "holies."

127. Why are there three "holies" and not four?

Because the holiness on high is three by three. It is thus written, "God is King, God was King, God will be King forever and ever." [137]

It is also written *(Numbers 6:24–26),* "May God bless you . . . May God shine upon you . . . May God lift. . . ." [138]

It is furthermore written *(Exodus 34:6),* "God *(YHVH),* God *(YHVH),*" The third one includes the rest of God's Attributes.

What are they? [As the verse continues], "God, merciful and gracious" — the thirteen Attributes [of Mercy].[139]

128. [The *Kedushah* is the verse *(Isaiah 6:3),* "Holy holy

holy is the Lord of Hosts, the whole earth is filled with His glory."

What is the meaning of "holy holy holy"? [And why is it] followed by, "the Lord of Hosts, the whole earth is filled with His glory"?

The [first] "holy" is the highest Crown.[140]

The [second] "holy" is the Root of the Tree.[141]

The [third] "holy" is attached and unified in them all.

[This is followed by], "the Lord of Hosts, the whole earth is filled with His glory."

129. What is the "holy" that is attached and unified?

What is this like? A king had sons, who in turn also had sons. When the [grand]sons do his will, he mingles with them, supports, them, and satisfies them all. He gives [his sons] everything good, so that they should be able to satisfy their children. But when the [grand]children do not do his will, then he only gives the fathers as much as they need.[142]

130. What is the meaning of, "the whole earth is filled with His glory"?

This is the earth that was created on the first day. It is on high, filled with God's glory and paralleling the Land of Israel.

And what is [this glory]? It is Wisdom, as it is written *(Proverbs 3:35),* "The wise shall inherit glory."

It is furthermore written *(Ezekiel 3:12),* "Blessed is God's glory from His place."

131. What is "God's glory"?

What is this like? A king had a matron in his chamber, and all his troops delighted in her. She had sons, and each day they came to see the king and to bless him.

They asked him, "Where is our mother?" He replied, "You cannot see her now." They said, "Let her be blessed wherever she is."

132. What is the meaning of "from His place"? This indicates that none know his place.

This is like a royal princess who came from a far place. People did not know her origin, but they saw that she was a woman of valor, beautiful and refined in all her ways. They said, "She certainly originates from the side of light, for she illuminates the world through her deeds."

They asked her, "From where are you?" She replied, "From my place." They said, "If so, the people of your place are great. May you be blessed, and may your place be blessed."

133. Is this "glory of God" then not one of His hosts? Is it not inferior? Why then do they bless it?

But what is this like? A man had a beautiful garden. Outside the garden but close to it, he had a nice section of field. On this section, he planted a beautiful flower garden.

The first thing that he would water would be his garden. The water would spread over the entire garden. It would not reach the section of field however, since it was not attached, even though it was all one. He therefore opened a place for it and watered it separately.

134. Rabbi Rahumai said:

Glory *(Kavod)* and Heart *(Lev)* both have the same [numerical value, namely 32].[143]

They are both one, but Glory refers to its function on high, and Heart refers to its function below.

"God's glory" and the "heart of heaven" are therefore both identical.[144]

135. Rabbi Yochanan said:

What is the meaning of the verse *(Exodus 17:11)*, "And it was when Moses would raise his hands, Israel would prevail, and when he would lower his hands, Amalek would prevail."?

This teaches us that the whole world endures because of the Lifting of Hands.[145]

Why?

Because the name of the power given to Jacob is Israel.

Abraham, Isaac and Jacob were each given a particular Power. The counterpart of the attribute in which each one walked was given to him.

Abraham did deeds of kindness. He prepared food for everyone in his area and for all wayfarers. He acted kindly and went out to greet them, as it is written *(Genesis 18:2)*, "and he ran to greet them." Not only that, but *(Genesis 18:2)*, "He bowed to the earth." This was a complete act of kindness.

God therefore granted him the same measure and gave him the attribute of Kindness *(Chesed)*. It is thus written

(Micah 7:20), "You give truth to Jacob, kindness to Abraham, as You swore to our fathers from days of yore."

What is the meaning of "from days of yore"? This teaches us that if Abraham did not do deeds of kindness, then he would not have been worthy of the attribute of Truth. Jacob would then not have been worthy of the attribute of Truth.

In the merit through which Abraham was worthy of the attribute of Kindness, Isaac became worthy of the attribute of Terror. It is thus written *(Genesis 31:53),* "And Jacob swore by the Terror of his father Isaac."

Does anyone then swear in this manner, mentioning his belief in the Terror of his father? But up until that time, Jacob had not been given any power. He therefore swore by the power that was given to his father. It is for this reason that it is written, "And Jacob swore by the Terror of his father Isaac."

What is it?

It is Chaos. It emanates from evil and astounds people.[146]

And what is that? It is that regarding which it is written *(I Kings 18:38),* "And fire came down and it consumed the burnt offering, and the stones, and the earth, and it evaporated the water that was in the trench." It is also written *(Deuteronomy 4:24),* "The Lord your God is a consuming fire, a jealous God."

136. What is Kindness?

It is the Torah, as it is written *(Isaiah 55:1),* "Ho, let all who are thirsty come for water, let he without silver come, [stock up and eat — come, stock up wine and milk, without silver and without payment]." [147]

[Kindness is therefore] silver. It is thus written, "come, stock up and eat — come, stock up wine and milk, without silver and without payment." He fed you Torah and taught you, for you have already earned it through the merit of Abraham, who did deeds of kindness. Without silver, he would feed others, and without payment, he would give them wine and milk.

137. Why wine and milk? What does one have to do with the other?

But this teaches us that wine is Terror and milk is Kindness.

Why is wine mentioned first? Because it is closer to us.[148]

Do you then think that this refers to actual wine and milk? We must say that it is the Form of wine and milk.

Through the merit of Abraham, who was worthy of the attribute of Kindness, Isaac was worthy of the attribute of Terror. And because Isaac was worthy of the attribute of Terror, Jacob was worthy of the attribute of Truth, which is the attribute of Peace.[149]

God bestowed him according to his measure. It is thus written *(Genesis 25:27)*, "Jacob was a complete man, dwelling in tents." The word "complete" means nothing other than peace. It is thus written *(Deuteronomy 18:13)*, "You shall be complete with the Lord your God," and the Targum renders this, "You shall be at peace *(sh'lim)*."

The word "complete" refers to nothing other than the Torah. It is thus written *(Malachi 2:6)*, "A Torah of truth was in his mouth." What is written in the very next phrase? It states, "With peace and uprightness, he walked before Me." "Uprightness" is nothing other than peace, as it is written *(Psalm 25:21)*, "Complete and upright."

It is therefore written *(Exodus 17:11)*, "And it was when Moses would raise his hands, Israel would prevail." This teaches us that the Attribute that is called Israel has in it a "Torah of Truth."

138. What is the meaning of "a Torah of Truth?"

It is that which teaches *(Moreh)* the Truth of [all] worlds, as well as His deeds in thought.

He erected Ten Sayings, and with them the world stands.[150] It is one of them.

In man He created ten fingers, paralleling these Ten Sayings.[151]

Moses raised his hands and concentrated to some degree on the Attribute that is called Israel, which contains the Torah of Truth. With his ten fingers, he alluded that he was upholding the Ten. For if [God] would not help Israel, then the Ten Sayings would not endure every day. It was for this reason that "Israel prevailed."

[The verse continues], "And when he lowered his hands, Amalek prevailed." Would Moses then do anything that would cause Amalek to prevail? But [this teaches us] that it is forbidden for a person to stand for [more than] three hours with his hands spread out to heaven.

139. His disciples asked: To whom are the hands raised?

He replied: To the heights of heaven. How do we know this? It is written *(Habakkuk 3:10)*, "The deep gives forth its voice, it lifts up its hands on high." This teaches us that the Lifting of Hands is only to the heights of the heaven.

When among Israel there are people who are wise and know the mystery of the Glorious Name, and they lift up their hands, they are immediately answered.[152]

It is thus written *(Isaiah 58:9)*, "Then *(AZ)* you will call and God will answer." If you call God "then" *(AZ)*, He will answer you immediately.

140. What is the meaning of "then" [— *AZ* — spelled *Alef Zayin*]?

This teaches us that it is not permissible to call *Alef* alone. [It can] only [be called] through the two letters that are attached to it, which sit first in the kingdom.[153]

Together with the Alef, they are then three. Seven of the Ten Sayings then remain, and this is the *Zayin* [which has the numerical value of seven].

It is also written *(Exodus 15:1)*, "Then *(AZ)* sang Moses and the children of Israel."

141. What are the Ten Sayings?

The first is the Highest Crown. Blessed and praised be its name and its people.

Who are its people?

They are Israel. It is thus written *(Psalm 100:3)*, "Know that the Lord is God, He made us, and not *(Lo)* we, His people." [Lo is spelled *Lamed Alef* and can be read, "to *Alef*.] The verse then reads, "to *Alef* are we."

[It is our duty] to recognize and know the Unity of Unities, who is unified in all His names.

142. The second one is Wisdom.

It is thus written *(Proverbs 8:22)*, "God procured me, the beginning of His way, before His works, from then *(Az)* ." A "beginning" is nothing other than Wisdom, as it is written (Psalm 111:10), "The beginning is wisdom, the fear of God."[154]

143. The third one is the quarry of the Torah, the treasury of Wisdom, the quarry of the "spirit of God."[155]

This teaches us that God carved out all the letters of the Torah, engraved it with spirit, and with it made all Forms. This is the meaning of the verse *(1 Samuel 2:2),* "There is no Rock *(Tzur)* like our God" — there is no Former*(Tzayir)*like our God.

144. These are three. What is the fourth?

The fourth is *(Deuteronomy 33:21),* "the charity of God," His merit, and His Kindness *(Chesed)* to all the world. This is the Right Hand of the Blessed Holy One.

145. What is the fifth? [156]

The fifth is the great fire of the Blessed Holy One. Regarding this it is written *(Deuteronomy 18:16),* "Let me see the great fire no more, lest I die."

This is the Left Hand of the Blessed Holy One.

What are they? They are the holy Chayot and the holy Serafim, to their right and their left. They are the "pleasant ones"[157] which ascend higher and higher, as it is written *(Ecclesiastes 5:7),* "And ones higher than they." [158]

It is also written *(Ezekiel 1:18),* "And as for their height, they had height, and they had fear, and their height was filled with eyes, around the four." And around Him are angels. Those around them also bow down before them, kneeling and declaring, "The Lord He is God, the Lord He is God."[159]

146. The sixth one is the Throne of Glory, crowned, included, praised and hailed.[160]

It is the house of the World to Come, and its place is in Wisdom. It is thus written *(Genesis 1:3),* "And God said, 'Let there be light,' and there was light."

147. And Rabbi Yochanan said:

There were two [types of] light, as it is written, "[let there be light,] and there was light." Regarding both of them it is written *(Genesis 1:4),* "[And God saw the light] that it was good."

The Blessed Holy One took one [of these types of light] and stored it away for the righteous in the World to Come. Regarding this it is written *(Psalm 31:20),* "How great is the *good* that You have hidden away for those who fear You, that You have accomplished for those who find shelter in You . . ."

We learn that no creature could look at the first light. It is thus written *(Genesis 1:4)*, "And *God* saw the light that it was good."

It is furthermore written *(Genesis 1:21)*, "And God saw all that He made, and behold, it was very good." God saw all that He had made and saw shining, brilliant good.[161]

He took of that good, and included in it the 32 paths of Wisdom, giving it to this world. This is the meaning of the verse *(Proverbs 4:2)*, "I have given you a doctrine of *good*, My Torah, do not abandon it." We say that this is the treasury of the Oral Torah.[162]

The Blessed Holy One said, "This Attribute is considered to be included in this world, and it is the Oral Torah. If you keep this Attribute in this world, then you will be worthy of the World to Come, which is the good stored away for the righteous."

What is it?

It is the force of the Blessed Holy One. It is thus written *(Habakkuk 3:4)*, "And the glow will be like light, [He has rays from His hand, and His hidden *force* is there] ." The glow that was taken from the first Light will be like [our visable] light if His children keep the "Torah and Commandment that I wrote to teach them."[163] It is thus written *(Proverbs 1:8)*, "Hear my son, the admonition of your father, and do not abandon the Torah of your mother."

148. And it is written *(Habakkuk 3:4)*, "He has rays from His hand, and His hidden force is there."

What is "His hidden force"?

This is the light that was stored away and hidden, as it is written *(Psalm 31:20)*, "[How great is the good] that You have hidden away for those who fear You, [,that You have accomplished for those who find shelter in You]."

What remains for us is that which "You have accomplished for those who find shelter in You." These are the ones who find shelter in Your shadow in this world, who keep Your Torah, observe Your Commandments, and sanctify Your name, unifying it secretly and publicly. The verse thus concludes, "in the sight of the sons of man."

149. Rabbi Rahumai said:

This teaches us that Israel had light. Torah is light, as it is written *(Proverbs 6:23)*, "For a commandment is a lamp, Torah is light, [and the way of life is the rebuke of admonition]."

And we say that a lamp is a commandment, illumination *(Orah)* is the Oral Torah, and light *(Or)* is the Written Torah. [How can we then say that the Oral Torah is light *(Or)*?]

Because this light has already been kept, it is called light.

What is this like? A room was hidden at the end of a house. Even though it is day, and there is bright light in the world, one cannot see in this room unless he brings along a lamp.

The same is true of the Oral Torah. Even though it is a light, it needs the written Torah to answer its questions and explain its mysteries.

150. Rabbi Rahumai said:

What is the meaning of the verse *(Proverbs 6:23)*, "And the way of life is the rebuke of admonition"?

This teaches us that when a person accustoms himself to study the Mystery of Creation and the Mystery of the Chariot, it is impossible that he not stumble. It is therefore written *(Isaiah 3:6)*, "Let this stumbling be under your hand." This refers to things that a person cannot understand unless they cause him to stumble.

The Torah calls it "the rebuke of admonition," but actually it makes one worthy of "the way of life." One who wishes to be worthy of "the way of life" must therefore endure "the rebuke of admonition."

151. Another explanation:

"Life" is the Torah, as it is written *(Deuteronomy 30:19)*, "And you shall choose life." It is furthermore written *(Deuteronomy 30:20)*, "For it is your life and your length of days."

If one wants to be worthy of it, he should reject physical pleasure and accept the yoke of the commandments. If he is afflicted with suffering, he should accept it with love. He should not ask, "Since I am fulfilling the will of my Maker and am studying the Torah each day, why am I afflicted with suffering?" Rather, he should accept it with love.

Then he will be completely worthy of the "way of life."

For who knows the ways of the Blessed Holy One? Regarding all things, one must therefore say, "Righteous are You, O God, and Your judgment is fair.[164] All that is done from heaven is for the good." [165]

152. You said [that the sixth one was] His Throne. Have we then not said that it is the Crown of the Blessed Holy One? We have said, "Israel was crowned with three crowns, the crown of priesthood, the crown of royalty, and the crown of Torah above them all." [166]

What is this like? A king had a pleasing, beautiful vessel and he was very fond of it. Sometimes he placed it on his head — this is the *Tefillin* worn on the head. At other times he carried it on his arm — in the knot of the *Tefillin* worn on the arm. Sometimes he lends it to his son so that it should remain with him. [167]

Sometimes it is called His Throne. This is because He carries it as an amulet on His arm, just like a throne.

153. What is the seventh? It is the heaven [called] *Aravot*. [168]

And why is it called heaven *(Shamayim)*? Because it is round like a head. [169]

We learn that it is in the center, with water at its right and fire at its left. It supports water *(Sa Mayim)* from fire and water, and brings peace between them.

Fire comes and finds the attribute of fire on its side. Water comes and finds the attribute of water on its side. It is therefore written *(Job 25:2)*, "He makes peace in His high places." [170]

154. Is it then the seventh? Is it nothing more than the sixth. [171]

But this teaches us that the Holy Palace is here, and it supports them all. It is thus counted as two. [172] It is therefore the seventh.

And what is it?

It is Thought that does not have any end or boundary. This place likewise does not have any end or boundary.

155. The seventh one is the east of the world. It is from where the Seed of Israel comes.

The spinal cord originates in man's brain and extends to the [sexual] organ, where the seed is. It is therefore written *(Isaiah 43:5)*, "From the east I will bring your seed, [and from the west I will gather you]."

When Israel is good, then this is the place from which I will bring your seed, and new seed will be granted to you. But when

Israel is wicked, [then I will bring] seed that has already been in the world. It is thus written *(Ecclesiastes 1:4)*, "A generation goes and a generation comes," teaching us that it has already come.[173]

156. What is the meaning of the verse *(Isaiah 43:5)*, "And from the west I will gather you"?

[This means that "I will gather you"] from the attribute that always points to the west.

Why is [west] called *MaAReV*? Because it is there that all seed is mixed together *(MitAReV)*.

What is this like? A king's son had a beautiful bride and he hid her in his chamber. He took riches from his father's house and constantly brought it to her. She, in turn, took everything, constantly put it away, and mixed it all together. Ultimately he seeks to see what he had gathered and accumulated.

It is therefore written, "And from the west I will gather you."

And what is his father's house?

It is that regarding which it is written, "From the east I will bring your seed." This teaches us that it is brought from the east and sowed on the west. He then gathers what he has sowed.[174]

157. What is the eighth one?

The Blessed Holy One has a single Righteous One *(Tzadik)* in His world, and it is dear to Him because it supports all the world. It is the Foundation *(Yesod)*.[175]

This is what sustains it, and makes it grow, increasing and watching it. It is beloved and dear on high, and beloved and dear below; fearsome and mighty on high, and fearsome and mighty below; rectified and accepted on high, and rectified and accepted below.

It is the Foundation of all souls.

Do you then say that it is the eighth? And do you say that it is the Foundation of all souls? Is it then not written *(Exodus 31:17)*, "And on the seventh day He rested and souled"?[176]

Yes, it is the seventh. This is because it decides between them. There are six, and three are below and three above, and it decides between them.[177]

158. Why is it called the seventh? Is it then the seventh?
It is not. But it is because the Blessed Holy One rested on the Sabbath with the attribute regarding which it is written *(Exodus 31:17),* "For six days God made the heaven and the earth, and on the seventh day He rested and souled." This teaches us that each day has a Saying that is its Master.[178]

This is not because it was created on that day, but because that is when it does the task to which it was assigned. Each one does its task and maintains its activities.

The seventh day therefore comes and does its task, making them all rejoice. Not only that, but it also causes their souls to grow, as it is written, "on the seventh day He rested and souled."

159. What is this "rest"? It is the absence of work. It is a cessation which is called *Shabbat* (meaning rest).

What is this like? A king had seven gardens, and the middle one contained a fountain, welling up from a living source. Three [of his gardens] are at its right, and three are at its left. When it performed its function and overflowed, they all rejoiced, saying, "It overflowed for our sake." It waters them and makes them grow, while they wait and rest.

Do we then say that it waters the seven? But it is written *(Isaiah 43:5),* "From the east I will bring your seed." This indicates that one of [the seven] waters it.

We must therefore say that it waters the Heart, and the Heart then waters them all.

160. Rabbi Berachiah sat and expounded:
Each day we speak of the World to Come. Do we then understand what we are saying?

In Aramaic, the "World to Come" is translated "the world that came."

And what is the meaning of "the world that came"?

We learned that before the world was created, it arose in thought to create an intense light to illuminate it. He created an intense light over which no created thing could have authority.

The Blessed Holy One saw, however, that the world could not endure [this light]. He therefore took a seventh of it and left it in its place for them. The rest He put away for the righteous in the Ultimate Future.[179]

He said, "If they are worthy of this seventh and keep it, I will give them [the rest] in the Final World."

It is therefore called "the world that came," since it already came [into existence] from the six days of creation. Regarding this it is written *(Psalm 31:20),* "How great is Your good that You have hidden away for those who fear You."

161. What is the meaning of the verse *(Exodus 15:27),* "And they came to Elim, where there were twelve wells of water and seventy date palms, and they encamped there by the water?"

What is so special about seventy date palms? In one small place there can be a thousand.

But [this teaches us that] they were worthy of their counterpart. They are likened to date palms.

It is written *(Exodus 15:23),* "And they came to Marah, and they could not drink of the waters of Marah, for they were bitter *(marah)."* This teaches us that the north wind confused them. It is thus written *(Exodus 15:25),* "And he cried out to God, and He showed him a tree. He cast it into the waters, and the waters became sweet."

God immediately placed His hand against the Satan and diminished him. It is thus written *(Exodus 15:25),* "There He gave them a decree and a law, and there He proved them."

This teaches us that at this time, the Satan attached himself to them in order to blot them out from the world. It is thus written *(Exodus 15:24),* "And the people complained to Moses saying, 'What shall we drink?'" [The Satan] continued to denounce Moses until he cried out to God and was answered.

What is the meaning of the verse, "And He showed him a tree"? This teaches us that the Tree of Life was near the water. The Satan came and removed it in order to denounce Israel and cause them to sin against their Father in heaven.

[The Satan] said to them, "Are you now then going into the desert? Even now [you have nothing] other than bitter water, but this has some benefit, since you can make some use of it. But when you enter the desert, you will not even find [water] with which to wash your hands and face. You will die from hunger and thirst, naked and having nothing."

The people came to Moses and repeated these words, but he put them off. When [the Satan] saw that he could not overcome them, he strengthened himself [to overcome] Israel and Moses.

The people came, and "they complained to Moses." They
said, "Even here we lack water. What will we drink in the
desert?"

The Satan had falsified the situation in order to cause the
people to sin. As soon as Moses saw the Satan, "He cried out to
God, and He showed him a tree." This is the Tree of Life that
the Satan had removed. He then "cast it into the water, and the
water became sweet."

The Blessed Holy One then gave the Satan a "decree and a
law," and it was there that He "proved" Israel. The Blessed
Holy One warned Israel saying *(Exodus 15:26)*, "If you listen to
the voice of the Lord your God, [and do what is upright in His
eyes, give ear to His commandments, and keep all His decrees,
then all the sickness that I brought upon the Egyptians, I will
not bring upon you, for I am God who heals you]."

162. What is this like? A king had a beautiful daughter,
and others desired her. The king knew about it, but could not
fight those who wanted to bring his daughter to evil ways. He
came to his house and warned her, saying, "My daughter, do
not pay attention to the words of these enemies and they will
not be able to overcome you. Do not leave the house, but do all
your work at home. Do not sit idle, even for a single moment.
Then, they will not be able to see you and harm you."

They have one Attribute which causes them to leave aside
every good way and choose every evil way. When they see a
person directing himself along a good way, they hate him.

What is [this Attribute]? It is the Satan.

This teaches us that the Blessed Holy One has an Attribute whose name is Evil. It is to the north of the Blessed Holy
One, as it is written *(Jeremiah 1:14)*, "From the north will Evil
come forth, upon all the inhabitants of the earth." Any evil that
comes to "all the inhabitants of the earth" comes from the
north.[180]

163. What is this One Attribute?

It is the Form of a Hand.

It has many messengers, and the name of them all is Evil
Evil.[181] Some of them are great, and some are small, but they
all bring guilt to the world.

This is because Chaos is toward the north. Chaos *(Tohu)* is
nothing other than Evil. It confounds *(Taha)* the world and

causes people to sin.[182]

Every Evil Urge *(Yetzer HaRa)* that exists in man comes from there.

And why is it placed to the left? This is because it does not have any authority any place in the world except in the north.

It is not accustomed to be anywhere except in the north. It does not want to be any place but in the north. If it remained in the south until it learned the routes of the south, how could it lead others astray? It would have to stay there for [several] days until it learned, and then it could not cause people to sin. It therefore is always in the north, to the left.

This is the meaning of the verse *(Genesis 8:21)*, "For the Urge of man's heart is evil from his youth." It is evil from his youth, and it does not incline [in any direction] other than the left, for it is already accustomed to be there.

It is regarding this that the Blessed Holy One said to Israel *(Exodus 15:26)*, "If you listen to the voice of the Lord your God, and do what is upright in His eyes, and give ear to His commandments" — and not to the commandments of the Evil Urge — and keep all His decrees" — and not the decrees of the Evil Urge — "[then all the sickness that I brought upon the Egyptians, I will not bring upon you,] for I am God who heals you."

164. What does the Evil Urge gain?

What is this like? A king appointed clerks over the lands of his kingdom, over his work and over his merchandise. Each and every thing had its clerk.

There was one clerk in charge of the storehouse containing good food. Another was in charge of the storehouse containing stones. Everyone came to the storehouse containing good food. The clerk in charge of the storehouse of stones came and saw that people were only buying from the other [clerk].

What did he do? He sent his messengers to tear down the weak houses [so that people would need stones to rebuild them]. They could not do so, however, to the strong ones. He said, "In the time that it takes to tear down one strong [house], you can tear down ten weak ones. People will then all come and buy stones from me, and I will not be inferior to the other."

It is thus written *(Jeremiah 1:14)*, "From the north will evil come forth, upon all the inhabitants of the earth." The verse then continues *(Jeremiah 1:15)*, "For I call all the families of the kingdom of the north — says God — and they will come, and each one will place his throne at the opening of the gates of Jerusalem . . ." Evil will be their business, and the Evil Urge will also constantly strive.

The word *Satan* means "turning aside," since he turns all the world aside to the balance of guilt.

How is this indicated? It is written *(Genesis 38:16)*, "And he turned aside to her," and the Targum renders this *VeSata*, [*Satah* being the root of Satan]. It is likewise written *(Proverbs 4:15)*, "Turn aside *(S'teh)* from it and pass on."

165. What is the significance of the "seventy date palms"?

They had accepted upon themselves the commandments, as it is written *(Exodus 15:26)*, "If you listen to the voice of the Lord your God." Immediately after this we find *(Exodus 15:27)*, "And they came to Elim *(Elimah)* [where there were twelve wells of water and seventy date palms]."

What is the meaning of *Elimah*? It is *Eli Mah* — "to me is what." [183]

"Where there were twelve wells of water." At first God gave it to them as wells, and in the end, he gave it back to them as stones. It is thus written [regarding the stones set up near the Jordan] *(Joshua 4:9)*, "twelve stones."

What is the reason? It is because the Torah was originally likened to water in the world. Only later was it put in a permanent place. Water, however, is here one day and elsewhere the next.

166. What are the seventy date palms?

This teaches us that the Blessed Holy One has seventy Structures.[184]

These draw from the twelve Simple Ones.[185] Just like water is simple, so are these simple.

How do we know that the date palm is a Structure? Because it is written *(Song of Songs 7:8)*, "Your structure is like a date palm."

Besides that, there are seventy kinds of date palms. It is therefore written that there were seventy date palms. One was not like the other, their functions were all different, and the taste of one was not like the taste of the other.

167. You said that the seventy date palms represent the seventy Structures. But have you not said that there are 72?

There are 71. Israel makes 72, but it is not included.

But did you not say that there were seventy?

One is the Officer of the Satan.

What is this like? A king had sons and bought slaves for them. The king then told his sons, "I am giving you all equally."

One of them replied, "I do not want to be with you, for I have the power to steal everything from you."

The king then said, "Because of this, you will not have a portion among them at all."

[The rebellious son] did what he could. He went out and lay in wait for [the slaves], showing them much gold, jewels and troops. He said, "Come over to me."

What did the king do? He amassed his armies together with the armies of all his sons. He showed them to the slaves and said, "Do not let him trick you into thinking that his armies are stronger than mine. Behold the troops of that son. He is deceitful and wants to rob you. Therefore, do not listen to him, for at first he will speak smoothly in order to entice you into his trap, but in the end he will laugh at you. You are my slaves, and I will do for you everything good if you turn away from him and do not listen to him."

He is the Prince of Chaos. It is thus written *(I Samuel 12:21)*, "Do not turn aside, for you will follow Chaos. It will not help or save, for it is Chaos." [It cannot help or save,] but it can do harm.

The advice that I give you is that you should *(Exodus 15:26)*, "Listen to the voice of the Lord your God, do what is right in His eyes, and give ear to His commandments, and keep all His decrees."

When you keep all His decrees, then, "All the sickness that I brought upon the Egyptians, I will not bring upon you."

Why did He say all this? In order to close all doors, so that he should not find you soft at times and hard at times.

When you keep all His decrees, then "all the sickness that I brought upon the Egyptians" — through My hand — "I will not bring upon you."

What is the meaning of "for I am God who heals you"? This means that even when he comes and strikes, I am God who will heal you.

168. Why do you call it the eighth? [186]

Because with it the eight are begun, and with it the eight numbers are completed. In function, however, it is the seventh one.

And what are [the eight] that were begun? This is the fact that a child enters the Covenant of Circumcision when eight days old.

Are they then eight? They are nothing more than seven. Why then did the Blessed Holy One say eight? Because there are eight directions in man.

What are they? They are as follows:

> The right and left hands
> The right and left legs
> The head, the body,
>   and the Covenant as an arbitrator
> And his wife, who is his mate.

It is thus written *(Genesis 2:24)*, "And he shall cling to his wife, and they shall be one flesh."

These are the eight, and they parallel the eight days of circumcision.

Are they then eight? They are nothing more than seven, since the body and covenant are one. It is therefore eight.

169. What is the ninth?

He said to them: The ninth and tenth are together, one opposite the other.[187]

One is higher than the other by 500 years.[188]

They are like two Wheels *(Ofanim)*. One inclines toward the north, while the other inclines toward the west. They reach down to the lowest earth.

What is the lowest earth? It is the last of the seven earths down below.[189]

The end of the Divine Presence of the Blessed Holy One is under His feet. It is thus written *(Isaiah 66:1)*, "The heaven is My throne, and the earth is the hassock for My feet."

The Victory *(Nitzachon)* of the world is there. It is thus written *(Isaiah 34:10)*, "for Victory of Victories *(Netzach Netzachim)*." [190]

170. What is the meaning of "Victory of Victories"?

There is a single Victory *(Netzach)*. Which is it? It is the one that inclines toward the west.

And what is secondary to it? This is the one that inclines toward the north.[191]

And the third one? This is the one that is below.

The third one? But you have said that the Chariot has two wheels. We must therefore say that the end of the Divine Presence is also called Victory.

This is the meaning of "Victory of Victories." "Victory" is one, and "Victories" is two, giving [a total of] three.

171. His disciples said to him: From above to below we know. But from below to above we do not know.[192]

He replied: Is it not all one — below to above and above to below?

They said: Our master, ascending is not the same as descending. One can run while descending, but cannot do so while ascending.

He replied: Go out and see.

He sat and expounded to them:

There is a Divine Presence below, just like there is a Divine Presence above.[193]

What is this Divine Presence? We have said that it is the light that was derived from the first Light, which is Wisdom. It also surrounds all things, as it is written *(Isaiah 6:3),* "The whole earth is filled with His glory."

What is its function?

What is this like? A king had seven sons, and he assigned each one a place. He said to them, "Sit here, one above the other."

The lowest one said, "I will not sit at the bottom. I do not want to be far from you."

[The king] replied, "I will surround you and see you all day long."

This is the meaning of the verse, "The whole earth is filled with His glory."

Why is He among them? This is so that He should support them and sustain them.

172. And what are the sons?

I have already told you that the Blessed Holy One has seven Holy Forms.[194]

All of them have a counterpart in man, as it is written *(Genesis 9:6),* "for in the form of God He made man." It is likewise written *(Genesis 1:27),* "In the form of God He made him, male and female He made them."

This is what they are:

The right and left legs
The right and left hands
The body, covenant and head.

But these are only six. You have said that there are seven.

The seventh is with his wife. It is thus written *(Genesis 2:24),* "And they shall be one flesh."

But she was taken from his ribs, as it is written *(Genesis 2:21),* "And He took one of his ribs."

He said: Yes, from his ribs.

Does He then have a rib?

Yes. It is written *(Exodus 26:20),* "the ribs of the tabernacle." The Targum renders this, "the side of the tabernacle."

And what is His side?

What is this like? A king had an idea to plant ten male trees in a garden. All of them were date palms. He said, "Since they are all the same kind, it is impossible for them to endure."

What did he do? He planted an *Etrog*[195] among them. This was one of those which he had intended to be male.

And why is the *Etrog* female? Because it is written *(Leviticus* 23:40), "The fruit of a beautiful tree, fronds of a date palm, [branches of a tree of leaves, and willows of the brook]."

What is the fruit of a beautiful *(hadar)* tree?

The Targum renders this verse, "The fruit of the *Etrog* tree, and the *Lulav.*"

173. What is the meaning of "beautiful"? It is the beauty of all things.

This is also the beauty of the *Song of Songs.* Regarding it, it is written *(Song of Songs 6:10),* "Who is she who looks forth as the dawn, fair as the moon, clear as the sun, terrible like an army with banners?"

This relates to the Female.

Because of her, the female was taken from Adam. This is because it is impossible for the lower world to endure without the female.

And why is the female called *Nekevah?* Because her orifices *(Nekev)* are wide. Also because she has more orifices than the male. What are they? They are the orifices of the breasts, the womb, and the receptacle.

174. And what is the reason that you said that the *Song of Songs* is beautiful?

Yes, it is the most beautiful of all the Holy Scriptures.

Rabbi Yochanan thus said: All Scripture is holy, and all the Torah is holy, but the *Song of Songs* is Holy of Holies.[196]

What is the meaning of Holy of Holies? It means that it is holy for the Holy Ones.

What are the Holy Ones? They are the counterparts of the six directions that are in man.[197] That which is holy for them is holy for everything.

175. What is this that is Holy? It is the *Etrog*, which is the beauty *(hadar)* of them all.

Why is it called beautiful *(hadar)*? Do not read *hadar,* but *HaDar* — "which dwells." [198]

This refers to the *Etrog* which is not bound together with the *Lulav*. Without it, the commandment of the *Lulav* cannot be fulfilled.

It is also bound with them all. It is with each one of them, and is unified with them all.

176. What does the *Lulav* parallel? It is the counterpart of the spinal cord.[199]

It is thus written *(Leviticus 23:40),* "[fronds of a date palm,] a branch of a tree of leaves, and willows of the brook."

The [leafy] branches [of the myrtle] must cover the majority [of the bunch]. If its branches do not cover its majority, it is invalid.

Why?

What is this like? A man has arms, and with them he protects his head. He has two arms, and his head makes three.

[It is therefore called] "a branch of a tree of leaves." A "branch" is to the left, and the "leaves" are to the right. It then comes out that the "tree" is in the center.[200]

And why is it called a "tree"? Because it is the Root of the Tree.[201]

177. What are "willows of the brook"? There are two [willow branches in the *Lulav,*] and these parallel the two legs in man.[202]

Why are the ["willows of the brook"] called *Arvey Nachal*?
Because the greater of the two is inclined toward the west
(ma-Arev) and draws its strength from there.

The one to the north is smaller than it by a journey of 500
years. It is on the northwest side, through which it functions.
It is named after it, since they are both mixed *(Arav)*.[203]

178. Another explanation:

[Willows of the Brook] are called *Arvey Nachal* because the
function of one is sometimes mixed *(ma-arav)* with that of the
other.

Why are they called Willows of the *Brook*? This is because
of the place in which they are fixed, which is called Brook. It is
thus written *(Ecclesiastes 1:7)*, "All the Brooks go to the sea,
but the sea is not filled."

What is this sea? We say that it is the *Etrog*.

How do we know that each of the seven Attributes is called
a Brook *(Nachal)*? Because it is written *(Numbers 21:19)*,
"From to Nachaliel, [from Nachaliel to Bamot, and from Bamot
to the valley that is in the Field of Moab, the head of the cliff,
and it looks down on the face of the Yeshimon]." Do not read
Nachaliel, but *Nachley El* — Brooks of God.

And all six then go on one path to the sea.

What is this path? It is the one that arbitrates between
them. It is thus written *(Habakkuk 3:5)*, "Before Him goes the
pestilence, and fiery bolts at His feet."

All of them go to that pipe, and from that pipe to the sea.[204]

This is the meaning of the verse, "From Gift to Brooks of
God." [Gift] is the place that is given, namely the brain. From
there they go to the Brooks of God.

"And from Brooks of God to Bamot." What is Bamot? As
the Targum renders it, *Ramta* — "heights." This is the *Segol*
that follows the *Zarka*.[205]

[The verse continues,] "And from Bamot to the valley that is
in the Field of Moab, the head of the cliff, and it looks down on
the face of the Yeshimon."

"And from the heights *(Bamot)* to the valley that is in the
Field of Moab." This is that which is prepared. And what is that
which was in the Field of Moab? Do not read Moab, but *May-av*
— "from a father." This is the father regarding which it is
written *(Genesis 26:5)*, "Because Abraham hearkened to My
voice, kept My trust, My commandments and My decrees . . ."

What is this field? It is the one that is at "the head of the cliff," and which also "looks down on the face of the Yeshimon." [Yeshimon] is interpreted to mean Heaven.[206]

Regarding that pipe, it is written *(Song of Songs 4:15)*, "A fountain of gardens, a well of living waters, flowing from Lebanon."

What is Lebanon? We say that this is Wisdom.[207]

What are the Willows of the Brook *(Nachal)*? We say that this is that which gives inheritance *(Nachalah)* to Israel. It refers to the two Wheels of the Chariot.[208]

179. We learned that there are Ten Spheres and Ten Sayings.[209]

Each Sphere has its Saying. It is not surrounded by it, but rather, it surrounds it.

This [physical] world is like a mustard seed inside a ring.

Why? Because of the Spirit that blows upon it, through which it is sustained. If this spirit were to be interrupted for even a moment, the world would be annihilated.

180. There are three Spheres in this world.[210]

How? This world inclines to the north and the south.

How? North west south. North west is the first sphere that revolves around us.

Do we then say that it is to the northwest? But we say that its strength is to the north. This is the left foot.

Above it is the second Sphere, which is entirely to the west.

Do we then say that it is to the west? But we say that its power is to the west. These are the Victories of the world.

Above it is the third Sphere, and its power is to the southwest.

What is the original power that you said was second? We say that this is the right foot.

And what is the power that is to the southwest? This is the Foundation of the world. Regarding this it is written *(Proverbs 10:25)*, "The Righteous is the Foundation of the world."

The second power stands behind the Chariot, while the first power stands in front of it.

The "Righteous, Foundation of the world" is in the center. It emanates from the south of the world, and is officer over the other two.

In its hand are also the souls of all living things. It is the Life of Worlds.

Whenever the word "creation" *(Beriah)* is used, it is done with it. Regarding it it is written *(Exodus 31:17),* "He rested and souled." [211]

This is the attribute of the Sabbath day. Regarding this it is written *(Exodus 20:8),* "Remember the Sabbath day and keep it holy."

But it is also written *(Deuteronomy 5:12),* "Keep [the Sabbath]." This is speaking of the seventh attribute. Regarding this seventh attribute it is written *(Leviticus 19:30),* "My sabbaths you shall *keep,* and My sanctuary you shall fear."

What is the seventh attribute? This is the Blessed Holy One's attribute of Goodness.

181. Why is it written, "My sabbaths you shall keep," [in the plural] rather than "My sabbath" [in the singular]?

What is this like? A king had a beautiful bride, and every week she would set aside a day to be with him. The king also had beautiful beloved sons. He said to them, "Since this is the situation, you should also rejoice on the day of my joy. For it is for your sake that I strive, and you also respect me."

182. What is the reason that [the Torah says] "remember" [in one place,] and "keep" [regarding the Sabbath in another]?

"Remember" *(zachor)* refers to the male *(Zachar).* "Keep" *(shamor)* refers to the bride.[212]

Why is it connected to, "and My sanctuary you shall fear"? This is because My sanctuary is holy. Why? "Because I am God who makes you holy" — from every side.[213]

183. Why do we say [in the blessing after food], "On all that He created . . . [Blessed] is the Life of Worlds." Why do we not say, "On all that You created"?

But we bless the Holy One, who grants His wisdom to this "Life of Worlds." It then provides for all.

184. What is the reason that we say [in blessings, "Blessed are you . . .] who made us holy with *His* commandments and commanded us" [in the third person]? Why do we not say, "that You made us holy with Your commandments, and You commanded us," [in the second person]?

This teaches us that all commandments are included in the Life of Worlds.

Because of His love for us, He gave us [the commandments] in order that they should make us holy and allow us to be worthy. Why? Because when we are in this world, we can become worthy of the World to Come, which is great.

In its hand is the treasury of souls. When Israel is good, these souls are worthy of emerging and coming to this world. But if they are not good, then [these souls] do not emerge.

We therefore say, "The Son of David will not come until all the souls in the Body are completed." [214]

What is the meaning of "all the souls in the Body"? We say that this refers to all the souls in man's body. [When these are completed] new ones will be worthy of emerging.

The Son of David (the Messiah) will then come. He will be able to be born, since his soul will emerge among the other new souls.

What is this like? A king had an army, and he sent them much bread to eat. They were so lazy that they did not take care of [the bread] which they did not eat [immediately]. The bread therefore became mouldy and went to waste.

The king investigated to find out if they had what to eat, and to see if they had eaten what he had sent them. He found that the bread had become mouldy and they were ashamed to ask for new bread. How could they tell the king, "We did not take care of [what you sent us,] but now we are asking for more"?

The king also became angry. He took the mouldy bread and ordered that it be dried and rectified as much as possible. He swore to the men, "I will not give you any more bread until you eat all this mouldy bread." He then returned the bread to them.

What did they do? They agreed to divide it up, and each one took his portion. The diligent one took his portion and placed it in the air, taking care of it and keeping it in good condition to eat. The other one took it and ate it lustfully. He ate what he could and laid the rest aside, not taking care of it since he had given up on it. It spoiled even more and became so mouldy that he could not eat it at all. He therefore starved to death.

He was then blamed for the sin of his body: Why did you kill yourself? Is it not enough that you ruined the bread the

first time? But I returned it to you and you ruined it [again].
You ruined your portion because you were too lazy to take care
of it. And not only that, but you also killed yourself.

[The soldier] replied, "My lord, what could I have done?"

He answered, "You should have taken care of it. And if you
claim that you were not able to, you should have watched your
friends and neighbors with whom you shared the bread. You
should have seen what they did and how they took care of it,
and you should have kept it like they did."

They also interrogated him: Why did you kill yourself? Is it
not enough that you ruined the bread? But you also went ahead
and killed the matter of your body. You shortened the days of
your life, or [at least] caused it. It may have been possible that
you would have had a good son. He could have saved you, and
[rectified] the damage that you and others did. Your suffering
will therefore be increased on all sides.

He became confused and replied, "What could I have done
when I did not have any bread? With what could I have sustained myself?"

They answered: If you would have strived and worked in
Torah, you would not reply foolishly and brazenly like this.
Because of your reply, it is obvious that you have not worked or
strived in Torah. It is thus written (Deuteronomy 8:3), "For not
by bread alone does man live, but from all that emanates from
God's mouth does man live." You should have searched and
probed and asked, "What is it through which man lives?"

What is this which "emanates from God's mouth"

From here they said, "An ignoramus cannot be pious." [215]

If a person does not act with kindness (Chesed) toward
himself, he cannot be called pious (Chasid.)

185. How can one do kindness to his Master?

By studying Torah. All study of Torah is a deed of kindness
toward one's Master. It is thus written (Deuteronomy 33:26),
"He rides the heavens with your help, [His pride is in the
skies]." God says, "When you study Torah for its own sake, then
you help Me and I can ride the heavens."

Then, "His pride is in the skies (Shechakim)."

What is Shechakim ? We say that it is in the innermost
chamber. The Targum thus renders it, "His word is in the
Heaven of Heaven."

Therefore, "not by bread alone does man live, but from all

that emanages from God's mouth does man life."

However, "the fool answers brazenly." [216]

"Abandon this brazenness, and do not reply in this manner!"

He is therefore punished. What is his punishment? We have already discussed it.[217]

186. What is the meaning of the verse *(Job 15:2),* "Should a wise man answer knowledge of spirit?" What is "knowledge of spirit"?

This is the Knowledge that is close to the spirit. Regarding this it is written *(Isaiah 11:2),* "And there will rest upon him a spirit of God, a spirit of wisdom and understanding, [a spirit of counsel and strength, a spirit of knowledge and the fear of God]."

[First comes] Wisdom, and then comes Understanding. And in Understanding is "counsel, strength, knowledge and the fear of God."

But you told us that "counsel" is deeds of Kindness, and that Understanding is the Attribute of Justice.

[One is above the other.][218]

Knowledge is Truth. Knowledge is therefore that with which one recognizes the truth.

"The fear of God " is the Treasury of the Torah.[219]

This is like I say, but one is above the other.[220]

Rabbi Akiba thus said: With whatever God created, He created its counterpart. It is thus written (Ecclesiastes 7:14), "Also one opposite the other has God made."[221]

What is the Treasury of the Torah? It is that regarding which it is written *(Isaiah 33:6),* "The fear of God is His treasury." A person must first be god-fearing, and then he can study Torah.

This is like a person who comes to buy date honey but does not bring a vessel in which to carry it. He says, "I will carry it in my bosom." He tries to carry it in his bosom but it was very heavy, and he is also afraid that it will tear and soil his clothing. He therefore throws it away on the road.

This person is then punished twice. First because he ruined good food, and second because he wasted his money.

187. The fear of God is the one that is higher.

It is in the palm of God's hand. It is also His Force.[222]

This palm *(kaf)* is called the pan of merit *(Kaf Zechut)*. This is because it inclines the world to the pan of merit.

It is thus written *(Isaiah 11:3)*, "I will grant him a spirit of the fear of God, and he will not judge by the sight of his eyes, he will not admonish according to what his ear hears." He will incline all the world to the pan of merit. From there counsel emanates, and from there health emanates to the world.²²³

[It is also written,] *(Genesis 49:24)*, "From there is the Shepherd, the Stone of Israel."²²⁴ This is the place that is called "There." Regarding this, it is written *(Habakkuk 3:4)*, "[He has rays from His hand,] and His hidden Force is *there."*

188. Once this thing comes, sharpen it. What is its sharpening? Tell us the meaning of the verse, "He has rays from His hand."

Why does it first say "rays" and then "His hand"? It should have said "His hands" [in the plural].

This is no contradiction. This is very much like the verse *(Exodus 32:19)*, "And Moses' anger flared, and he threw the tablets from his hands." The way this is written, however, it would be read "His hand" [in the singular.].²²⁵

It is likewise written *(Exodus 17:12)*, "And his hands was faithful until the sun set." The verse says *Emunah* ("was faithful" — in the singular) and not *Emunot* ("were faithful" — in the plural).

They replied: Our master, we are pointing out a contradiction in order to receive an answer, and you are covering our eyes. Did you not teach us, master, that you must answer first things first and last things last?²²⁶

[He said:] And what have you then asked? [The meaning of,] "He has rays from His hand." By the divine service, I have just explained it to you with my words.

They were ashamed.

When he saw that they were ashamed, he said to them: Is it not true that [at first] there was water, and that fire emanated from it?²²⁷ Water therefore included fire.

And Master, what is the meaning of "rays"?

He replied: There are five rays. These are the five fingers on man's right hand.²²⁸

189. And master, you are the one who told us in Rabbi

Yochanan's name that there are only two "arms of the world."[229]

He replied: Yes. But here "rays" allude to the two rays that are below them.

And what are they?

He said: With the anger of your head.

And what is above?

He said: The fear of God.

190. And what is the fear of God?

It is the first light.

Rabbi [Meir] thus said: Why is it written *(Genesis 1:3)*, "And God said, 'let there be light,' and there was light"? Why does it not say, "and it was so"? [230]

But this teaches us that the light was very intense, so that no created thing could gaze upon it. God therefore stored it away for the righteous in the Ultimate Future.

This is the measure of all merchandise *(Sechorah)* in the world. It is also the power of the precious stones that are called *Socheret* and *Dar*.[231]

And upon what is the attribute of *Dar*?

This teaches us that God took a thousandth of its radiance, and from it He constructed a beautiful precious stone. In it He included all the commandments.

Abraham came, and He sought a power to give him. He gave him this precious stone, but he did not want it. He was worthy and took Kindness as his attribute, as it is written *(Micah 7:20)*, "Kindness to Abraham." [232]

Isaac came, and He sought a power, but He gave it to him and he did not want it. He was worthy and took the attribute of Strength, which is [called] Terror. It is thus written *(Genesis 31:53)*, "And Jacob swore by the Terror of Isaac his father."

Jacob came and wanted it, but it was not given to him. They said, "Since Abraham is above and Isaac is below him, you will be in the center and take all three."

What is the center?

It is peace, as it is written *(Micah 7:20)*, "You give Truth to Jacob." Truth is identical with Peace, as it is written *(Esther 9:30)*, "Words of Peace and Truth." It is likewise written *(II Kings 20:19)*, "For peace and truth will be in my days." [233]

This is the meaning of the verse *(Isaiah 58:14)*, "I will feed

you with the inheritance of Jacob your father." This is a complete inheritance *(Nachalah)*, comprising Kindness, Terror,
Truth and Peace.[234]

It is therefore written *(Psalm 118:22)*, "The stone despised
by the builders has become the chief cornerstone." This is the
Stone that was despised by Abraham and Isaac, the builders of
the world, and that then became the chief cornerstone.

191. And why did they despise it? Is it not written
(Genesis 26:5), "Because Abraham hearkened to My voice, and
kept My watch, My commandments, My decrees and My Torahs."

What is the meaning of "My watch"?

It refers to what the Attribute of Kindness said: As long as
Abraham was in the world, I did not have to do my job. Abraham stood there in my place and "kept my watch." It is my
task to bring merit to the world, and even when people are
guilty, I bring them merit. I also bring them back, directing
their hearts to do the will of their Father in heaven.

All this Abraham did, as it is written *(Genesis 21:33)*,
"And he planted a tamarisk in Beersheba, and he called there
in the name of the Lord, God of the world." He would share his
bread and water with all the people in the world, bringing them
merit. Seeking to convince them, he would say, "Whom then
are you serving? Serve the Lord, God of heaven and earth." He
would preach to them until they would repent.

How do we know that he would also bring merit to
those who were guilty?

It is written *(Genesis 18:17)*, "Shall I then cover from
Abraham what I am doing? Abraham is becoming a great,
mighty nation, and all the nations of the earth will be blessed
through him." [235]
[God said,] "I will give him merit. I know that he will seek
mercy for them and be worthy."

Is it then possible to say that the Blessed Holy One did not
know that they could be saved? But He told this [to Abraham]
to bring him merit. From here they said, "If one comes to purify
himself, they help him. If one comes to defile himself, they open
for him." [236]

What is the meaning of, "they open for him"? It refers to
those that are always open.[237]

192. [It is written that Abraham kept] *(Genesis 26:5)*, "My commandments, My decrees, and My Torahs." He said, "Since I do not want [the precious stone], I will keep all the commandments that are included in it." [238]

What is the meaning of "My Torahs"? This teaches us that he knew and kept even the decisions *(Horah)* and discussions that are taught on high.

193. And what is the meaning of the verse *(Genesis 49:24)*, "From there is the Shepherd, the Rock of Israel."

From "There" is nourished the Rock of Israel.[239]

What is the meaning of "from There"? We say that this is the Supernal Righteous One *(Tzadik)*.[240]

What is it?

It is [the precious stone called] *Socheret*. And the stone that is below it is called *Dar*.

And what are the rays mentioned in the verse *(Habakkuk 3:4)*, "He has rays from His hand"?

These are the five fingers of the right hand.[241]

194. Rabbi Rahumai said:

This I received [from the tradition]. When Moses wanted to know about the glorious fearsome Name, may it be blessed, he said *(Exodus 33:18)*, "Show me please Your glory." He wanted to know why there are righteous who have good, righteous who have evil, wicked who have good, and wicked who have evil. But they would not tell him.

Do you then think that they did not tell him? Can one then imagine that Moses did not know this mystery? But this is what Moses said: "I know the ways of the Powers, but I do not know how Thought spreads through them. I know that Truth is in Thought, but I do not know its parts." He wanted to know, but they would not tell him.

195. Why is there a righteous person who has good, and [another] righteous person who has evil?

This is because the [second] righteous person was wicked previously, and is now being punished.

Is one then punished for his childhood deeds? Did not Rabbi Simon say that in the Tribunal on high, no punishment is meted out until one is twenty years or older.[242]

He said: I am not speaking of his present lifetime. I am

speaking about what he has already been, previously.

His colleagues said to him: How long will you conceal your words?

He replied: Go out and see. What is this like? A person planted a vineyard and hoped to grow grapes, but instead, sour grapes grew. He saw that his planting and harvest were not successful so he tore it out. He cleaned out the sour grape vines and planted again. When he saw that his planting was not successful, he tore it up and planted it again.

How many times?

He said to them: For a thousand generations. It is thus written *(Psalm 105:8)*, "The word that He commanded for a thousand generations.

It is in relation to this that they said, "Lacking were 974 generations. The Blessed Holy One stood up and planted them in each generation." [243]

196. Rabbah said: If the righteous wanted, they could create a world.[244] What interferes? Your sins, as it is written *(Isaiah 59:2)*, "Only your sins separate between you and your God." Therefore, if not for your sins, there would not be any differentiation between you and Him.

We thus see that Rabba created a man and sent it to Rav Zeira. He spoke to it, but it would not reply. But if not for your sins, it would also have been able to reply.

And from what would it have replied? From its soul.

Does a man then have a soul to place in it?

Yes, as it is written *(Genesis 2:7)*, "And He blew in his nostrils a soul of life." If not for your sins, man would therefore have a "soul of life." [Because of your sins, however] the soul is not pure.

This is the difference between you and Him. It is thus written *(Psalm 8:6)*, "And You have made him a little less than God."

What is the meaning of "a little"? This is because [man] sins, while the Blessed Holy One does not. Blessed be He and blessed be His Name for ever and ever, He has no sins.

But the [Evil] Urge comes from Him.

Can we then imagine that it comes from Him? But it originated from Him until David came and killed it. It is thus written *(Psalm 109:22)*, "My heart is hollow within me."

David said: Because I was able to overcome it *(Psalm 5:5)*, "Evil will not sojourn with You."

How was David able to overcome it? Through his study, since he never stopped [studying] day or night. He therefore attached the Torah on high. For whenever a person studies Torah for its own sake, the Torah attaches itself to the Blessed Holy One.

They therefore say, "A person should always study Torah, even not for its sake, since if [he studies it] not for its sake, he will eventually come to [study it] for its sake." [245]

What is this Torah that you are discussing?

It is the Bride who is adorned and crowned, and who is included in the commandments. It is the Treasury of the Torah. It is the betrothed of the Blessed Holy One, as it is written *(Deuteronomy 33:4)*, "Moses commanded us the Torah, the heritage *(Morasha)* of the congregation of Jacob." Do not read "heritage" *(Morasha)* but "betrothed" *(Me'urasa)*.

How is this so? When Israel engages in the Torah for its own sake, then it is the betrothed of the Blessed Holy One, then it is the heritage of Israel.

197. Rabbi Amorai sat and expounded:

Why was Tamar worthy of being the mother of Peretz and Zerach? [246]

It was because her name was Tamar. Tamar was [also] the sister of Amnon. She was therefore made for this.

Why were they called Peretz and Zerach?

Peretz was named after the moon. The moon breaks out *(paratz)* at times, and will be built up in the future. Zerach was named after the sun, which always shines *(zarach)* in the same manner.

But Peretz was the first-born. Is then the sun not greater than the moon?

This is no difficulty, as it is written *(Genesis 38:28)*, "One put out a hand," [indicating that Zerach's hand emerged before Peretz was born]. It is then written *(Genesis 38:30)*, "Then his brother, upon whose hand was the scarlet thread, emerged, and he was named Zerach."

[Zerach] was supposed to have been the first-born. But God saw that Solomon would descend [from Peretz], and He had such great joy that He made [Zerach] return.

198. Why was she called Tamar and not any other name? Because she was female.

Can we then say that [it was something special that] she was female?

But it is because she included both male and female. For [Tamar means a date palm, and] every date palm includes both male and female.[247]

How is this? The frond *(Lulav)* is male. The fruit is male on the outside and female on the inside.

And how? The seed of the date has a split like a woman. Paralleling it is the power of the moon above.

The Blessed Holy One created Adam male and female, as it is written *(Genesis 1:27)*, "Male and female He created them." Is it then possible to say this? Is it then not written *(Genesis 1:27)*, "And God created man in His image, in the image of God He created him"? It is only then later written *(Genesis 2:18)*, "I will make him a helper opposite him," and *(Genesis 2:21)*, "And He took one of his ribs, and closed the flesh under it." [We therefore see that the male was created first, and only later the female.]

But we must say that the Torah uses [three different words]: "formed" *(yatzar)*, "made" *(asah)*, and "created" *(bara)*.[248]

When the soul was made, the word "made" is used.[249] [The word "created" is then used:] "Male and female He *created* them." The word "formed" was used when the soul was combined with the body and the spirit was brought together.[250]

How do we know that "forming" means bringing together? For it is written *(Genesis 2:19)*, "And the Lord God formed (gathered) all the beasts of the field and all the flying things of the heaven, and He brought them to the Man to see what he would call each thing."

This explains the verse *(Genesis 5:2)*, "Male and female He created them." It is also written *(Genesis 1:28)*, "And God blessed them."

199. The soul of the female comes from the Female, and the soul of the male comes from the Male.

This is the reason why the Serpent followed Eve. He said, "Her soul comes from the north, and I will therefore quickly seduce her." [251]

And how did he seduce her? He had intercourse with her.

200. His disciples asked: Tell us how this took place.

He replied: The wicked Samael made a bond with all the host on high against his Master. This was because the Blessed Holy One said [regarding man] *(Genesis 1:26)*, "And let him rule over the fish of the sea and the flying things of the heaven." [252]

[Samael] said, "How can we cause him to sin and be exiled from before God?" He descended with all his host, and sought a suitable companion on earth. He finally found the serpent, which looked like a camel, and he rode on it.

He then went to the woman and said to her *(Genesis 3:1)*, "Did God also say, from all the trees of the garden [you shall not eat]?" [He said, "I know that He did not forbid all the trees,] but I will seek more — I will add in order that she should subtract."

She replied, "He did not stop us from anything besides *(Genesis 3:2)*, "the fruit of the tree that is in the middle of the garden. God said, 'Do not eat from it and do not touch it, lest you die.' "

She had added two things. She said, "from the *fruit* of the tree that is in the middle of the garden," while [God] had only said *(Genesis 2:17)*, "from the Tree of Knowledge." She also said, "do not touch it lest you die," [while God had only spoken of eating it].

What did Samael do? He went and touched the tree. The tree cried out and said, "Wicked one, do not touch me!" It is thus written *(Psalm 36:12)*, "Let not a foot of pride overtake me, and let not the hand of the wicked move me. There have the workers of iniquity fallen — they are thrust down, they cannot rise."

He then said to the woman, "See, I touched the tree and I did not die. You can also touch it and not die."

The woman went and touched the tree. She saw the Angel of Death approaching her and said, "Woe is to me. Now I will die and the Blessed Holy One will make another woman and give her to Adam. I will therefore cause him to eat with me. If we die, we will both die, and if we live, we will both live."

She took the fruit of the tree and ate it, and she also gave some to her husband. Their eyes were opened and their teeth were set on edge. He said, "What is this that you have given me to eat? Just as my teeth were set on edge, so will the teeth of all [future] generations be set on edge."

[God then] sat down in true judgment, as it is written *(Psalm 9:5)*, "[You have upheld my cause, You have sat on the throne as a] righteous Judge." He called to Adam and said, "Why do you flee from Me?"

[Adam] replied *(Genesis 3:10)*, " 'I heard Your voice in the garden' — and my bones trembled. 'I was afraid because I was naked, and I hid.' I was naked of works, I was naked of commandments, and I was naked of deeds." It is therefore written, "because I was naked, and I hid."

What was Adam's garment? It was a skin of fingernail. As soon as he ate from the fruit of the tree, this skin of fingernail was removed from him, and he saw himself naked. It is thus written *(Genesis 3:11)*, "Who told you that you were naked? [Did you eat from the tree that I commanded you not to eat from it?]"

Adam said to the Blessed Holy One, "Master of all worlds: When I was alone, did I ever sin before You? But the woman that You placed with me enticed me from your word." It is thus written *(Genesis 3:12)*, "The woman that you placed with me [gave it to me, and I ate]."

The Blessed Holy One said to her, "Is it not enough that you sinned? But you also caused Adam to sin."

She replied to Him, "Master of all worlds: The serpent enticed me to sin before You."

[God] took the three of them, and decreed upon them a sentence of nine curses and death.

He then cast the wicked Samael and his group from their holy place in heaven. He cut off the feet of the serpent and cursed it more than all the other animals and beasts of the field. He also decreed that it must shed its skin every seven years.

Samael was punished and made the guardian angel over the wicked Esau.

In the Future, when God uproots the Kingdom of Edom, he will lower him first.[253] It is thus written *(Isaiah 24:21)*, "God will punish the host of the heights of high."

This statement, death and punishment all came because she added to the commandment of the Blessed Holy One. Regarding this it is said, "Whoever increases diminishes." [254]

May God enlighten our eyes with the light of His Torah,
May He place in our hearts His fear,
May we be worthy to greet Him

He will enlighten the heart
Waken the heart with understanding
Make the heart shine with brilliance.

PART TWO
Commentary on Bahir

BY ARYEH KAPLAN

Numbers refer to paragraphs in text

Commentary on Bahir

1. This paragraph has already been discussed in the Introduction, in the section on Tzimtzum. It speaks of a basic dichotomy, where God must be both imminent and transcendental — He must fill all creation, yet, at the same time, must be utterly divorced from it.

The Light discussed here refers to the Divine Essence, as perceived in the mystical state. Due to the Constriction *(Tzimtzum)*, we do not see this Light when we look toward God, and He therefore seems to be surrounded with darkness. Creation must exist as an independent entity, and therefore cannot be totally infused with the Divine Presence. At the same time, however, it cannot be said that this Essence does not infuse all creation, since "there is no place empty of Him." Therefore, when we look toward God, this Light must actually be there. This is the dichotomy.

Rabbi Nehuniah resolves this by explaining that the Constriction only exists with regard to creation, but not with respect to the Creator. Although we see Him surrounded by darkness, He sees Himself surrounded by Light — since for Him, even this darkness is actually light.

In this discussion, the author makes use of a dialectic involving thesis, antithesis and synthesis. The same concept is alluded to in the last of the Thirteen Principles of Exegesis of Rabbi Ishmael (who was a disciple of Rabbi Nehuniah): "Two verses that oppose one another until a third verse is brought to reconcile them" (Introduction to *Sifra*). It is this dialectic that results in the basic triplet structure so often found in Kabbalah. See *Sefer Yetzirah* 3:1 and below **127**.

Besides a philosophical teaching, however, Rabbi
Nehuniah was also providing an important lesson for initiates
into the mysteries. The vision may be one of clouds and gloom,
but for God, even this darkness is light.

This is alluded to by the word *Shechakim*, the Hebrew
word for "skies" in the verse from Job 37:21 as well as *Psalm
18:12* (*see* **74**). This word *Shechakim* always alludes to the
sefirot Netzach and Hod, the sefirot involved in prophecy and
the mystical vision (*cf.* **185**). One verse says that there is
brilliance in this vision: "It is brilliant in the skies
(Shechakim)," while the other verse says, "thick clouds of the
skies *(Shechakim)*" (Psalm 18:12).

2. Although *Tohu* and *Bohu* usually have the simple connotation of chaos and desolation, they are here described as the
basic ingredients of creation.

God gives existence to all things, and is therefore the
ultimate Giver. Creation, on the other hand, must receive its
very existence from God, and is therefore the ultimate receiver.

Another important principle is the fact that God is an
absolutely simple Unity, and cannot be described by any qualities whatsoever. Every concept that is necessary for creation
must therefore also be created. As we see, two of the most basic
of these are the concepts of giving and receiving. In Kabbalistic
terminology, the concept of giving is referred to as "Light,"
while that of receiving is called a "Vessel."

Both Tohu (Chaos) and Bohu (Desolation) allude to these
primeval Vessels. Tohu refers to the first Vessels, which were
shattered, while Bohu refers to these Vessels after they were
restored and rectified.

The original Vessels consisted of the Ten Sefirot in their
most primitive form. In this state, they could not interact with
each other, and hence, could not give anything to each other.
All they could do was receive from God.

In order to receive God's Light, however, a Vessel must in
some way be connected to God. The basic difference between
the spiritual and the physical is the fact that space does not
exist in the spiritual, and hence, there is no way in which the
Sefirot can be physically connected to God. The only possible
relationship is therefore resemblance. Hence, in order to re-

ceive God's Light, the Vessel must, at least to some degree, resemble God.

This presents a difficulty, however. If God is the ultimate Giver, while the Vessel only receives, the two are then absolute opposites. Therefore, in order for a vessel to properly receive, it must also give.

What is therefore needed is a vessel that gives as well as receives. The ultimate such vessel is man. If man is to receive God's Light, he must first resemble God by being a giver. This he does by keeping God's commandments, and thereby providing spiritual sustenance to the supernal worlds. Before he can do this, however, he must also resemble God by having both free will and free choice, and this is only possible when both evil and good exist.

The first stage of creation is called the Universe of Chaos or Tohu. This is a state where the Vessels, which were the primitive Ten Sefirot, could receive God's Light, but could neither give nor interact. Insofar as they did not resemble God, these Vessels were incomplete, and therefore could not hold the Light. Since they could not fulfill their purpose, they were overwhelmed by the Light and "shattered," this being the concept of the "Breaking of Vessels."

It is for this reason that these Vessels are called Tohu, which comes from a root meaning "confounded." When a person is confounded, it means that he is perceiving an idea that his mind cannot hold. Similarly, the vessels of Tohu-Chaos received a Light that they could not hold. Just like confusion and confoundment shatter the thought process, so these Vessels were shattered.

The broken pieces of these Vessels fell to a lower spiritual level and subsequently became the source of all evil. It is therefore said that Tohu-Chaos is the source of evil (*see* **11**).

The reason why the Vessels were originally created without the ability to hold the Light was so that evil should come into being, thus giving man the freedom of choice, which, as we have seen, was necessary for the rectification of the Vessels. Furthermore, since evil originated in the highest original Vessels, it can be rectified and re-elevated to this level.

This Breaking of Vessels is alluded to in the Midrash, which states that "God created universes and destroyed them"

(Bereshit Rabbah 3:7*)*. It is also alluded to in the Torah in the
account of the Kings of Edom, at the end of Genesis 36. The
death of each of these kings is said to infer the shattering of a
particular Vessel and its fall to a lower level, such a fall being
referred to as "death." For the reason why they are called
"kings," see **49.**

The word Tohu is spelled *Tav Hu,* Tav being the last letter
of the Hebrew alphabet. Since Malkhut-Kingship is the last of
the Sefirot, it is represented by the letter Tav. Tohu — *Tav Hu*
— therefore refers to the realm of these "kings."

After having been shattered, the Vessels were re-rectified
and rebuilt into Personifications *(Partzufim),* enumerated in
62. Each of these Personifications consists of 613 parts, paralleling the 613 parts of the body, as well as the 613 commandments of the Torah. These Personifications were then able to
interact with each other. More important, through the Torah
they were also able to interact with man, and therefore became
givers as well as receivers.

In the rectified state, the Vessels were adequate to receive
God's Light. In Kabbalistic terminology, this state is called the
Universe of Rectification (Tikkun). As here, it is also called
Bohu-Desolation.

Since the vessels of Bohu can interact, there is said to be
"peace" between them. Bohu is therefore seen as the source of
peace **(11).**

Bohu is translated as "desolation," or more precisely,
"emptiness" *(see* Targum). This represents the "emptiness" of a
Vessel ready to receive. The word Bohu can also be read as two
words, *Bo Hu,* literally, "in it is it" or "it is in it." This is also
because it is something that can hold the Light "in it."

Kabbalists also speak of Tohu as the intermediate state
between potential and realization *(see* Raavad, Introduction to
Sefer Yetzira). In their initial stage the Vessels only had
potential existence, in the Infinite Being, and in this state,
they could not be comprehended at all. Their state of realization, on the other hand, is that of Bohu. Tohu is the intermediate state between these two.

For initiates, this also contains a lesson for those who
would enter the mystical realm. The Husks (Klipot), derived
from Tohu-Chaos, are the forces that "confound people," and

cause them to have misleading visions. A complete vessel is a vision that contains a complete, understandable idea, whereas a broken vessel is one that is confounding and confusing. The state toward which one must strive is therefore Bohu, for it is what contains the true vision — "it is in it."

3. The first letter of the Torah is Bet, the second letter of the Hebrew alphabet. It is also the first letter of the word *Berakhah,* meaning "blessing."

When the Torah is discussed, it normally refers to the Five Books of Moses, or in a broader sense, to the entire theological structure based on these Books. In a Kabbalistic sense, however, the word "Torah" refers to the entire spiritual blueprint of creation.

When the Kabbalists speak of God's eminence and transcendence, they say that He "fills all worlds and surrounds all worlds" (*Zohar* 3:225a). The letter Bet refers to the interface between these two concepts (14), and hence the name of the letter Bet is related to the word *Bayit,* meaning "house."

The concept whereby God "fills all worlds" is indicated by the word "Blessing." Whenever God reveals His Essence in any thing, He is said to "bless" that thing, and the verse therefore states that "the *filling* is God's blessing." The vehicle for this blessing is nothing other than the Torah.

In order for a totally transcendental God to relate to His creation, a series of Ten Sefirot (Emanations) had to be brought into existence. The first two of these Sefirot are Keter-Crown and Chakhmah-Wisdom. The first Sefirah is called the Crown, since a crown is worn above the head. The Crown therefore refers to things that are above the mind's abilities of comprehension. Wisdom is therefore the first thing that the mind can grasp, and is therefore called a "beginning." Since Chakhmah-Wisdom is the second Sefirah, it is alluded to by the second letter of the Hebrew alphabet, which is the letter Bet. (*See* **64, 77**).

4. The word *Berakhah* (blessing) is closely related to the word *Berekh,* meaning "knee." Just as bending the knee lowers the body, so the concept of *Berakhah* lowers God's Essence so that He can relate to the universe and be comprehended through His acts.

The "Blessing" is therefore our highest comprehension of God, which is the "Place to which every knee bends." It is the house *(Bayit)* which one must seek out before he can find the King. This again alludes to the Sefirah of Chakhmah-Wisdom, which is represented by the letter Bet.

An important concept here, which shall be encountered many times, is the Kabbalistic idea that before there is an "awakening from on high," there must first be an "awakening from below." That is, before any spiritual sustenance is granted, there must first be some effort on the part of the recipient. This is closely related to the concept that every recipient of God's Light must also be a giver, as discussed in **2**.

The word "Blessing" primarily refers to sustenance given as a result of "awakening from below." The primary means of such "awakening" is the Torah and its commandments.

5. Here Rabbi Rahumai explains that the Sefirah Chakhmah-Wisdom, represented by the Bet, is the transition between God's transcendence and His imminence. It not only surrounds, but is also the "filling."

Wisdom is the conduit of God's Essence, and it therefore sustains all things. As the link between Creator and creation, it is the vehicle containing the potential for all things. The Talmud thus says, "Who has Wisdom? He who sees the unborn" *(Tamid* 32a). Chakhmah-Wisdom is the concept through which God initially perceived all creation (and it therefore parallels the eyes), and is hence said to have given Him advice. This is alluded to in a Midrash, which states that God sought advice from the Torah before He created the universe *(Pirkey Rabbi Eliezer* 3).

It has already been stated that the Torah is likened to the Sea (3). The Torah is represented by water, since it flows from the highest spiritual sources to infuse the lowest spiritual levels and even the physical world, which is beneath them all. Here, however, the analogy is used in a different sense, and the Torah is likened to a spring of water flowing from bedrock. The bedrock represents the power of Tzimtzum-Constriction, which holds back the Divine Light. As discussed in the Introduction. after the process of Tzimtzum, a thread of Light was drawn into the Vacated Space. This "thread of Light" is the "spring."

In order to hold something, a vessel has to be able to prevent it from flowing. A sieve cannot hold water. The same force that acts as a Vessel to hold God's light therefore also serves to hold it back and constrict it. This is the concept of Bohu, as discussed in 2. Here it is represented as a rock, and the scripture likewise speaks of "Stones of Bohu" (Isaiah 34:11).

Of the Ten Sefirot, the last seven correspond to the seven days of the week. These inferior seven are called Attributes *(Midot)*. Above these seven are the three superior Sefirot, called Mentalities *(Mochin)*, consisting of Keter-Crown, Chakhmah-Wisdom and Binah-Understanding.

The Torah stems from God's Wisdom, and is therefore two levels above the inferior seven. It is therefore said that the Torah was created two "days" before the seven days of creation.

In the Kabbalah, the following parallels are found:

Chakhmah-Wisdom	Thousands	Eyes	Atzilut	Yud
Binah-Understanding	Hundreds	Ears	Beriyah	Heh
The Next Six Sefirot	Tens	Nose	Yetzirah	Vav
Malkhut-Kingship	Units	Mouth	Asiyah	Heh

These four levels thus correspond to the four letters of the Tetragrammaton (YHVH). They also correspond to the four universes: Atzilut-Nearness, the universe of Sefirot; Beriyah-Creation, the universe of souls and the Throne; Yetzirah-Formation, the universe of Angels; and Asiyah-Making, the physical universe and its spiritual shadow.

Since the level of Chakhmah-Wisdom is that of thousands, each day becomes a thousand years. It is also the level of Eyes, and it is therefore written, "a thousand years in Your *eyes....*" When it reaches the level of the six days of creation, it is then breathed through the *nose.*

As discussed above, before any blessing or sustenance is granted, there must first be an "awakening from below" (4). David therefore says that when he exalts God, His name is also blessed, that is, brought down to shine on all creation (see *Tshuvot Rashba* 5:51).

The word Praise *(Tehillah)* here represents the Sefirah of Malkhut-Kingship, which is the lowest Sefirah and the ultimate recipient and Vessel. This Sefirah is also related to

David, who initiated the concept of Kingship in Israel. It is
through this attribute that God is called King, and the verse
therefore states, "I will raise You high, my God, O King."

God's purpose in creation was that He should give of His
good to His handiwork. When this purpose is fulfilled through
"awakening from below," God's purpose is fulfilled, and, as it
were, He is "elevated."

6. The example here stresses the "awakening from below"
involved in the concept of blessing. Rain coming from above
represents God's sustenance that descends from the aspect in
which He "surrounds all worlds." The wetness of the ground is
that which comes from the aspect where He "fills all worlds."
Still, "water" must also come from below, from the spring. This
alludes to the fact that the "awakening from below" is primarily through the Torah. This is also the concept of Praise, which
begins from the bottom with Kingship and ascends upward (see
171).

For the symbolism of the tree, see **119**.

7. Even though it was stated earlier (in **3**) that the sea
alludes to the Torah, here it is said to refer to the World to
Come. This is no contradiction, since the Torah is the emanation of God's Light, and hence in itself is the main reward of the
World to Come. This reward will be the revelation of God's
glory, which is the "Filling."

The present physical world is alluded to by the south, since
the south parallels the Sefirah of Chesed-Love. While the reward of the World to Come must be earned, that which is given
in the present world is a gift of Love.

8. When God changed Abram's name to Abraham, He did
so by the addition of the letter Heh. According to tradition, the
number of parts in the human body is 248 (Ohalot 1:8). When
God added this Heh to Abraham's name, He gave him dominance over the final five parts of his body, namely, the two eyes,
two ears, and the sexual organ, as mentioned in the Talmud
(Nedarim 32b).

The letter Heh has the numerical value of five, and alludes
to the five levels of the soul (**53**). The fact that this letter was

added to Abraham's name indicates that these five levels were given over to him.

Another connotation of the letter Heh is that of holding. The numerical value of Heh is five, alluding to the five fingers of the hand (*see* **188, 193**). This is also indicated by the way the letter Heh is used as a prefix and suffix. At the end of a word it indicates the feminine sense, and is also used as a suffix to indicate the feminine possessive. As a prefix, it is the word "the," grasping and specifying a particular object. In both these contexts, the letter Heh has the context of delineating and holding.

This is also the connotation of the two Heh's in the Tetragrammaton, which is spelled Yud Heh Vav Heh. The first Heh corresponds to the Sefirah of Binah-Understanding, and this is the "hand" with which God gives the reward of the World to Come. The final Heh is the Sefirah of Malkhut-Kingship, and this is the hand that He gives us so that we should be able to accept this reward. Thus, through this Heh, Abraham became worthy of the World to Come. It is likened to the sea, since like the sea, it is a receptacle.

The "form" of God in which He created man is actually God's blueprint form for man (*see* **82, 172**). This "form" or "blueprint" consisted of God's first throught in creation, and hence is the highest level of creation. In later Kabbalistic writings, it is referred to as Adam Kadmon (Primeval Man). This blueprint contains 248 parts, and when Abraham was perfected through the commandment of circumcision, he became its precise counterpart.

9. The grammatical form *Rash* is actually found in a number of places, such as Deuteronomy 1:21, 2:24, 2:31, I Kings 21:15.

The author is stating that God must be included in all of man's works, that is, they must all be for God's sake, and not merely for any anticipated future reward. One can then "inherit God," since the principle future reward is the perception of the Infinite Being.

The Yud in the Tetragammaton refers to Chakhmah-Wisdom, while the Heh is Binah-Understanding. God had already given Abraham the Heh, and therefore it may be thought

that the Yud is to remain hidden, and not given in the World to
Come. God therefore says, "Take everything," both the Yud
and the Heh. The son in this parable, in one sense, refers to
Abraham.

The example also teaches that God Himself must be
sought, and no merely reward. If the son would have sought the
treasuries and not have asked for the King, he would not have
received all. It was only after he had sought the King himself
that he received all the treasures.

The Yud and Heh also correspond to the "two thousand
years" mentioned in 5.

10. In this verse, it is Wisdom (the Torah) that is speaking, as is obvious from Proverbs 8:1. In 5, the verse Proverbs
8:30 was discussed, and the author now returns to an earlier
similar verse in this chapter.

In Hebrew, the word *Olam,* which means "universe" and
"eternity," is derived from the same root as *Elam,* meaning
"concealment." The "universe" thus conceals God, and does not
allow Him to be seen directly.

Eternity is the ultimate concealment, since the human
mind cannot penetrate infinite time, nor can it fathom the
timelessness of true eternity. This "concealment" alludes to
Keter-Crown, which is above Chakhmah-Wisdom and is its
source (*see* **49**). Keter-Crown is thus alluded to by the word
Kedem, which means "before." Keter-Crown represents God's
will, which is the source of the Torah.

The Crown is therefore worn above the "head," since the
"head" represents Chakhmah-Wisdom and Binah-
Understanding, which are aspects of conscious mentality. The
Torah is Wisdom, and is therefore the "head" of creation.

It might be thought that the Torah was created only to
rectify creation as it already exists. If this were so, the Torah
would have been created after the earth. But actually, the
Torah was the blueprint of creation, and therefore preceded it.

The word *BeReshit* — "In the beginning" — refers to Wisdom. *Elohim,* one of the Hebrew names of God, refers to Understanding, since when we use the word "God," we are actually
speaking of our understanding of Him. In this same verse,
Shamayim (heavens) indicates the next six Sefirot, and for this
reason the word *Shamayim* is a plural word. "Earth" is
Malkhut-Kingship. Hence, the verse, "In the beginning God

created the heavens and the earth," alludes to the four basic levels of creation (*see* comment on **5**).

The word "created" in this verse remains redundant in this scheme, and it is therefore questioned. The author answers that the word "created" indicates that Chakhmah-Wisdom contained the potential of all that would be brought into existence.

Before creation, only the Infinite Being existed, and therefore all was sameness and homogeneity. Sameness is therefore the highest concept that the mind can comprehend with regard to the Infinite Being, and it is therefore the essence of Chakhmah-Wisdom.

Creation, however, is at the opposite pole than the Creator, since the Creator gives existence, while creation accepts it. Therefore, before creation could be brought into existence, the concept of differentiation had to be brought into being. This is the essence of Binah-Understanding. It is for this reason that the word *Binah* shares the same root as *Bein*, meaning between. The Talmud also states that Understanding refers to "understanding one thing from something dissimilar" *(Sanhedrin 93b)*.

On the level of "Beginning" or Wisdom, all that exists is undifferentiated potential. When it enters the realm of *Elohim* (God) or Understanding, it can be differentiated into Heaven and Earth.

11. The name of God used in the verse from Ecclesiastes is also *Elohim*, which refers to Binah-Understanding. It is through understanding that the mind differentiates things, so Understanding is the more general concept of differentiation. The verse, "Also one opposite the other was made by God *(Elohim)*," thus is stating that opposite stem from the concept of *Elohim*, namely Binah-Understanding.

For a discussion of Desolation and Chaos, see comment on on **2**.

Michael is the angel that oversees Love, the concept of giving freely, while Gabriel is the angel of Justice, the restraint of Love, as well as receiving without giving. These represent two opposites, and their only reconciliation is Bohu-Desolation, the concept of free will, which allows a recipient to also be a giver.

As will be discussed, the angels are in the universe of

Yetzirah-Formation, which is a reflection of Atzilut-Nearness, the universe of the Sefirot. Michael is the counterpart of the Sefirah of Chesed-Love, while Gabriel is that of Gevurah-Strength. God's name *El* is associated with Chesed-Love, and Michael literally means *Mi KaEl* — "Who is like El." (Cf. *Bamidbar Rabbah 2:6*). Gabriel is *Gavri El,* "The Strength of God."

Peace is most closely related to Daat-Knowledge, which is a quasi-Sefirah, intermediate between Chakhmah-Wisdom and Binah-Understanding (*see* note 220). Daat-Knowledge descends to become the Sefirah of Tiferet-Beauty. The "Prince of Peace" is the angel corresponding to Tiferet-Beauty, and is identified as the archangel Uriel (*see* **108**).

12. "Creation" generally is said to refer to the very first step, creating "something from nothing. "Making" on the other hand, refers to the completion of a concept.

It is therefore written that God "creates evil." This refers to the Universe of Tohu-Chaos, which was the first step of creation, and was "something from nothing." The ultimate realization of creation is the concept of peace, where all opposites are resolved, and the verse therefore states "He makes peace."

The most important realization of peace is the reconciliation between the ultimate opposites, Creator and creation. This was only accomplished through the creation of Evil (*see* commentary on **2**).

13. Here again, the concept of "creation" means "something from nothing," while "formation" is "something from something." Light emanates from God's essence, and is therefore "something from something." Darkness, on the other hand, is a completely novel concept, and has no relationship to God. It is therefore "created" — "something from nothing." (see *Moreh Nebuchim 3:10*).

This paragraph also contains an allusion to the Tzimtzum, the original Constriction discussed in the Introduction. All creation was originally filled with the Light of the Infinite Being, and therefore, "darkness," which is the restraint and constriction of this Light, was something completely novel. It is for this reason that the word "created" is used with regard to darkness. The thread of Light that entered this darkness of the

Vacated Space, however, had its origin in the original Infinite Light, and is therefore said to be "formed."

In general, thought is said to be on the level of Creation, since thought is "something from nothing." Speech, on the other hand, emanates from thought — "something from something" — and is therefore on the level of Formation. When the verse states, "God said, let there be light," the phrase "God said" indicates the level of speech, which is also the level of Formation.

In no place in the account of creation, however, does it state that "God said" that darkness should be created. Darkness therefore does not involve speech, but only thought, which is the level of Creation. The scripture therefore states, "And darkness on the face of the deep" (Genesis 1:2), without any mention of a saying.

The concept of darkness is also one of separation, as the Torah states, "He divided between light and darkness" (Genesis 1:4), in the case of "becoming well" a person likewise separates himself from his disease *(Or HaGanuz).*

14. God encompasses all things, even space and time, and is not encompassed by them. This is also true of Chakhmah-Wisdom, which is the concept of Beginning — without end — before space and time were created.

Regarding the significance of the Bet, see comment on **3.**

15. The two main organs of human expression, the mouth and the sexual organ, are thus "open" in front. The Bet thus represents Chakhmah-Wisdom, the first Sefirah through which God expresses Himself.

Chakhmah-Wisdom is only a Sefirah, however, an emanation of God's glory, and it should not be considered in any way to be co-equal to God. It therefore has an indentation above its protruding tail, indicating a receptacle, and alluding to the fact that the Bet receives existence from an even higher power, namely the Alef.

The Alef is the first Sefirah, which is Keter-Crown. This is totally hidden, and only serves to receive from God, holding back His light so that it does not overwhelm creation. The Alef is therefore open in the back.

Even Keter-Crown must receive existence from the Infinite Being which is infinitely higher than this Sefirah. This is then most certainly true of Chakhmah-Wisdom, which is secondary to Keter-Crown.

Even though Keter-Crown is the very highest conceivable element of creation, it is infinitely lower than the Infinite Being. The Zohar thus states that even though Keter is the most brilliant light, it is utter darkness when compared to the Infinite Being *(Tikuney Zohar 70)*. Therefore, even the Alef begins with a Bet, that is, in the form of the Alef, there is a diagonal Bet (see Illustration).

16. The question here is that since the light can only be granted as a matter of free will, how is it certain that man will be worthy of it? God answers with the verse from Samuel, indicating that He brings about things so that in the end all will be worthy of this Light, and "none will be cast away."

The "Light" created before the world also alludes to the fact that the World to Come was created before the universe *(see* **160***)*.

This Light is represented by a crown, since with regard to the World to Come it is taught that "the righteous will sit with their crowns on their heads" *(Talmud, Berakhot 17a)*. This means that the highest Light, which emanates from Keter-Crown, will then be comprehended by man.

17. The Torah emanates from Chakhmah-Wisdom, while Alef alludes to Keter-Crown, which is higher than Wisdom. Keter-Crown is not perceivable in this world, and therefore the highest actual level that can be perceived is Chakhmah-Wisdom.

The alphabet contains the letters as abstract concepts, and therefore, it can begin with the Alef. But the Torah is concerned with the actual perception of God, and must therefore begin with Bet, which alludes to Chakhmah-Wisdom.

18. The letter Bet has a "tail" pointing backward. (*see* **15**).

19. Gimel alludes to Binah-Understanding, which is the Hand that gives Wisdom (*see* comment on **8**). Wisdom is meaningless unless it is understood, while through Understanding, one can bestow Wisdom to another.

20. The Gimel consists of a head, body and a tail. It receives from the head, and dispenses wisdom through its tail.

21. The principle conclusion here is that there are two types of angels. One type stands before God and praises Him, while the second type are His messengers. The first type was created on the second day of creation, while the second type was made on the fifth day. *(Cf. Bachya on Genesis 28:12)*.

22. Michael is the angel of water and the south, while Gabriel is the angel of fire and the north *(see* **11.***)*.

The Tree here refers to the entire array of Sefirot *(see* **6, 119**). It especially alludes to the final seven Sefirot.

"All" refers to the Sefirah of Yesod-Foundation. The final seven Sefirot are alluded to in the verse, "Yours, O God, are the Greatness, the Strength, the Beauty, the Victory and the Splendor, for All in heaven and earth, Yours O God is the Kingdom . . ." (I Chronicles 29:11). This verse names the Sefirot, and here, Yesod-Foundation is referred to as "All." (Also *see* **78**).

This Sefirah is called All, since through it must flow *all* spiritual sustenance. This Sefirah also parallels the sexual organ in man. It is through the sex act that new human beings are born, and souls transmitted to the world. Yesod-Foundation parallels this function insofar as it is the source of all souls *(see* **180**).

23. *See* **5.** As usual, "heavens" here refer to the six Sefirot from Chesed-Love to Yesod-Foundation. The "earth," in which the tree is rooted, is Malkhut-Kingship, the lowest Sefirah, and the final Heh in the Tetragrammaton YHVH. The spring dug in the earth is Binah-Understanding, the first Heh in the Name *(see* comment on **8, 10**).

The Tree is "heaven," and it is planted in the "earth."

24. The basic question here is what was created first, the "heaven," which is the Light and the power of giving, or the "earth," which is the Vessel, and the power of receiving. Rabbi Yannai declares that without a vessel there can be no light, and the vessel was therefore created first.

He then goes on to explain that even though the heaven was created first, it was not given a name until after the earth was created. Before the earth was created, the heaven was not complete, and therefore could not be named.

The earth is the Feminine concept of receiving, while the

heaven is the Male concept of giving. Thus, when the earth was created, the supernal sexual union could also exist, and the Sefirah of Yesod-Foundation, which parallels the sexual organ, could come into being. When this happened, heaven could be given a name, but until this took place, worlds were created and destroyed.

The "Pedestals" are Netzach-Victory and Hod-Splendor. The "attachment" is Yesod-Foundation.

The verse therefore states "you *founded* the earth," indicating that Yesod-Foundation came into being with the earth.

25. This alludes to the concept of Constriction (Tzimtzum) discussed in the Introduction. First a Vacated Space was formed in the Infinite Light, and into this space was drawn a "Thread of Light." Since this thread is actually nothing more than an extension of the original Light, the author states that it was light that had been hidden.

26. The letters Alef Yud Shin spell out *Ish,* the Hebrew word for man. The allusion is to the Supernal Man (*see* **117**).

The Alef is the Sefirah of Keter-Crown, as in (*see* **17**). Yud is the first letter of YHVH, and alludes to the channel from Keter-Crown to Chakhman-Wisdom. Shin is the channel from Chakhmah-Wisdom to Binah-Understanding.

These letters can also be understood in a simpler sense. Alef never occurs as a suffix, while as a prefix, it indicates the first person future — "I will." God is the absolute "I," and the statement "I will" indicates His yet unrealized potential. This is the level of Keter-Crown, the Alef that precedes the Bet of *Bereshit,* and the yet unrealized potential of the "crown" in the World to Come. Furthermore, Keter-Crown is the level above comprehension, and therefore, we cannot speak of it at all. Only God Himself can speak of Keter-Crown, and it is He who says of it, "I will." It is the same sense that the name associated with Keter-Crown is Ehyeh Asher Ehyeh, which means "I will be what I will be" (Exodus 3:14). Alef has the value of one, indicating the unity of this level.

As a prefix Yud means "he will," while as a suffix it means "my." It therefore indicates God's potential of which we can speak, the level of Chakhmah-Wisdom of which we can say "He will." When God speaks of Himself, He calls Himself Ehyeh (I will be), while when we speak of Him, we call Him YHVH, which has the connotation of "He is-will be" (*see* Rashbam on Exodus 3:14). The Yud is therefore the first letter of the Tetragrammaton, since it is the first level of our understanding.

As a suffix, Yud means "my," since, even though it can be perceived by us, it is still a level that belongs solely to God. This is also the level of Atzilut-Nearness, which we experience as Nothingness. Yud also has the numerical value of ten, indicating the Ten Sefirot which are in Atzilut.

As a prefix, Shin indicates the word "that," and thus is a letter that connects and specifies. In form, it has three heads on top, coming down to a single point. The three heads indicates the three basic concepts, thesis, antithesis and synthesis (*see* 1). All this exists to bring about a single goal, the Kingship of God, indicated by the single point at the bottom. Shin is therefore "all the world," and it is the answer to the why of creation.

God is called a "Man," since we anthropomorphize our understanding of Him in the three ways indicated by the letters Alef, Yud and Shin. First of all, we see Him as an absolute Unity, represented by the Alef. We then see Him as expressing Himself through the Ten Sefirot so that we can perceive His glory, this being the Yud. Finally, we see Him in His multitude of deeds with a unity of purpose, represented by the Shin.

27. Dalet, the fourth letter of the Hebrew alphabet is usually said to represent Malkhut-Kingship, the last of the Ten Sefirot. While each of the other nine give to the one below it, Malkhut-Kingship, being the lowest, cannot give. Since it cannot give, it does not resemble God in any manner, and in this sense is called poor. Like the absolutely destitute, it only receives, but cannot give.

28. See illustration and note 10.

As mentioned earlier, Gimel is Binah-Understanding, the first Heh in YHVH, while Dalet is Malkhut-Kingship, the final Heh. Since both Gimel and Heh refer to the same Sefirah, they should be in proximity. The author answers this difficulty by stating that Dalet and Heh also refer to the same Sefirah, namely Malkhut-Kingship, and therefore the Heh must follow the Dalet.

The author therefore states that "in the head, Gimel is in the place of Heh." That is, when referring to Binah-Understanding, Gimel and Heh represent the same Sefirah, and Binah-Understanding is in the head. But "in the tail, Dalet is in the place of Heh." In the Sefirah of Malkhut-Kingship, which is the tail of all Sefirot, the Dalet and Heh represent the same Sefirah.

29. Since the two Heh's in YHVH have different connotations, there must be something that connects them. This is the letter Vav.

As a prefix, the letter Vav means "and" and hence is a connective. In Hebrew, the word *Vav* also means a hook.

In the Tetragrammaton, the Yud relates to the thing that is given, the first Heh to the hand that gives, and the final Heh to the hand that receives (*see* **8**). In this context, the Vav is the arm that stretches out to give, and the letter is therefore written in the shape of an arm. This is also the inner meaning of the fact that a cubit, an arms length, consists of six handbreadths, alluded to by the Vav, which has a numerical value of six.

30. The numerical value of Vav is six, corresponding to the six directions of the physical universe. Physical space has three dimensions, and each dimension implies two directions. The six directions are east, west, north, south, up, and down.

Here, the letters of the Tetragrammaton are given their significance in the space-time continuum, which is paralleled in the spiritual world. The Yud represents Chakhmah-Wisdom, which is the thing that is given, while the initial Heh is Binah-Understanding, the "Hand" that holds it so as to give it. In a space-time sense, the Yud is the past, which is the thing that is given, while the initial Heh is the future, which holds what the past gives to it. At the interface between past and future is the three dimensional space continuum, consisting of six directions and represented by the letter Vav. These are the first three letters of the Tetragrammaton, YHV.

These concepts also have their parallel in a conceptual, spiritual sense. The most primary relationship possible is that which exists between Creator and creation, namely the cause-effect relationship. Cause and Effect are represented by Keter-Crown and Malkhut-Kingship, the first and last of the Ten sefirot.

Once we have the concepts of cause and effect, another

concept comes into being, namely that of opposites. In order to speak of opposites, however, we must also be able to speak of similarities. Two new concepts thus come into being, namely similarity and oppositeness. In the language of philosophy these are thesis and antithesis, while in Kabbalistic terminology, these two are Chakhmah-Wisdom and Binah-Understanding, the Yud and initial Heh of the Tetragrammaton.

Once we speak in terms of similarity and opposition, we have created yet another concept, namely that of relationship. In philosophic terms, this is the synthesis between thesis and antithesis. In our present terminology, it is the Vav of the Tetragrammaton.

At this point in the logical sequence, we have five concepts, namely cause and effect, which are Keter-Crown and Malkhut-Kingship; similarity and opposition, which are Chakhmah-Wisdom and Binah-Understanding; and relationship. The concept of relationship is expressed by Zer Anpin (Small Face), discussed in **53, 81, 140.**

Until the concept of relationship was introduced, only four abstract points existed, namely, Keter-Crown and Malkhut-Kingship, and Chakhmah-Wisdom and Binah-Understanding. It is with the concept of relationship that there comes into being a three-dimensional conceptual continuum, having six directions. This is represented by the Vav, currently under discussion.

In this representation, each of the original four abstract concepts gives rise to a relationship. Accordingly, Chakhmah-Wisdom gives rise to Chesed-Love, Binah-Understanding gives rise to Gevurah-Strength, Keter-Crown gives rise to Tiferet-Beauty, and Malkhut-Kingship gives rise to Yesod-Foundation.

As discussed above (in **2**), in a spiritual sense, similarity is closeness, while opposition is distance. In order to give, however, the giver must be close to the recipient, and thus, in a spiritual sense, there must be an element of similarity between giver and recipient. Therefore, Chakhmah-Wisdom, which is the concept of similarity, gives rise to Chesed-Love, which is the concept of giving. Conversely, Binah-Understanding, which is differentiation, gives rise to Gevurah-Strength, the concept of withholding.

Tiferet-Beauty is similarly derived from Keter-Crown, which is the concept of cause. In order to be a cause, something must give the precise amount of existence or motivation required for the effect. This is the concept of measured giving, represented by Tiferet-Beauty. However, since Tiferet-Beauty is the synthesis between Chesed-Love and Gevurah-Strength, it is usually represented as being below these two.

Malkhut-Kingship, the concept of effect, is usually said to be the feminine element of creation. Since Yesod-Foundation is derived from Malkhut-Kingship, it is naturally drawn to it and is motivated to attach itself to it. It is for this reason that Yesod-Foundation is said to parallel the sexual organ.

We thus have four new concepts, namely, Chesed-Love, Gevurah-Strength, Tiferet-Beauty, and Yesod-Foundation. These are derived from the original four.

Now that we have introduced the concept of relationship, these four concepts are no longer merely abstract points in conceptual space, but are connected by the concept of "relationship." The two pairs are like two crossing lines, yielding the four directions of a two-dimensional continuum.

We can arbitrarily depict this in terms of physical space. Since a cause is normally considered to be "above" its effect, the dimension linking Keter-Crown and Malkhut-Kingship can be designated as the up-down dimension. The Wisdom-Understanding relation can similarly be designated as the right-left or east-west dimension. This then yields a two dimensional conceptual space.

But since the concept of relationship exists, we must also speak of the relationship between the two dimensions themselves. In the conceptual space depiction, we can say that a line can be drawn between the two existing lines.

We immediately see that the cause-effect, Crown-Kingship relationship was the primary relationship. The thesis-antithesis, Wisdom-Understanding relationship was only introduced so as to make the cause-effect relationship possible.

The Crown-Kingship relationship can therefore be called the primary dimension, while the Wisdom-Understanding relationship is a secondary dimension. This yields a totally new concept, namely the qualities of being primary and secondary. These in turn form a new, third dimension, to which can be assigned the forward-backward direction. In a Kabbalistic sense, this is the dimension linking Netzach-Victory and Hod-Splendor.

With the introduction of these two new concepts, Zer Anpin is completed with its six Sefirot, namely, Chesed-Love, Gevurah-Strength, Tiferet-Beauty, Netzach-Victory, Hod-Splendor, and Yesod-Foundation. These are the six directions of a conceptual continuum, represented by the Vav, currently under discussion.

These six Sefirot, together with the original four, then yield the Ten Sefirot.

The six conceptual directions represented by the Vav correspond to the six physical directions in the space continuum. Furthermore, as the *Sefer Yetzira* explains, Wisdom-Understanding delineates the time dimension, while Crown-Kingship represents the spiritual, moral dimension between good and evil. Creation thus consists of five dimensions, or ten directions.

Since Keter-Crown is closest to God, it is said to represent good. Conversely, Malkhut-Kingship is furthest from God, since it is a receiving effect, and it is therefore said to represent evil.

In this context, Chakhmah-Wisdom is said to represent the past, while Binah-Understanding is the future. Wisdom is similarity and unity, and there is only one past. Understanding is dissimilarity and plurality, and there are many possible futures. It is the fact that there are many possible futures that makes free will possible. Hence, Binah-Understanding is said to be the ultimate root of free will, and therefore, of evil.

Since the past fertilizes the future, Wisdom and the past are male, while Understanding and the future are female. It is therefore taught that "God gave the female additional Understanding" *(Bereshit Rabbah 18:1)*. Furthermore, we have knowledge of the past, but not of the future. The future, which is the feminine element, is therefore deficient in knowledge, and it is therefore taught that "women are weak in knowledge" *(Kiddushin 80b)*. This is also related to the reason why women are exempt from time dependent commandments.

The author asks, "Is not Vav a single letter?" All the six Sefirot of Zer Anpin are actually a single concept, namely "relationship."

He answers that the "heavens" are spread out. Even though it is a single concept, it is represented by six independent concepts, it is represented by six independent concepts, which are its six Sefirot.

It is for this reason that the Hebrew word for heaven, *Shamayim,* is always in the plural. It is the plural of the word *Sham,* meaning "there." It therefore literally refers to all places that can be considered "there." The concept of "there," however, while a single concept, also implies all directions. The heavens are therefore said to be "spread out."

31. The allusion of a garden has already been used a numer of times (**5, 6, 23**). The paradigm of gardens is Eden, and hence the question is posed, where is it and what is its spiritual significance?

The reply is that it is on earth. This indicates that the original Garden of Eden was physical, here on earth, and that it was not merely a spiritual entity.

In a conceptual sense, however, this has a deeper meaning. The concept of the Garden is in the conceptual Earth, that is, in the Sefirah of Malkhut-Kingship, the last Heh of the Tetragrammaton.

The first three letters of the Tetragrammaton have already been discussed, and now it is the final Heh that must be explained. As stated earlier, it is the ultimate effect, the ultimate purpose of creation — "the final deed that was in the first thought."

God's purpose in creation was to bestow good and the place where this good is bestowed is in the Garden of Eden. It is for this reason that man's ultimate reward in the afterlife is called "Garden of Eden" *(Gan Eden).* Since God is the ultimate good, the good that He bestows is His own Essence. As discussed earlier, this is realized through Malkhut-Kingship.

32. The word *Et* is spelled Alef Tav, the first and last letters of the Hebrew alphabet. It therefore implies a transition from beginning to end. Rabbi Ishmael therefore states that its main purpose is to indicate the transitive sense of the word "created."

Rabbi Akiba, on the other hand, replies that the very fact that *Et* contains the Alef Tav implies that it superimposes the entire alphabet between the subject verb and predicate noun, adding all things that pertain to that noun (Cf. *Or Torah, Bereshit*).

The Talmud states that Rabbi Akiba learned this rule from Nahum Ish Gamzu, a colleague of Rabbi Nehunia. Rabbi Ishmael, on the other hand, was a disciple of Rabbi Nehunia who did not accept this rule, and who taught a completely different method of exegesis *(Shavuot 26a)*.

One of the things that Rabbi Akiba "adds" to the "earth" is the Garden of Eden, strengthening the position that the garden is on earth.

33. Alternatively, this verse can be read, "He threw from the heavens the land of the beauty of Israel." This would indicate that the "land" or "earth" was originally in heaven.

The question then arises, how can it be said that the Garden of Eden was on earth, when "the land of the beauty of Israel" was originally in heaven. This also raises a question against Rabbi Yanai's statement that the earth was created before the heaven (**24**), since the earth was originally in heaven.

Another problem involves the usual identification of "earth" with Malkhut-Kingship. Here it is seen to be identified with "the beauty of Israel," which is the Sefirah of Tiferet-Beauty. This is one of the six Sefirot associated with Zer Anpin, which is usually called "heaven" (*see* **30**).

The answer is that the true meaning of this verse is actually "He cast from heaven to earth the beauty of Israel."

The "crown" in this paragraph represents the Sefirah of Keter-Crown, while the "cloak" is alluded to in the verse, "He wraps Himself in light as a garment" (Psalms 104:2), quoted above (**30**). This "cloak" or garment is the light of Chakhmah-Wisdom and Binah-Understanding when they descend to protect the lower Sefirot from evil.

34. All the letters up to Vav have already been discussed, while Zayin will be explained later (**53**). The discussion skips to Chet, the eighth letter of the Hebrew alphabet.

In the reply, there is a reference to *Ruch-ot* (directions or winds), and hence, this discussion is in the context of the word *Ruach* (spirit or wind), as it occurs in Genesis 1:2. This verse has already been discussed (**2**), and the discussion is continued here.

The letter Chet is the final letter of the word *Ruach,* and under it is the vowel point Patach. The final Chet is unique in this respect, since in all other cases the vowel is read after its accompanying letter, while the Patach is always read before its primary Chet at the end of a word.

The Kabbalists state that the letter Chet represents the Sefirah of Yesod-Foundation, which parallels the male organ. This organ contains two ducts, one for reproduction, and one for discharging waste, and these are represented by the two legs of the Chet (*Shaar RaShBY,* on *Zohar 1:3a*). The duct involved in reproduction is the source of good, while that involved in discharging waste is the source of evil.

The primary concept of the Chet is that of an opening from below, and this is indicated by the form of the letter, which is actually closed on three sides, and open on the bottom. This is reinforced by the Patach under the Chet, since the word Patach literally means "opening."

The author states that the Chet in the word *Ruach* alludes to the three directions or winds — *Ruch-ot* in Hebrew — which are closed. These closed directions are south, east and west, corresponding respectively to the Sefirot of Chesed-Love, Tiferet-Beauty, and Yesod-Foundation. The only open direction is the north, which corresponds to Gevurah-Strength.

The concept of Chesed-Love is that of freely giving, while that of Gevurah-Strength is that of restraint. When it is said that Strength is restraint, it is in the sense of the teaching, "Who is strong, he who restrains his urge" *(Avot 4:1).* It is obvious that man can restrain his nature, but if man can do so, then God certainly can. God's nature, however, is to do good, and therefore, when He restrains His nature, the result is evil. The Sefirah of Gevurah-Strength is therefore seen as the source of Evil.

North is associated with evil in many places (*see* **162, 163, 199**). It is said to be "open," since the existence of evil opens the door for free will.

THE TRIPLET ARRAY OF THE TEN SEFIROT

KETER-CROWN

BINAH-UNDERSTANDING   CHAKHMAH-WISDOM

GEVURAH-STRENGTH   CHESED-LOVE

TIFERET-BEAUTY

HOD-SPLENDOR   NETZACH-VICTORY

YESOD-FOUNDATION

MALKHUT-KINGSHIP

THE VOWELS AND THE SEFIROT

Vowel	Form		Sound	Sefirah
Kametz	**T**	bottom	ah, aw	Keter-Crown
Patach	**-**	bottom	ah	Chakhmah-Wisdom
Tzerey	**••**	bottom	ay	Binah-Understanding
Segol	**⸫**	bottom	eh	Chesed-Love
Shva	**⁝**	bottom	schwa	Gevurah-Strength
Cholem	**•**	upper left	oh	Tiferet-Beauty
Chirek	**•**	bottom	ee	Netzach-Victory
Kibutz	**⸪**	bottom	u	Hod-Splendor
Shurek	**•**	center left	oo	Yesod-Foundation
No Vowel				Malkhut-Kingship

(*See* Tikuney Zohar 70, 129a, b)

The "stormy wind," "great cloud," and "burning fire," mentioned by Ezekiel are said to represent the three Husks (*Klipot*) of evil (*Zohar 2:203a*). These Husks are the source of all evil, and in this verse, are associated with the North.

The Husk closest to the physical world is fire, and it is this that destroys and punishes. It is for this reason that the punishment of Gehenom is said to be fire (see *Etz Chaim, Shaar Kitzur ABYA 4*).

The Sefirah of Gevurah-Strength corresponds to the second day of creation. The Talmud states that in the account of creation, the phrase, "it was good," does not occur on the second day, since it was on this day that the fires of Gehenon were created (*Pesachim 54a*).

There is a constant tension between Chesed-Love and Gevurah-Strength, these being the attributes of mercy and justice respectively. When Israel does God's will, then the attribute of mercy is on the ascendancy.

35. The attribute of strict justice would demand immediate punishment for any sin. The attribute of mercy, however, delays punishment, giving man a chance to repent.

36. (*See* notes and illustration) The letter Dalet consists of two lines, one from right to left on top, and the other straight down on the right side. The first line connects Chakhmah-Wisdom to Binah-Understanding, while the second line connects Chakhmah-Wisdom to Chesed-Love. The vowel associated with Chakhmah-Wisdom is Patach, while Segol is associated with Chesed-Love.

The word Dalet means door, while the word Patach means opening. Since Chakhmah-Wisdom represents our highest perception of the Divine, it is God's opening to reveal Himself.

Segol is related to the word *Segulah,* a remedy that works for no apparent reason. Segol thus parallels the Sefirah of Chesed-Love, which gives freely, even without reason. The Sefirah of Gevurah-Strength, on the other hand, restrains, and only gives that which is earned with strict justice.

The two "doors of the world" are Patach and Segol. Patach is a natural opening, while Segol is the opening that gives even without reason. Both are in the door that is the Dalet. (*see* **89, 178**).

37. The opening (Patach) between Chakhmah-Wisdom and Binah-Understanding also allows for the existence of Gevurah-Strength, which, as mentioned above, is both north and evil. (*see* note 19).

The level of the Throne is Binah-Understanding. It is called a Throne because, in general, the concept of sitting is that of lowering. Therefore, when we say that God "sits," we actually mean that He is lowering His essence so as to be concerned with His universe and comprehended by it. The Throne is the vehicle through which God "sits" and thus lowers Himself, and this is the concept of Binah-Understanding, through which we comprehend God. This Throne is mentioned in Ezekiel 1:26 and Isaiah 6:1.

Understanding is normally in the head. But its counterpart in the lower Sefirot is Gevurah-Strength, which parallels the left arm. Thus, this Throne is sometimes on the "head," and sometimes on the "arm." This then parallels the Tefillin worn on both the head and the left arm (Deuteronomy 6:8).

Alluded to here are the Tefillin worn by God, mentioned in the Talmud *(Berakhot 7a).* When we wear Tefillin, they parallel those of God, and they bring us near to God insofar as they help us to resemble Him. Of course, God's Tefillin are not physical, but refer to special concepts associated with the appropriate Sefirot.

In a sense, our wearing Tefillin thus "lowers" God toward us, and allows us to partake of His essence. This, however, is the concept of a Throne, as mentioned above. This might seem to indicate that we should make the Tefillin in the form of a chair and sit on them, but this would not be properly respectful.

The author then states that God wears His Tefillin in the open Mem. This is the concept of Binah-Understanding, the supernal Mother, when She descends to encompass and protect the lower Sefirot, which are Her "children." This descent is the mystery of the supernal Womb (see **84**). The Tefillin worn on the head thus have straps which descend and encompass the body.

The numerical value of Mem is forty, alluding to the forty days in which the embryo is formed in the Womb. These forty also parallel the Ten Sefirot in each of the four boxes of the head Tefillin (see **50**).

38. The main theme here is the fact that God has maximum pleasure when evil is transformed into good. Man was given free will so as to overcome evil, this being the purpose of creation. When evil is overcome, this purpose is fulfilled, and this is God's "pleasure."

In a deeper sense, the more one overcomes evil, the more he makes use of his free will, and in doing so, the more he resembles God.

In this paragraph, it is evident that the opposite of evil is peace. (see **11, 12.**).

40. The vowel point Cholem corresponds to the Sefirah of Tiferet-Beauty, which is the essence of Zer Anpin, the Supernal Man.

This is also the concept of the soul. In general, the vowel points are considered to be the souls of the letters (**116**). In the case of the Cholem, however, the vowel point also often includes the letter Vav. It is thus a vowel point associated with a letter, alluding to the soul as manifest in the body. Furthermore, the fact that the letter Vav is used indicates connection (see comment on **29**).

If primary attention is given to the soul, then the body is

also strong in the World to Come. This is speaking of the body after the resurrection, which is strengthened to such an extent by the soul that it becomes immortal (see *Derekh HaShem 1:3:13*). The main strength of the body is the fact that it resembles the Supernal Man, represented by the Cholem.

The Cholem is placed on the head of the Vav, indicating that the main domain of the soul is in man's mind. But if one perverts the soul, then there is sickness in the head.

41. The Cholem indicates the manifestation of the soul in the body. The most common form of this manifestation is a dream. (See *Derekh HaShem 3:1:6*).

42. The Vowel point Chirek parallels the Sefirah of Netzach-Victory.

As discussed earlier, Netzach-Victory represents the primary purpose in creation, while Hod-Splendor is that which is secondary (**30**). Evil is a result of the secondary elements of creation, since its purpose is only to allow free choice to exist, and thus bring about the primary purpose, which is man's attachment to God. Since Evil is associated with the "backward side" *(Acharayim)* or "Other Side" *(Sitra Achara)*, it derives its primary nourishment from Hod-Splendor. *(See Etz Chaim, Shaar HaYereach 5)*.

It is for this reason that the Hebrew word for Splendor, *Hod,* also has the connotation of *Hodaah,* which means submission. Hod-Splendor is submissive in the sense that it allows Evil to exist. This does not contradict the fact that the ultimate source of evil is Gevurah-Strength, since in the array of Sefirot, Hod-Splendor is an offshoot of Gevurah-Strength.

The primary purpose, however, is all good, and therefore detests Evil. This is represented by the Chirek, which parallels Netzach-Victory. It is therefore stated that one should repel himself from evil so that good should attach itself to him.

The Chirek is therefore a single dot, indicating that there is basically one primary purpose.

The main concept of "ice" *(Kerach)* mentioned here is smoothness. The root *Karach* thus also has the connotation of baldness.

Water is usually associated with Chesed-Love, and it is in this sense that water is mentioned in the first day of creation, since the first day also parallels Chesed-Love. The realization of the potential of water, however, took place on the fifth day, which parallels Hod-Splendor, when the fish and other sea creatures were created. In this context, water has the connotation of change and free will, this being the concept of Hod-Splendor, the secondary level of creation. Sea creatures were the first animals created, and these partake of this concept of change and free will.

Ice, on the other hand, is frozen water, and indicates the concept of water when it is transformed into a state of permanence. This is related to Netzach-Victory, since the word *Netzach* also has the connotation of permanence and eternity. This alludes to man's permanent state, which is in the World to Come, where "the righteous sit, delighting in the radiance of the Divine Presence" *(Berakhot 17a).* The angels seen by Ezekiel are always in such a state, and regarding them it is therefore written, "above their head was a likeness of fearsome ice" (Ezekiel 1:22).

Hair is something that comes from a living creature, but in itself, is not alive. It thus represents an extreme lowering of status, non-life emanating from life. It is also a self-made garment that conceals the living creature.

God-s primary purpose in creation was that He should be able to reveal Himself to His handiwork, this being the greatest possible good that He can bestow. This is then the level of Netzach-Victory, the primary purpose. It is impossible to accomplish this, however, without constriction, lowering and concealment, since no created thing could tolerate God's unrestricted Light. Therefore, as a secondary concept, God must constrict His essence, and lower and conceal His light. This is alluded to by "hair." It is also the level of Hod-Splendor, the secondary purpose.

Baldness, the removal of hair, alludes to the Ultimate Future, when no concealment will be necessary and man will experience God to the greatest degree possible. At this time, the primary purpose, represented by the Chirek and Netzach-Victory, will be revealed.

The words "and cleanses" is the last of the Thirteen Attributes of Mercy mentioned in God's revelation to Moses. This alludes to God's ultimate cleansing of all evil, where His primary purpose will be revealed.

45. This follows the previous discussion, since it speaks of a type of fire that consumes water.

The first Voice is Chesed-Love, and is therefore represented by water.

The second Voice is Gevurah-Strength. The first verse, from Isaiah, shows that Gevurah-Strength is represented by a hand, but does not indicate which hand. The next verse, in its entirety reads, "My hand has founded the earth, My right hand has spread out the heavens." This indicates that an unspecified "hand" refers to the left hand. Hence, the second Voice, Gevurah-Strength, parallels the left hand (*see* **145**).

The third Voice is Hod-Splendor, as indicated by the verses quoted.

The fourth Voice is Yesod-Foundation, and this is always alluded to by the bow.

The fifth Voice is Tiferet-Beauty, which makes peace between fire and water (*see* **11**).

The sixth Voice is Netzach-Victory, which also has the connotation of permanence and eternity. It is thus alluded to in the word "eternity."

The seventh Voice is Malkhut-Kingship, which is alluded to by "Glory."

This ordering differs from the conventional ordering of the Sefirot insofar as Hod-Splendor and Yesod-Foundation are transposed with Tiferet-Beauty and Netzach-Victory.

46. This teaches another aspect of Netzach-Victory, namely that it is the source of revelation and prophecy. This is the same as the fire of Elijah, mentioned in **44.**

Netzach-Victory and Hod-Splendor parallel the two feet, which stand on the earth. Similarly, these two Sefirot relate to the level that is below them. It is thus that all revelation comes from these Sefirot. Hence, this "great fire" was on earth, and it was from it that the word emerged.

47. This indicates that they saw only the Sefirot, but not God Himself. Furthermore, they saw only the lowest seven of the Ten Sefirot. They did not see the "throat," indicating that they had no perception of anything above the "neck," namely the Sefirot of Chakhmah-Wisdom, Binah-Understanding, and Keter-Crown. These are discussed in **49.**

48. It is this section that the concept of the Ten Sefirot is introduced. The inferior seven Sefirot parallel the seven days of creation, and have already been discussed in **45.** Besides the seven days, creation also involved Ten Sayings *(Avot 5:1).* Similarly, even though the revelation at Sinai involved Ten Commandments, it consisted of seven Voices.

The question then arises, since creation involves a concept of ten, why is it usually expressed in terms of seven?

The answer given is that the ten "were expressed with a single word." The Ten represent an internal concept, which is expressed externally as a single idea. This is because the Ten represent a complete structure. The seven, on the other hand, are an incomplete structure, and are therefore seen as separate entities (See *Etz Chaim, Shaar HaMelachim 5*).

Thus, in speech, creation involved a concept of Ten Sayings *(see* **118, 138, 140, 179**). This was an internal concept, externalized in a single act of creation. When creation was expressed, however, it was an action of seven days.

49. The Ten are divided into two groups, seven Voices and ten Sayings. The lowest of the Ten Sefirot are usually called Attributes *(Midot),* while the highest three are called Mentalities *(Mochin).* An Attribute is something that is externalized, while a Mentality or mental process is completely internal. Similarly, a "voice" is externalized, while a "saying" without voice is not.

The Ten Kings mentioned here are the same as those in **27.** The Sefirot are called Kings in many places in Kabbalistic literature, especially in their state in the Universe of Chaos before the rectification *(see* comment on **11**). These are alluded to by the Kings of Edom at the end of Genesis 36. They are called "kings," since a king only takes from his subjects, and does not contribute to the economy of his kingdom. Similarly, these Sefirot of the Universe of Chaos could only receive, but could not give.

Of the three Sefirot mentioned here, only Chakhmah-Wisdom and Binah-Understanding are mentioned explicitly. With regard to Keter-Crown, we are merely warned not to speculate into its mysteries.

50. In Kabbalistic terminology, the word "glory" always

refers to a garment (cf. *Shabbat 113a*). It also alludes to the Sefirah of Malkhut-Kingship.

A garment serves two purposes, to conceal and to reveal. With respect to God, the concept of "garment" conceals His true Essence, while at the same time, attenuating it so that it can be revealed.

The verse, "the beginning of Your word is truth *(EMeT)*," speaks of the three steps preceding the seven days of creation. The word *Emet* is spelled Alef Mem Tav, which are the first, middle, and last letters of the Hebrew alphabet. As such, they refer to the concepts of past, present and future. These parallel the Sefirot of Chakhmah-Wisdom, Keter-Crown, and Binah-Understanding, which are hidden.

As discussed earlier, Chakhmah-Wisdom parallels the past, while Binah-Understanding is the future (*see* comment on **30.**). Keter-Crown is the eternal present, since it exists on a plane that is totally above time. This level, however, is totally beyond comprehension, and is therefore represented by the quasi-Sefirah Daat-Knowledge, which is the concept of the interface between Chakhmah-Wisdom and Binah-Understanding. This is the temporal present, which is the interface between past and future. The internal concept of Keter-Crown is thus externalized as Daat-Knowledge (*see* **186**).

Although translated "the beginning of Your word," the literal translation of this verse is "the head *(rosh)* of Your word." It thus refers to the three highest Sefirot, which constitute the "head."

The Sefirot which are called "Kings" at the end of Genesis 36 are primarily the lower seven. These are the Sefirot which we can probe. Furthermore, the Sefirah through which the others are revealed is always Malkhut-Kingship. Hence, "the glory of kings is to reveal a word."

The four basic steps of creation also imply four universes, each with its own inhabitants. The inhabitants of the lower three universes are species of angels. They are given in the following Table:

THE FOUR LEVELS		
Level	*Universe*	*Inhabitants*
Chakhmah-Wisdom	Atzilut-Nearness	Sefirot *(Emanations)* Partzufim *(Personifications)*
Binah-Understanding	Beriyah-Creation	Serafim (Archons)
The Next Six	Yetzirah-Formation	Angels (Chayot, Cherubim, *etc.*)
Malkhut-Kingship	Asiyah-Making	Ophanim (Wheels)

The "glory of kings" refers to the level of Malkhut-Kingship, which is the Universe of Asiyah-Making. The angels of this Universe, which are the spokesmen of expression, are called Ophanim.

51. Here the Sefirot are discussed in greater detail. Since Keter-Crown cannot be probed, the first Sefirah discussed is Chakhmah-Wisdom.

Chakhmah-Wisdom is alluded to by the first word of the Torah, *BeReshit*, "in the beginning." It is thus referred to by the verse, "the *beginning* is Wisdom" (*see* **49**).

The second Sefirah discussed is Binah-Understanding. This has already been identified with souls from the verse, "the soul *(Neshamah)* of Shadai gives them Understanding" (**49**). Here it is also identified with the concept of Spirit *(Ruach)*, and is thus alluded to in the verse, "the Spirit of God fluttered on the face of the waters" (Genesis 1:2).

In Kabbalistic teachings, Binah-Understanding is said to be the source of souls, and it is therefore called the Supernal Mother *(Ima Ila'ah)*. As mentioned above, the level of Binah-Understanding is the Universe of Beriyah-Creation, and it is in this Universe that Neshamah souls originate.

As discussed earlier, Chakhmah-Wisdom is the past, while Binah-Understanding is the future, and therefore, the concept of time originates from the confluence of these two Sefirot. The complete concept of time is therefore defined only on the level of Binah-Understanding. Since man can only function within the framework of time, his soul originates from this level, which is where time originates.

The next level is that of Chesed-Love, which is the fourth Sefirah. Chesed-Love is likened to water (*see* comment on **43.**) One reason for this is because water flows freely downward from a high place, and the influence of Chesed-Love likewise descends freely from its high place.

On a more basic level, water is the essence of change. Once time is defined by Chakhmah-Wisdom and Binah-Understanding, the concept of change can also be defined. The liquid state is the essence of change, while the solid state is permanence.

Chesed-Love, which parallels water, is said to be below "spirit," which is Binah-Understanding. This is based on the verse, "the *spirit* of God fluttered on the face of the *water*" (Genesis 1:2).

This level of Chesed-Love, paralleling water, is the first of the lower seven Sefirot, corresponding to the seven days of creation. It is therefore the primary building block of creation, and it is thus written, "I have said, the world is built on Chesed" (Psalms 89:3). It is likewise written "He spread the earth on the water" (Psalm 136:6). Since the concept of Chesed-Love begins the Torah on the first day of creation, it is through this that man is initiated into the Torah.

The verse from Isaiah here is actually the verse from which the Talmud derives the teaching that the Torah is likened to water (see *Bava Kama 17a*).

52. Since gold is more valuable than silver, the question arises as to why silver is mentioned first in the scripture. It is answered that silver is Chesed-Love, while gold is Gevurah-Strength, the fifth Sefirah. The reason given is because silver is less valuable, it is therefore placed at the right, where it is "easy to take out" and distribute. Gold, on the other hand, is more valuable, and is placed to the left and withheld.

In Kabbalistic usage, the right hand is Chesed-Love, while the left hand is Gevurah-Strength (*see* **144, 145**). In general, the right hand implies giving, while the left is withholding. It is thus taught that "the left pushes away, while the right draws close" *(Sotah 47a).*

53. The first six of the inferior seven Sefirot, from Chesed-Love to Yesod-Foundation, are personified as Zer Anpin (Small Face), the archetype of the masculine personification. (see 81, 140). This masculine Personification is the 'Man on the throne" seen by Ezekiel: "And on the likeness of the throne was the likeness of the appearance of a Man" (Ezekiel 1:26). Even though the seven inferior Sefirot also include Malkhut-Kingship, the feminine element, the author is now speaking of a level before the female is taken from the male. This level corresponds to Adam before Eve was taken from him.

The "Male" represented by the Zayin is in the Universe of Atzilut-Nearness, while the Throne is in the Universe of Beriyah-Creation, which is also the world of souls. In this sense, the Heh is a throne for the Zayin.

In another sense, the Heh also represents Binah-Understanding, which is the Mother of the Male, and is also the root of souls (51). It is the first Heh of the Tetragrammaton (see comment on 29).

The soul contains five levels, and these correspond to the Sefirot and Universes in the manner presented in the following Table.

THE FIVE LEVELS OF THE SOUL

Sefirah	Universe	Soul Level
Keter-Crown	Adam Kadmon	Yechidah-Uniqueness
Chakhmah-Wisdom	Atzilut-Nearness	Chayah-Vitality
Binah-Understanding	Beriyah-Creation	Neshamah-Breath
The Next Six	Yetzirah-Formation	Ruach-Wind Spirit
Malkhut-Kingship	Asiyah-Making	Nefesh-Soul

Of these five, only the lowest three enter into man's being. The higher two, Chayah-Vitality and Yechidah-Uniqueness, are considered to be Envelopments (Makifin), which do not directly influence man. One reason for this is that the highest of two levels exist on a realm above time (see comment on 51). These levels will only enter into man's being in the World to Come.

The concept of these parts of the soul can be understood by the analogy of a glassblower. A breath leaves the glassblower's lips, travels through his blowing tube as a wind, and finally rests in the object that he is forming, shaping it as he desires.

The breath is the Neshamah-Breath, which has this literal meaning. It is alluded to in the verse, "And God blew in his nostrils a breath *(Neshamah)* of life" (Genesis 2:7). This is transmitted down to man in the form of a "wind," which is the level of Ruach-Windspirit. When it rests in man, it is called Nefesh-Soul, which comes from the root *Nafash,* meaning "to rest."

In this scheme, the level of Chayah-Vitality would represent the breath before it even leaves the Blower, while it is still an integral part of his life force. The level of Yechidah-Uniqueness would be the very desire that wills Him to breath.

It has already been noted that Bet represents Chakhmah-Wisdom, which is the sustenance of all things (5).

The key to this teaching is the letter Heh, which is lower than its throne Zayin, and at the same time, is above it. Similarly, even though gold is more valuable than silver, it is manifest on a lower level.

The reason for this involves an important concept. God's primary purpose in creation was to give. Since creation cannot accept all that God has to give, He must also restrain. The concept of restraint therefore fulfills a secondary function in creation. Silver and Chesed-Love represent giving, and are thus on a higher level than gold and Gevurah-Strength, which represent restraint.

But even though giving is higher than restraint, that which is withheld is always greater than that which is given. Indeed, the reason why it is held back is precisely because it is too high to be given. Thus, that which is given is silver, while that which is withheld is the more valuable gold. This is evidenced by the five levels of the soul, where the two highest are held back.

In the sense that it is represented here, the word *HaZahav* ("the gold," HZHV) is actually a reversal of the Tetragrammaton YHVH, with the Zayin replacing the Yud.

54. The above concept is developed more fully here. The King is Chakhmah-Wisdom, while his daughter is Malkhut-Kingship, the archetypal feminine element. She is bound to the Male, and for this reason he is represented by the letter Zayin, as above. It is this Daughter that gives birth to all creation.

In order for creation to be independent of the King, He must divorce Himself from it. Yet, at the same time, He must also remain intimately connected with it, this being the primary paradox of creation (see 1). The King therefore constrains Himself, but leaves a "window" through which He can communicate with His daughter. The window restrains, but it can be opened.

The window is the letter Heh, which is said to represent the five levels of the soul. Even though God conceals Himself from man, the soul is the window to God.

The verse thus says that the King's Daughter is hidden, not only from the King, but also from us. The garment that hides her is gold, the concept of restraint.

55. As discussed earlier (in **51, 53**), the highest level of the soul that we experience is Neshamah-Breath, which is the level of Binah-Understanding. It is only in the Future World that we will reach the level of Chakhmah-Wisdom, which is the level of Chayah-Vitality.

The Bet refers to Chakhmah-Wisdom, which is two levels above the seven days of creation. These two levels are the two thousand years.

The questioner understands these two thousand to infer that "thousands of times more than it was," actually means two thousand. He is answered that "thousands" can also mean seven thousand.

This can also be interpreted to mean that just as the sun rules over the world for seven thousand years, so shall the moon.

56. The first five Sefirot, Keter-Crown, Chakhmah-Wisdom, Binah-Understanding, Chesed-Love (silver), and Gevurah-Strength (gold), have now been discussed. Since a window can be closed as well as opened, the gold is the Attribute of Justice.

57. The seven lower Sefirot are alluded to by "heaven" and "earth." "Heaven" are the six, while "earth" is Malkhut-Kingship (see **30**).

The Sabbath represents the level of Malkhut-Kingship, which is the level of Nefesh-Soul. As mentioned above, the word Nefesh comes from a root meaning "to rest."

As we shall see, the dimension defined by Keter-Crown and Malkhut-Kingship is the dimension of "soul."

The level of the body is to work to earn sustenance, while the level of the soul is to receive it as a free gift. During the six days of labor we must earn everything that we obtain with "motivation from below," while on the Sabbath it is given as a free gift. This "sustains souls."

58. The Sabbath represents Malkhut-Kingship, the primary female element, and the womb from which all souls originate. In Kabbalistic teachings, "word" also alludes to Malkhut-Kingship.

The "covenant" is the Sefirah of Yesod-Foundation, which parallels the male sex organ. It is through the coupling of Male and Female that souls are begotten. The covenant of Abraham involved circumcision of the male sex organ, since Abraham and his children would then be able to transmit souls begotten by the supernal Male and Female (*see* **82, 168**).

This covenant is said to be between the "ten fingers and ten toes." The ten fingers allude to the Ten Sefirot that gives (*see* **138**). This is the concept of "motivation from above." The ten toes, on the other hand, represent the Ten Sefirot that receive from below, just as the feet are supported by the ground beneath them.

The concept that unifies these two sets of ten is the sexual organ, which begets souls. As mentioned above (**53**), the soul is the "window" to God, and is thus the channel through which the "hands" give and the "feet" receive.

Once Abraham was given this great ability to bring down the highest souls through the covenant of circumcision, he was ashamed, for he had already begotten Ishmael while uncircumcised. God then told him that he would be the "father of many nations," and that even though Ishmael was already born, his main fulfillment would be through Isaac.

59. In this context, water refers to Chakhmah-Wisdom, while fire is Binah-Understanding (*see* HaGra on *Sefer Yetizrah 1:11, 12*). This is also alluded to in the word *EMeT* — "Truth." (*see* **50**). Even though it is usually said that water is Chesed-Love and fire is Gevurah-Strength, here they allude to Chakhmah-Wisdom and Binah-Understanding. This is no contradiction, since Chakhmah-Wisdom is the root of Chesed-Love, while Binah-Understanding is the root of Gevurah-Strength (**29**).

"Heaven" alludes to the six Sefirot of Zer Anpin, which correspond to the six days of creation. These are born out of the union of Chakhmah-Wisdom and Binah-Understanding, the supernal Father and Mother, fire and water.

"Heaven" is "there is water," since the highest of these six Sefirot is Chesed-Love, which is represented by water. The six also contain Gevurah-Strength, however, and it is therefore "water combined with fire."

The concept of "peace and love" is that of rectification (2). Once the Sefirot can interact and communicate with each other, they can be rectified to form Personifications *(Partzufim)*. The most important of these Personifications is Zer Anpin (Small Face), which consists of these six Sefirot, and is alluded to in the word "Heaven." *(see* **11, 153**).

60. The seven here again refer to the lower seven Sefirot, consisting of Zer Anpin together with Malkhut-Kingship, the Female. The reply is that they must look carefully at the verse. "Righteous" always refers to the Sefirah of Yesod-Foundation, since it is written, "The *Righteous* is the *Foundation* of the world" (Proverbs 10:25). *(see* **61**).

In Kabbalistic teachings, "Judgment" is Zer Anpin itself. Thus, six of the seven Sefirot are "Judgment," which are the six of Zer Anpin. The Sefirah of Yesod-Foundation, which is the male sex organ, also includes the Female, as discussed below *(see* **67, 82**).

61. The letter Tzadi here is meant to represent the Sefirah of Yesod-Foundation, the Righteous One *(Tzadik)*. The Yud represents Chakhmah-Wisdom, the first letter of YHVH. The Nun has a numerical value of fifty, which represents the "fifty gates of Understanding," and hence, the Nun alludes to Binah-Understanding. This is the first Heh of YHVH. Heh has the numerical value of five, and when multiplied by the ten of Yud yields fifty.

When Chakhmah-Wisdom and Binah-Understanding come together in the union between the supernal Father and Mother, then there can also be a union between the Male and Female, Zer Anpin and Malkhut-Kingship. The union between Chakhmah-Wisdom and Binah-Understanding, the Father and Mother, is called Daat-Knowledge indicates union and intercourse, as in the verse, "And Adam *knew* his wife"

(Genesis 4:1). This is also the mystery of the Talmudic adage, "There can be no erection without Knowledge" *(Yevamot 53b)*. The letter Tzadi is doubled, indicating that it is male and female *(see 83)*. The Tazdi thus represents Yesod-Foundation, the sexual organs of both the male and the female. Both are aroused when the Mentalities, Chakmah-Wisdom and Binah-Understanding are brought together.

62. Another reason why Binah-Understanding is represented by "fifty gates" is that it extends downward through five Sefirot to Hod-Splendor. Netzach-Victory and Hod-Splendor, however, are the source of prophecy, the level of the "seers."

It was in this "field of the seers" that Balaam built seven altars, paralleling the seven Sefirot here under discussion.

The author states that this field is like a carriage — a conveyance — and it is identified with the "heart" of the Blessed Holy One. It is well established in Kabbalah that the "heart" represents the Sefirah of Binah-Understanding, since it is taught that "the heart understands" *(Berakhot 61a)*.

Whenever the expression "Blessed Holy One" is used, it stands for the Personification of Zer Anpin (Small Face). There are five basic Personifications *(Partzufim),* constructed out of the Sefirot in the Universe of Rectification, and they are listed in the following Table.

THE PERSONIFICATIONS

Sefirah	*Partzuf—Personification*
Keter—Crown	Atika Kadisha—The Ancient Holy One
	Arikh Anpin—Great Face (Long Suffering)
Chakhmah—Wisdom	Abba—Father
Binah—Understanding	Imma—Mother
The Next Six	Zer Anpin—Small Face (Short Temper)
Malkhut—Kingship	Nukvah—The Female (Rachel)

An important question is raised by the Ari (Rabbi Yitzchak Luria). If Binah-Understanding is a mental process, why is it said to be in the heart, and not in the head?   The heart is actually the Personification of Imma-Mother, which is Binah-Understanding, where She reveals Herself in Zer Anpin.

Each of these five Personifications also consists of Ten Sefirot. The Yesod-Foundation of Imma-Mother extends into the "chest" of Zer Anpin, this being the concept of the heart. This Yesod-Foundation of Imma-Mother is the Tzadi, mentioned in the previous paragraph.

Even though the Seers perceive with Binah-Understanding, it is channeled through Netzach-Victory and Hod-Splendor, which are the two "feet" of Zer Anpin. Just as feet are in contact with the ground below them, so Netzach-Victory and Hod-Splendor are in contact with minds below them. The heart, which is Binah-Understanding, extends through Netzach-Victory and Hod-Splendor, the two "feet," and therefore causes Zer Anpin to "stroll."

The statement that Binah-Understanding extends to Hod-Splendor, the left foot, may seem to contradict the statement that it extends to the "chest" of Zer Anpin. However, the Yesod-Foundation of Imma-Mother, the Personification of Binah-Understanding, extends to the "chest," while Hod-Splendor of Imma-Mother extends to Hod-Splendor of Zer Anpin.

63. In a variant reading, the answer is, "Mother, thus Ben Zomah is outside . . ." He is therefore replying that Binah-Understanding is Imma-Mother (*see* **104**).

The Thirty-two Paths are said to pertain to the heart, and therefore pertain to Binah-Understanding. In *Sefer Yetzirah,* however, they are called the Thirty-two Paths of Wisdom, and thus would appear to pertain to Chakhmah-Wisdom rather than to Binah-Understanding. The Ari reconciles this difficulty with the Zoharic statement that "Father and Mother never separate *(Zohar 3:290b)*. Therefore, Yesod-Foundation of Abba-Father (Chakhmah-Wisdom) is always in conjunction with Yesod-Foundation of Imma-Mother (Binah-Understanding). Furthermore, while Yesod-Foundation of Imma-Mother extends to the heart of Zer Anpin, Yesod-Foundation of Imma-Mother extends to the heart of Zer Anpin, Yesod-Foundation of Abba-Father extends to Yesod-Foundation of Zer Anpin. Yesod-Foundation of Abba-Father (Chakhmah-Wisdom) is concealed by Yesod-Foundation of

Imma-Mother (Binah-Understanding), and therefore, the first place where Abba-Father is revealed in Zer Anpin is where Imma-Mother ceases to be revealed. This is in Zer Anpin's heart, and therefore, this is the place where the Thirty-Two Paths of *Wisdom* are revealed.

In Kabbalistic literature, these Thirty-Two Paths represent the thirty-two times that God's name Elohim occurs in the first chapter of Genesis. Elohim is the Name that parallels the Sefirah of Binah-Understanding. Here, the author states that "with them the world was created."

The concept of the heart, which consists of the letters Lamed Bet, also represent the Torah as a whole. The first letter of the Torah is a Bet, while the final letter is a Lamed.

As discussed earlier (in **30**), the Ten Sefirot represent the ten basic directions of a five-dimensional hyperspace. Keter-Crown and Malkhut-Kingship define the good-evil dimension, Chakhmah-Wisdom and Binah-Understanding define the time dimension, while the other six define the three dimensional space continuum. Two to the fifth power is thirty-two, and therefore, this is the number of corners in a five-dimensional hypercube (*see* **95**).

Although the source of revelation is Netzach-Victory and Hod-Splendor, all revelation ultimately comes through Malkhut-Kingship, which is the Female. This is also the Divine Presence *(Shekhinah).* Therefore, it is primarily through the Daughter that the Thirty-two Paths are revealed.

The concept of the Female, however, is divided into two concepts, which in Kabbalistic teachings are represented by Jacob's two wives, Leah and Rachel. Rachel is the Female concept that stems from Malkhut-Kingship proper. Leah, on the other hand, is actually Malkhut-Kingship of Imma-Mother (Binah-Understanding), and as such, represents the lowest level of Imma-Mother, which is in the place of Malkhut-Kingship. Normally, Leah is seen as being above Rachel.

Since both Zer Anpin and Rachel come from the womb of Imma-Mother, they are represented as brother and sister. They are also husband and wife, this being the meaning of "my sister, my bride" (Song of Songs 4:9, 5:1). The Female is also the "daughter" of Zer Anpin, since, like Eve, she was derived from the rib of her mate. Furthermore, since one aspect of the Female is Leah, who is actually the lowest level of Imma-Mother, she is actually in part also Zer Anpin's mother.

It is therefore written, "Say to Wisdom, you are my sister, and call Understanding mother" (Proverbs 7:4). In the next section, wisdom is also called God's daughter.

64. Judgment is Zer Anpin (**60**). This is explained further in **67.**

65. In Hebrew, Solomon is Shlomoh, from the root *Shalom,* meaning "peace" (*see* I Chronicles 22:9). As discussed earlier, Peace is the attribute of Daat-Knowledge, which is the concept of union and reconciliation, especially between male and female. The word *Shalom* — peace — comes from the same root as *Shalem,* which means perfect and complete. In particular, neither the male nor the female is complete without the other.

Shalom (ShaLOM) is spelled with a Vav, while Shlomoh *(ShLoMoH)* is spelled with a Heh. As discussed earlier, the Vav represents the Male, while Heh is the Female. Shlomoh-Solomon is therefore the concept of "Peace" in Malkhut-Kingship, the Female. Shlomoh-Solomon is therefore said to be "The *King* to whom Peace belongs" (*Shavuot 35b,* Rashi on Song of Songs 1:1). God therefore told Solomon that his name was like the name of "My Glory," since Glory always refers to the Sefirah of Malkhut-Kingship.

Wisdom was then given to Solomon through the "daughter" which is also the Sefirah of Malkhut-Kingship. It is an important Kabbalistic teaching that Malkhut-Kingship is the Sefirah through which all others are revealed. Since Solomon made himself a counterpart of Malkhut-Kingship, he could draw through it.

Shlomoh is literally Shalom Heh — peace of the female Heh, which is both Binah-Understanding and Malkhut-Kingship. Solomon was thus the one who brought the element of Daat-Knowledge, which is Peace, to the Female, which is Malkhut-Kingship. Daat-Knowledge is the bond between Chakhmah-Wisdom and Binah-Understanding, and specifically, is the means through which Chakhmah-Wisdom influences Binah-Understanding. Hence, Solomon brings Chakhmah-Wisdom down to Malkhut-Kingship, and through it was in turn given wisdom.

66. The "Congregation of Israel" refers to the souls of Israel, both past and future. Although they frequently intervene for mankind, they do not do so when man sins. This is related to the teaching that God consulted with the souls of the righteous at the time of creation *(Bereshit Rabbah 8:7).*

67. The seven Sefirot alluded to in this verse also work to punish man when he sins *(see 60).*

Here it is evident that the primary purpose of the seven Sefirot of Zer Anpin and the Female is to control providence. They act as a feedback mechanism, dealing with man according to his deeds.

At the beginning of *Etz Chaim* ("Tree of Life"), the Ari makes the following statement: "When it arose in His Will to create the universe, to bestow good to His handiwork, that they should recognize His greatness, and be worthy of being a vehicle for the supernal, to cleave to Him."

The five concepts mentioned correspond to the five levels of creation and to the five Personifications *(Partzufim):*

"It rose in His will"	Arikh Anpin	Keter-Crown
"to bestow good"	Abba-Father	Chakhmah-Wisdom
"that they may recognize Him"	Imma-Mother	Binah-Understanding
"a vehicle for the supernal"	Zer Anpin	The Next Six
"to cleave to Him"	Female	Malkhut-Kingship

Arikh Anpin is thus the hidden Will of God, which cannot be probed. It represents God's own motivation in creating the world, which is beyond the realm of human understanding and wisdom.

The highest purpose that can be probed is that God created the universe in order to bestow good to His handiwork. This is the level of Abba-Father and Chakhmah-Wisdom.

The purpose that His handiwork should "recognize Him" is then the level of Binah-Understanding. It is because of this purpose, that, to some degree, we can "understand" God.

Zer Anpin is what is usually referred to as the "Supernal Man," and it is with regard to Zer Anpin that it is written that "God made man in His image" (Genesis 1:27). In the spiritual realm, when two things resemble each other, they are said to be in proximity, and one can be a vehicle for the other. Therefore, since man is a counterpart of Zer Anpin, it is through Zer Anpin that man can become a vehicle for the supernal.

Man then binds himself to the Female, just as the male cleaves to the female in a physical sense. The Female is the Divine Presence *(Shekhinah)*. This binding is the ultimate delight of the World to Come, and it is thus taught, "In the World to Come . . . the righteous will sit, with their crowns on their heads, delighting in the radiance of the Shekhinah" *(Berakhot 17a)*.

It was explained above, in **30,** that Keter-Crown is cause, Malkhut-Kingship is effect, Chakhmah-Wisdom is similarity, Binah-Understanding is difference, while the six Sefirot of Zer Anpin represent connection.

Keter-Crown is the Supernal Will, the cause of all things. Chakhmah-Wisdom is similarity, since it represents the fact that God wishes to bestow of His good, and make His handiwork as much like Him as possible. Binah-Understanding is difference, and this is comprehending God, since this involves understanding how He is different from all other things. Zer Anpin is relationship, this being the concept of being a "vehicle" for the supernal. Finally, Malkhut-Kingship is effect, since the ultimate effect of the entire process is that man should be attached to God.

Earning reward is therefore through Zer Anpin, while receiving it is through the Female. Zer Anpin therefore consists of the six Sefirot and corresponds to the six working days, while the Female corresponds to the Sabbath.

Another important teaching of the Kabbalistic philosophers is that all of man's reward and punishment is the result of his deeds. Therefore, since man is the counterpart of Zer Anpin, each individual has a portion there, and each individual's deeds have an effect on the "body" of Zer Anpin. Conversely, Zer Anpin is directly linked to man, overseeing and guiding the providence that effects him. Through Zer Anpin, man's deeds have an important bearing on providence. It is for this reason that Zer Anpin is called "Judgment" **(60)**.

The author therefore concludes by stating that when a person repents, he also elevates the seven. Everything that takes place in Zer Anpin is a direct result of man's activities.

The author furthermore states that there can be no judgment without Wisdom **(64)**. Chakhmah-Wisdom is the level where God "bestows good," and all of God's judgment is motivated by this purpose.

68. *Maaseh Merkava,* the Works or Mysteries of the Chariot, usually refers to the mystical experience (*see* **88**). The Chariot experience is therefore said to be a "vision" *(Tzefiyah),* which is related to the word for "seers," *Tzofim,* mentioned above in **62**. A person has such a vision by becoming a vehicle or Chariot *(Merkava)* to the divine, this being the level of Zer Anpin, as above.

The concept of prayer is basically that of attachment to God. Engaging in the Merkava, the mystical experience, however, is an even higher level of attachment. It refers to a vision of the Godly, and the verse therefore says, "I heard a report of You."

We have seen (in **5**) that the concept of Praise *(Tehillah)* refers to Malkhut-Kingship. Prayer *(Tefillah),* on the other hand is called "the service of the heart" *(Taanit 2a).* Since we are currently speaking of the heart, this concept of prayer is introduced.

69. It is clearly evident here that "hearing" is on the level of Binah-Understanding, a concept that has already been introduced (*see* **5**). The level of "hearing" on high is the attribute through which God "hears" prayer.

According to the Kabbalah, Ezekiel's vision of the Chariot was in the Universe of Yetzirah-Formation, which is the level of Zer Anpin (*see* **50, 53**). The vision mentioned here is therefore Binah-Understanding as revealed in Zer Anpin, which, as mentioned above, is the concept of the "heart" (**62**).

Fear is not from "the days," which are the Sefirot of Zer Anpin, but from Binah-Understanding.

70. The Talmud thus states that Alef Bet has the meaning of *Aluf Binah* — "Learn Understanding" *(Shabbat 104a; Tikuney Zohar 70–130a).*

As already discussed, Alef represents Keter-Crown (*see* **15, 17, 26, 117, 140**). The word Alef *(ALePh)* therefore has the same letters as *PeLeA,* meaning hidden, since Keter-Crown is the concealed Sefirah.

Even though the eyes, ears, nose and mouth are said to represent different Sefirot (as in **5**), they are all in Keter-

Crown. The Crown is that which is above and outside the head, and these organs are all windows opening into the head. Actually, then, the Ear is Binah-Understanding of Arikh Anpin, the Personification of Keter-Crown (*see* **79**).

It is taught that each letter nourishes the following one. Since Alef is the first letter, it therefore nourishes them all.

The letter Alef also has the shape of a brain, again alluding to Keter-Crown.

The Alef also consists of a Yud on the upper right, a Yud on the lower left, and a diagonal line separating the two Yud's (*see* Fig. 1). The upper Yud is the upper right part of the brain, which is Chakhmah-Wisdom. The lower Yud is the left leg, which is Hod-Splendor, the source of inspiration and prophecy. The line has the shape of a Vav, which represents the six intervening Sefirot.

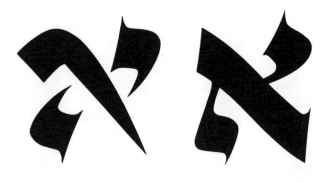

Fig. 7. The *Alef* consists of two *Yuds* and a *Vav*.

The two Yuds each have a numerical value of ten, while the Vav has a value of six. Therefore the two Yuds and the Vav have a total numerical value of twenty-six, which is also the numerical value of the Tetragrammaton YHVH. The verse, "YHVH at their *head*," is therefore introduced.

The Name of YHVH is usually said to be the Name that is specific to Zer Anpin. The four letters, however, also allude to the four levels, where Yud is Chakhmah-Wisdom, Heh is Binah-Understanding, Vav is Zer Anpin, and the final Heh is Malkhut-Kingship.

Besides this, however, there is another connotation of the Name YHVH, and this is only evident when the letters are spelled out. The Kabbalists state that there are four such possible spellings, illustrated in Table 4. These four spellings have the numerical values of 72, 63, 45 and 52. They represent the four levels as they exist in Adam Kadmon (Primeval Man), which is the Universe that corresponds to Keter-Crown. (*see* Introduction to *Shaar HaHakdamot*).

THE FOUR SPELLINGS OF YHVH

Spelling				Value	Level
ה י	ו י ה	ה י	ד ו י	YUD HY VYV HY	72	Chakhmah—Wisdom
ה י	ו א ו	ה י	ד ו י	YUD HY VAV HY	63	Binah—Understanding
א ה	ו א ו	א ה	ד ו י	YUD HA VAV HA	45	The Next Six
ה ה	ו ו	ה ה	ד ו י	YUD HH VV HA	52	Malkhut—Kingship

The Name used here is spelled out in such a manner so as to add up to 45. This spelling corresponds to the six Sefirot of Zer Anpin, as they are reflected in Adam Kadmon. Even though the Sefirot and Personifications are in the Universe of Atzilut-Nearness, which is below Adam Kadmon, they also have counterparts in Adam Kadmon, which are reflected by the spellings of the Tetragrammaton.

The name adding up to 45 is thus Zer Anpin, the Supernal Man. Therefore, 45 is also the numerical value of *ADaM*, the Hebrew word for man. This is also the Blessed Holy One, as above (*see* **62**).

The "Holy Palace" is usually said to be Malkhut-Kingship (see *Sefer Yetzirah* 4:3). Actually, however, it is the confluence of Keter-Crown, Chakhmah-Wisdom, Binah-Understanding, and Malkhut-Kingship, but it is primarily expressed in Malkhut-Kingship.

71. The King here is said to be "talented, hidden and concealed." The Hebrew for "hidden" here is *MuPhla,* from the root *PeLA,* which alludes to Keter-Crown. As mentioned earlier, *PeLA* therefore has the same letters as *ALpHh.*

The "house" mentioned here is the letter Bet, beyond which one may not look.

The word *Shanim* — "years" — has the same letters as the word *Sh'nayim,* meaning "two." This alludes to the second Sefirah, which is Chakhmah-Wisdom, the Bet.

72. Regarding the pearl, see **72, 190.** The "pearl" usually refers to the level of Malkhut-Kingship, but it can also be "embraced with the hands and placed on the head," which is the level of Keter-Crown.

Day is usually said to represent Zer Anpin, while night is the Female. Day is therefore the "great light," the sun, which is Zer Anpin, while the moon is the Female. Since "day" is Zer Anpin, and "years are made from days," years are also in Zer Anpin. Actually, time is completed with the Sefirah of Binah-Understanding, and only begins to function within the realm of Zer Anpin (see *Pardes Rimonim 18:3*).

"Life" indicates the Sefirah of Yesod-Foundation, and it denotes the sexual organ when it is "alive," that is, during intercourse. Years are constructed through a measuring of the sun and moon, day and night, a confluence of male and female.

73. This verse is discussed at length in **155.**

The word for day, *Yom,* has the same root as *Yam,* which means west (and sea). This is the direction of Yesod-Foundation, the concept of "life" and the "pearl."

The question then arises that the pearl has been identified with day, the "great light," the sun. This is in the east, the direction of Tiferet-Beauty. Furthermore, "seed" comes from the east.

The author answers that "day" actually refers to a day of twenty-four hours, consisting of both day and night. This is the confluence of Zer Anpin and the Female mentioned above. Zer Anpin is to the east of the Female, facing the west, and the "seed" therefore comes from the east. "Earth and heaven" also refer to Malkhut-Kingship and Zer Anpin, as above.

74. This verse has already been discussed in **1.**
The concept of *Shechakim* usually refers to the Sefirot of Netzach-Victory and Hod-Splendor. As discussed earlier, these two Sefirot are the source of prophecy, vision and inspiration. The concept of a vision both reveals and hides, allowing only what is fitting to be seen. The vision therefore contains "thick clouds," since we only see God through a "thick cloud." This is also the significance of the "thick clouds" at the revelation at Sinai.

Immediately below Netzach-Victory and Hod-Splendor, the *Shechakim,* is the Sefirah of Yesod-Foundation, which is called Righteous *(Tzedek).* This is the concept of "the righteous, the Foundation of the world."

There are two modes through which God judges the world, the Attribute of Judgment *(Midat HaDin),* and the Attribute of Mercy *(Midat HaRachamim).* The Attribute of Judgment demands a single, fixed, unmitigated response for any wrong, while the Attribute of Mercy admits a number of mitigated responses. Therefore, Judgment comes from the Female, which is derived from a single Sefirah, Malkhut-Kingship, and therefore has just one single response. Zer Anpin, on the other hand, is constructed from six Sefirot, and therefore allows an infinite blend of responses. It is therefore the source of the Attribute of Mercy.

Actually, however, all providence ultimately comes from the Sefirah of Malkhut-Kingship, this being the definition of the word. But in order for Malkhut-Kingship to act in a mode of Mercy, it must be bound to Zer Anpin, this being the concept of the Supernal Union. This Union, however, takes place through Yesod-Foundation, the sex organ, which is also called Righteous *(Tzadik).*

Yesod-Foundation, however, has two modes, one of celibacy, and one of intercourse. The Righteous is one who is "separated from sex," and therefore, when it is in this mode, it is called, "the Righteous, the Foundation of the world." The word "world" here is *Olam,* also having the connotation of *Elam* — 'Hidden" **(10).** Therefore, Yesod-Foundation is called Righteous when the sex organ is hidden and not expressed. Similarly, Joseph is called Righteous *(Tzadik)* precisely because he refused to have intercourse with Potiphar's wife.

When Yesod-Foundation is in this mode, there is no union

between Zer Anpin and the Female. The Female is then in a mode of Judgment.

In the second mode, Yesod-Foundation is called *Chai* — "alive." It is said to be "alive" when it is functioning during intercourse.

If a person pursues righteousness, then he arouses its counterpart on high and brings about the supernal union. He then "may live and occupy the land." When the verse says that he will "live," it means that he will bring Yesod-Foundation into its mode of *Chai,* which is that of union. He will then occupy the "Land," which always alludes to the Sefirah of Malkhut-Kingship, which is the Female.

75. The word "glow" *(Nogah)* usually refers to the twilight, which is the light of day shining into the night. As discussed above, day is Male, while night is Female, The "glow" of twilight is therefore when the Male intrudes into the Female. It therefore represents the sexual organ of the Female, and is thus said to be "opposite Him"

It is then explained that the first "righteousness" refers to the Divine Presence *(Shekhinah),* which is Malkhut-Kingship, the Female. The reference is to the sexual organ of the Female.

The other "righteousness" is the male organ, which is the Sefirah of Yesod-Foundation. It frightens the righteous, "for there is no man righteous on earth, who does good and does not sin" (Ecclesiastes 7:20). It is more frightening, since sexual righteousness, while possible for a woman, is next to impossible for a man.

The author then asks if this "righteousness" is charity. Charity is the concept of giving something freely, without its being earned.

He replies that it is not. The concept of a free gift is like a "coat of mail, " worn on the "body." The "body" is Tiferet-Beauty, which is the concept of measured giving *(see* **30**).

If God were to bestow His good freely without its being earned, it would not be a perfect good. For one thing, since it was not earned, it would be the "bread of shame" *(Magid Mesharim, Bereshit).* Furthermore, since the recipient is receiving without giving, he does not at all resemble God when he receives, and this itself is a concept of shame. Therefore, in order that this good be perfect, it must be earned. This is the concept of "righteousness" *(Tzedek),* where a fair reward is given for a fair job of earning it.

This concept of "righteousness" is said to be in the "head," which is defined as "truth" *(EMeT).* "Truth" has already been defined in this context, as consisting of Chakhmah-Wisdom Binah-Understanding, and Daat-Knowledge **(50)**. As already defined, however, Chakhmah-Wisdom and Binah-Understanding are respectively the concepts of similarity and difference **(30)**. The only way in which man can receive God's good is by being similar to Him, which is the concept of Chakhmah-Wisdom. But, at the same time, if God gives and man receives, then God and man are poles apart, and are ultimately different.

The Solution of this dichotomy is the concept of "righteousness" and fairness, which indicates that man must earn this good. The mens of this earning is the Torah, which, in the context of this verse, is "Your word." This is also alluded to by the fact that the final letters of the first three words of the Torah, *BeReshit Bara Elohim,* spell out the word *EMeT* –"truth"*(Baal HaTurim ad loc.).* In this context, however, the order is reversed, and the letters of *EMeT* appear as *Tav, Alef, Mem,* representing Binah-Understanding, Chakhmah-Wisdom, and Daat-Knowledge, respectively, in that order. The order is that of the paradox and its resolution.

For the relation between Truth and Peace, see **2, 137, 190.** It has been discussed that Fire and Water are Binah-Understanding and Chakhmah-Wisdom, and these are reflected in Gevurah-Strength and Chesed-Love. Likewise, Truth, which is the confluence of Chakhmah-Wisdom and Binah-Understanding, is reflected in Peace, which is the confluence of Chesed-Love and Gevurah-Strength.

As mentioned above, although Keter-Crown is the highest Sefirah, it is concealed, and therefore only expressed internally. Externally, it is represented by Daat-Knowledge, the confluence between Chakhmah-Wisdom and Binah-Understanding. Truth alludes primarily to Keter-Crown, while Daat-Knowledge is Peace. Genuine Truth is hidden and is only internal. Each person knows his own truth, and no one can probe the truth of another. All that one can have is Knowledge of another person, and, in the highest sense, this comes about from intimacy.

Daat-Knowledge is the confluence of Male and Female, Father and Mother. This is the concept of Peace (see **186**). It is Peace that reconciles opposites, and it is therefore the concept that allows for the union between man and woman. This is referred to as "Peace of the household" *(Shalom Bayit)*.

Half of King Hezekiah's days were associated with the attribute of David, which is Malkhut-Kingship, the Female. The other half were associated with Peace and Truth, the attributes that unify the six Sefirot of Zer Anpin into a single unity, this unification being the result of the union between Abba-Father and Imma-Mother. Zer Anpin is the Male, the other half of his days.

The concept of the daily cycle is that of Peace, since it reconciles day and night which are two opposites.

76. The concept of "holiness" is that of separation. God is thus called "holy" insofar as He is utterly divorced from any concept associated with His handiwork.

"Holiness" therefore alludes to the three highest unknowable Sefirot. These are the concept of the "Holy" in the "Holy Palace" (*see* **70**). This level is called "holy" since it is utterly divorced from our conceptions.

The concept that connects these three highest Sefirot to the lower seven is called Daat-Knowledge. It thus has the connotation of attachment and connection, as in "Adam knew his wife." The "years" mentioned here are the seven lower Sefirot, where time exists. The prophet says, "in the midst of years make it known," that is, through Daat-Knowledge, the highest levels should be revealed in the lower seven Sefirot.

The seven lower Sefirot include Male and Female. When the concept of Knowledge exists between them, the Male and Female are united.

This is the meaning of "God saw and He knew." As the result of the deeds of humanity, His "children," Zer Anpin and the Female can come together, this being the concept of His "knowing" Her. Thus, when the "children" do the King's will, He remembers their Mother.

On a higher level, when the lower seven Sefirot are in a state of rectification, then Chakhman-Wisdom and Binah-Understanding, the Father and Mother, are also bound together by Daat-Knowledge. When they are thus joined, the concept of Daat-Knowledge also binds them to the lower seven Sefirot.

77. This concept is similar to that of **34.**

The word *Rachem,* which we translate as "love," and which is often translated as "mercy," actually comes from the same root as *Rechem,* meaning "womb." Hence, a more precise translation would be "mother-love," the love that a mother has for the fruit of her womb.

Although Malkhut-Kingship is the root of the Attribute of Justice, this Sefirah is also the "womb" from which all souls flow. As mentioned earlier, Atzilut-Nearness is the Universe of the Sefirot, while Beriyah-Creation is the Universe of Souls. The lowest Sefirah of Atzilut-Nearness is Malkhut-Kingship, and it is therefore the Sefirah that is closest to the Universe of Souls, giving birth into it. It is in this sense that it is called a "womb."

It was King David who said, "I love *(Rachem)* You, O God my strength." The attribute of David is Malkhut-Kingship, as discussed many times in the Kabbalistic texts. Since David communed with God through this concept of "mother-love," which is Malkhut-Kingship, this attribute was given to him (*see* **75**).

David's son, Solomon, also represents the attribute of Malkhut-Kingship (**65**). It was through this attribute that God gave wisdom to Solomon.

Solomon represents the union between Male and Female, the concept that brings "peace" *(Shalom)* to the Female. The elements of Zer Anpin are then able to work through the Female, which is the Divine Presence *(Shekhinah),* which oversees all providence.

The element of Zer Anpin which is most desired to be in operation is that of Chesed-Love, which is the attribute of Abraham (*see* **135, 190, 191**). It is therefore said that the "seed" should be that of Abraham, which means that the "seed" that Zer Anpin introduces into the Female should derive from Chesed-Love. This is accomplished through Daat-Knowledge, and the verse therefore ends, "In the midst of years make it known."

78. According to the Talmud, the daughter's name was actually Bakol, meaning "With All."

The word "All" always refers to the Sefirah of Yesod-Foundation, which is the sexual organ (see 22). BaKol is literally Bet Kol, where Bet is the second letter of the Hebrew alphabet, and hence indicates the number two. Therefore, BaKol is the "second All," that is, the second sexual organ, namely that of the Female.

God gave Abraham the commandement of Circumcision, which was the rectification of the male sex organ, thus assuring that he would have "seed." In a physical sense, this meant that he would be able to have children through Sarah, and that he would have descendants until the end of time. It also implied that he would have access to the souls that are begotten by the attribute of Yesod-Foundation. In a purely spiritual sense, however, it meant that Abraham's attribute, which is Chesed-Love, would have "seed" and enter Malkhut-Kingship, the Female, thus influencing all providence.

It is therefore written that God blessed Abraham "with All," that is, with the Sefirah of Yesod-Foundation, which is called "All." But the blessing actually was that his attribute should enter into Malkhut-Kingship, the Daughter. It is thus taught that God blessed Abraham with a daughter.

The verse then quoted is, "All that is called by My Name for My Glory." Again, as always, "Glory" refers to Malkhut-Kingship. "My Name" is Sh'mi, literally Shem Yud, "the Name of Yud," the Yud being the aspect of Chakhmah-Wisdom, the first letter of the Tetragrammaton. The attribute of "All" transmits the Yud, which is Chakhmah-Wisdom, to Glory, which is Malkhut-Kingship, the Female. The meaning of this is that Yesod-Foundation is the attribute that brings Chakhmah-Wisdom to Malkhut-Kingship, this being the same aspect as that discussed with regard to Solomon in the previous section.

It is therefore written that God "blessed" Abraham. As discussed earlier, "blessing" always refers to Chakhmah-Wisdom (3).

On a deeper level, the Sefirah of Chesed-Love is directly derived from Chakhmah-Wisdom (30). The "blessing," which is Chakhmah-Wisdom, is therefore to Abraham, who is the personification of Chesed-Love.

Both here and in 65, Chakhmah-Wisdom is called a "daughter." This might seem surprising, since Chakhmah-

Wisdom is a male element, while "daughter" is usually said to refer to Malkhut-Kingship.

The Hebrew word for "daughter," however is *BaT*, spelled Bet Tav. As mentioned above, Bet is Chakhmah-Wisdom, while Tav is Malkhut-Kingship. The concept of "Daughter" is therefore the channeling of Chakhmah-Wisdom to Malkhut-Kingship.

The verse concludes, "I created it, I formed it, and I made it." "My Glory" is Malkhut-Kingship, the lowest level of Atzilut-Nearness. The lower three universes are then mentioned explicitly: Beriyah-Creation, Yetzirah-Formation, and Asiyah-Making. It is actually from this verse that the mystery of the Four Universes is derived in Kabbalah texts (See *Mesechta Atzilut 5*).

In Genesis 26:24, God calls Abraham, "My slave." The King to whom the slave belongs is the Sefirah of Malkhut-Kingship, the Divine Presence (Shekhinah). It was to this attribute that Abraham first bound himself as a slave. The Talmud therefore states that Abraham was the first one who addressed God by His name *Adonoy,* which is the Name associated with Malkhut-Kingship (see Table).

THE SEFIROT AND NAMES OF GOD

Sefirah		*Name*
Keter—Crown	אהיה אשר אהיה	Ehyeh Asher Ehyeh
Chakhmah—Wisdom	יה	Yah
Binah—Understanding	יהוה (אלהים)	YHVH (read Elohim)
Chesed—Love	אל	El
Gevurah—Strength	אלהים	Elohim
Tiferet—Beauty	יהוה (אדני)	YHVH (read Adonoy)
Netzach—Victory	אדני צבאות	Adonoy Tzevaot
Hod—Splendor	אלהים צבאות	Elohim Tzevaot
Yesot—Splendor	שדי (אל חי)	Shaddai (El Chai)
Malkhut—Kingship	אדני	Adonoy

This Sefirah then gave Abraham over to its "older brother," which refers to the Sefirah of Yesod-Foundation, the lowest element of Zer Anpin. God then revealed Himself as Shaddai, the Name associated with Yesod-Foundation. He

then gave Abraham the commandment of circumcision, which
is the rectification of Yesod-Foundation, the male organ.

This "older brother" called Abraham his "friend," through
the aspect of "seed." This is the aspect of Yesod-Foundation.
The beautiful "vessel" given to Abraham was then this "daughter," as discussed above.

The concept here is the process through which "motivation
from below" brings about "motivation from above." Abraham
bound himself to the aspect of Malkhut-Kingship, and all such
binding is, in itself, an aspect of Yesod-Foundation. He was
then given the Attribute of Yesod-Foundation, which was the
covenant in his body, and he was then worthy of experiencing
Malkhut-Kingship "in his place."

Regarding the "treasuries of kings," see **89.**

79. This verse literally says, "I heard Your hearing." It is
well established that "hearing" refers to Understanding, and
therefore, when the prophet said, "I heard Your hearing," it
means that he understood God's Understanding. That is, with
his own understanding, he delved into the Sefirah of Binah-
Understanding. This is infinite, as it is written, "There is no
probing His Understanding" (Isaiah 40:28).

Ozen, the Hebrew word for ear, is spelled Alef Zayin Nun.
The concept of the Alef is explained above (**70**).

Of the highest three Sefirot, the only one which can in any
way be grasped is Binah-Understanding. It is therefore taught
that the Torah uses anthropomorphic allegories to "satisfy the
ear," since this is the highest level of our comprehension (see
Etz Chaim, Shaar AChaP 2). It is for this same reason that we
say, "Hear O Israel" (Deuteronomy 6:4).

Seeing and hearing respectively correspond to Chakhmah-
Wisdom and Binah-Understanding. We can only grasp the
Divine with understanding, but not with wisdom. The highest
level of our comprehension is therefore Binah-Understanding,
the level of the "Ear," but even here, there is a reflection of
Keter-Crown in the Alef of *Ozen.*

The author states that Alef is the root of the Ten Commandments. On the simplest level, this is because Alef is the first
level of the Decalogue. On a deeper level, just as Alef is the first
letter of the first of the Ten Commandments, it also represents
the first of the Ten Sefirot, which is Keter-Crown.

80. The important lesson here is that the name of each thing is its spiritual essence, and it is very closely related to its physical being.

81. The example here is the root of a tree. The symbolism of the "tree" is well developed in the Bahir, and the "root of the tree" is the root of all existence. It is related to the letters Shin and Resh. Regarding the Shin, see **26, 118.**

The final lesson here is that every branch of the Tree can be the root of a new "tree." It can be brought back to its "ground" and rooted again.

After the Alef, which represents Keter-Crown and its revelation in Binah-Understanding, comes the Zayin, which represents the next seven Sefirot. These are discussed in the next section.

82. Here we find the basic explanation of all the anthropomorphisms in the Bible and other writings. Even though we know that God is absolutely incorporeal, having neither body, shape nor form, it is taught that "He borrows terms from His creatures to express His relationship to His creation (*Mekhilta* on Exodus 19:18). These terms are used allegorically, but at the same time, each has a definite meaning in terms of the Sefirot. (See Table).

SEFIROT AND ANTHROPOMORPHIC REPRESENTATION

1. Keter-Crown	
2. Chakhmah-Wisdom	skull, mind
3. Binah-Understanding	right brain
4. Chesed-Love	left brain, heart
5. Gevurah-Strength	right hand
6. Tiferet-Beauty	body, torso
7. Netzach-Victory	right foot, right kidney, right testicle
8. Hod-Splendor	left foot, left kidney, left testicle
9. Yesod-Foundation	sexual organ
10. Malkhut-Kingship	mouth (of organ), mate

The verse that states that man is created in "God's image" therefore means that man parallels the Sefirot in the structure of both his body and soul. This is especially true with respect to the Personification *(Partzuf)* of Zer Anpin, which is the Supernal Man.

It was stated earlier, however, that the Sefirot of Zer Anpin are represented by the Vav *(see* **130***)*. This is because it is formed out of six Sefirot, and the question then arises, how can we say that it has seven parts. It is answered that Malkhut-Kingship is also included, since Yesod-Foundation and Malkhut-Kingship are connected.

The word Ear *(Ozen),* has the connotation of communion. In a time of communion, when the Male and Female are bound together, the Vav becomes a Zayin.

The teaching here still seems difficult to understand. In reckoning the seven, instead of counting the "mate" as the seventh element, it is given as the "head."

Actually, however, this is related to Bat, the "Daughter," where Chakhmah-Wisdom is drawn down through Malkhut-Kingship. Only when Zer Anpin is connected to his Bride does he have Chakhmah-Wisdom, and only then is he said to have a head. This is related to the Talmudic teaching that a man is incomplete as long as he does not have a wife.

The form of the Vav is that of a line, which a small square to the left. That of the Zayin is a line, with a full square on top, extending both to the right and the left. When Zer Anpin is represented by the Vav, He only has the left-brain, which is Binah-Understanding. When represented by the Zayin, both right and left brains are present, indicating that he has both Chakhmah-Wisdom and Binah-Understanding.

When both Chakhmah-Wisdom and Binah-Understanding exist, their confluence creates Daat-Knowledge, which binds them to the body. Therefore the "head" can also be counted. But when only Binah-Understanding is present, there is no Daat-Knowledge, and, since the head cannot effect the body, it is not counted in the mode of the Vav.

83. The letter Nun has the form of an enlongated Zayin, and has the numerical value of fifty.

THE SEFIROT

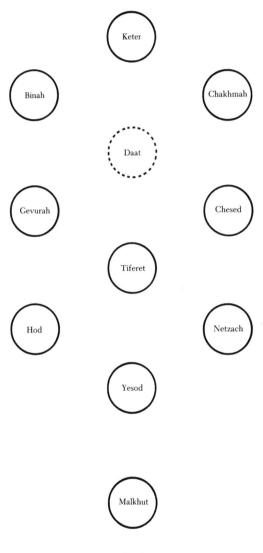

Fig. 8.

If we look at the Diagram, we see that there are four Sefirot in the center line: Keter-Crown, Tiferet-Beauty, Yesod-Foundation, and Malkhut-Kingship. When the quasi-Sefirah, Daat-Knowledge, is also included the center line has five elements. This is the significance of the Nun. Each of these five elements is multiplied by ten, yielding fifty, which is the numerical value of Nun.

This is the concept of the spinal cord, which unites the body with the brain.

Above, it was said that the Nun is Binah-Understanding (**61**). This is because Keter-Crown is only comprehended through Binah-Understanding, this being the concept of the Ear. It is for this reason that the "head" of the Nun is inclined slightly toward the left, indicating the dominance of Binah-Understanding. Nun is also the final letter of *Ozen,* which means "ear."

This is the concept of the Son, *Ben* in Hebrew, where the Chakhmah-Wisdom associated with the Bet flows through the Nun to be expressed. The Son usually refers to Zer Anpin.

There are two letters Nun in the Hebrew alphabet, a bent one in the middle of a word, and a straight one at the end of a

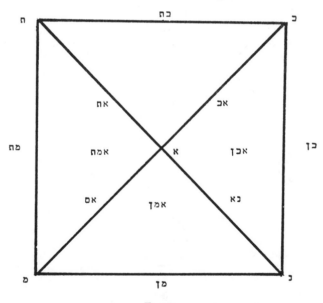

Fig. 9

word. In the bent Nun, instead of going straight down the middle, the line inclines slightly to the right, and then bends sharply to the center. That is, it bends toward Netzach-Victory, and ends at Yesod-Foundation. Yesod-Foundation is the Sefirah that bestows to another, and therefore, such a Nun is in the middle of a word, where it can bestow to the next letter. The straight Nun, on the other hand, "includes male and female," and since it extends all the way down the middle, includes Malkhut-Kingship as well. Just as Malkhut-Kingship is an endpoint, so is the final Nun.

84. The letter Mem represents the present, which is the womb of the future (*see* **37,50**). In its external aspect, it represents Daat-Knowledge, while in its internal aspect, it is Keter-Crown. Mem has a numerical value of forty, which consists of four steps, each step containing ten elements. These four steps are Keter-Crown, Chakhmah-Wisdom,Binah-Understanding, and Daat-Knowledge.

In the next section, we see that the open Mem, which occurs in the middle of a word, is the female, while the closed Mem, which is at the end of a word, is the male. The letter Mem itself, however, is spelled Mem Mem, with both the open and closed Mem, and it therefore includes both the male and the female. The reason for this is because it contains both Chakhmah-Wisdom and Binah-Understanding, Father and Mother.

The Mem is the womb open from below to give birth. The Tet, on the other hand, is the womb that is open from above to receive from the Male.

In another sense, there are two female Sefirot, Binah-Understanding, the supernal Mother, and Malkhut-Kingship, the supernal Bride. The Mem is the womb of Binah-Understanding, while the Tet is the womb of Malkhut-Kingship. Since Binah-Understanding is one of the three un-fathomable upper Sefirot, it can only be viewed from the outside. Malkhut-Kingship, on the other hand, is the womb of the universe, and hence is visible only on the inside. We are inside the letter Tet, looking upward through its small opening on top.

85. As mentioned earlier, water represents the concept of change, and this is also the primary concept of birth.

The teaching here includes the entire mystery of Mikvah, the ritual pool used for purification. The Mikvah contains forty Sah's (measures) of water, forty being the numerical value of Mem. The Mikvah thus represents the womb. When a person enters the Mikvah, it is like he re-enters the womb, and when he emerges, it is like he is reborn.

The concept of the Mem is that of the present, while water represents change. It is the present that is the arena of all change.

The concept of water contains both male and female aspects. These are alluded to in the water above and below the firmament respectively *(Genesis 1:7, Yerushalmi, Berakhot 9:2)*. Masculine water is active change, while feminine water is passive change, the two being action and reaction respectively.

87. As discussed earlier, hearing is Binah-Understanding, while seeing is Chakhmah-Wisdom. Both are derived from thought, which is Keter-Crown.

88. The concept of thought is like that of "up." No matter how high one reaches, one can still go further. Therefore, with respect to thought, the word "rise" is used.

While there is no limit as to how high one can go, on a finite body, such as the planet earth, there is a limit how far down one can go. Depending on the subject, there is a limit to how deeply it can be probed.

Knowledge is the expression of the mind. No matter how deep the expression, it can ultimately be fathomed. But the mind itself cannot be fathomed.

Similarly, the Merkava-Chariot is merely an expression of the Divine, and not the Divine itself. It is therefore called a "vision." This vision consists of elements in the seer's mind interacting with the unseeable. The seer is therefore said to be above the vision, since it emanates from elements in his own mind.

The concept of this covering *(Succah,* coming from the same root as *Sechuta)* has already been mentioned in passing **(74)**, from the verse, "He made darkness His hiding place . . . His *Succah,* the darkness of waters, thick clouds of the skies *(Shechakim),* (Psalms 18:12). As mentioned, *Shechakim* refer to the Sefirot of Netzach-Victory and Hod-Splendor, the two

Sefirot which are the source of vision and inspiration. This however, only comes through the concept of *"Succah."* The word *"Succah"* has the connotation of both "seeing" and "covering," and therefore it is a cover through which one can see.

When we speak of God's "thought," we are speaking of a level where He "surrounds all worlds." On the other hand, when we speak of the Merkava-Chariot, we are speaking of a level where He "fills all worlds." We therefore can look down into our own soul to see Him.

89. Segol is a vowel point, discussed above (**36**). Besides being a vowel point, however, Segol is also a cantellation note.

The four levels of expression are Letters, Ornaments, Vowels, and Cantellations (see *Etz Chaim, Shaar TNTA 1*) (*Also see* Table five).

LEVELS OF EXPRESSION

Level	*Expression*
Asiyah-Making	Letters— *Otiot*
Yetzirah-Formation	Ornaments — *Tagin*
Beriyah-Creation	Vowels — *Sekudot*
Atzilut-Nearness	Cantellations — *Ta'amim*

As a cantellation, Segol is associated with Malkhut-Kingship, as is the Zarka. Segol is the mode of "above to below," while Zarka is "below to above." These are respectively the concepts of "motivation from below," and "motivation from above."

The word Segol comes from the same root as *Segulah,* meaning "treasury." It is called the "Treasury of Kings," since it accepts from all the "Kings" that are above it. The "Kings" refer to the Sefirot, as discussed above in **27** and **49**.

The word Zarka comes from the root *Zarak,* meaning to "throw." It therefore represents the concept of "motivation from below," like something that is "thrown" upward. When something is thrown upward, however, it falls down again, and thus, a "motivation from below" results in a "motivation from above." The latter is the "Treasury of Kings."

Zarka is the first of the cantellation notes, and it is followed by Segol. First must come "motivation from below," and only then is it followed by "motivation from above."

90. There are two praises of the angels. The first is "Holy, holy, holy, the Lord of Hosts, the whole earth is filled with His glory" (Isaiah 6:3). This speaks of God's imminence, where His Glory, which is the aspect of Malkhut-Kingship, fills all creation. The second praise is the one quoted here, "Blessed be God's glory from His place" (Ezekiel 3:12). This indicates His transcendence, where even His Glory, which is Malkhut-Kingship, the lowest level, must be blessed from afar. These two levels are the ones discussed above (in 2), Where it was said that God both fills all worlds and encompasses all worlds.

The word "bless" indicates the aspect in which God fills all worlds (*see* 3). This, however, comes from God's "place," that is, from the aspect where He is the place of the universe," encompassing all creation. Thus, when it is said, "Blessed be God's glory from His place," it means that the aspect in which He "surrounds all worlds" must be brought down so that He should "fill all worlds."

Between the aspect of His "filling all worlds" and His "surrounding all worlds" are the universes themselves, where God is hidden through the concept of Tzimtzum-Constriction (see *Likutey Moharan 64:2*). The concept of Zarka is then to cross this abyss, and since one cannot reach across it, it must be "thrown." We then bring the Light from the aspect of "surrounding all worlds" to that of "filling all worlds," which we can perceive through gazing in the Markava. This is the *Segulah,* the treasure.

Both filling and surrounding involve the word Glory *(Kavod),* which represents Malkhut-Kingship. These two aspects are respectively represented by Zarkal and Segol, the two cantellations indicating Malkhut-Kingship. One "throws" thought to reach the level of "surrounding," while the other is the "treasure" of "filling."

The author states this in highly mysterious language, which is also reproduced in the Talmud *(Chagigah 13b).* The concept of a Crown is something that surrounds, just like a crown encompasses the head. When God is called "Owner of heaven and earth," it means that He oversees all things with His providence, this being the concept of "filling." We thus bring the crown, which is "surrounding," to that of the head, which is Chakhmah-Wisdom and blessing, which is the concept of "filling." The entire verse is: "Blessed be Abraham to God most High, Owner of heaven and earth." The concept of "Owner" thus involves "blessing."

91. The accent is at the end of a word, indicating that it is actually the lowest level. But the concept of the "Crown," the surrounding, rises higher and higher without end, like the concept of "up," discussed above.

The reason for this is that Keter-Crown is very closely related to Malkhut-Kingship, this being the concept of the "Crown of the King." Even though one is the highest Sefirah and the other is the lowest, they are connected through the concept of, "Their beginning is imbedded in their end" *(Sefer Yetzirah 1:7)*. Furthermore, all creation, even the highest levels, are nothing more than Malkhut-Kingship of the Infinite Being, this being the mystery of the verse, "Your Kingship *(Malkhut)* is a Kingship of all worlds" (Psalms 145:13).

The stone mentioned here is called *Dar,* discussed in **190**.

92. The discussion now returns to the Thirty-Two Paths, first introduced in **63**. Here they are said to parallel the thirty-two threads of the Tzitzit.

The Tzitzit are the ritual tassels or fringes mentioned in Numbers 15:38. They are worn in the Tallit, as well as in the "small Tallit" *(Tallit Katan),* which is worn all day. The word Tzitzit comes from the root "Tzutz," meaning to gaze, since they are meant to be the object of contemplation and meditation. The Torah thus says regarding them, "You shall gaze upon them and remember all of God's commandments, . . . and not stray after your heart and after your eyes . . ." (Numbers 15:39).

The Tallit covers the entire body, while the Tzitzit-fringes hang down around the legs. As discussed earlier, the two legs parallel the Sefirot of Netzach-Victory and Hod-Splendor, which are the source of prophecy and vision. The Tzitzit-fringes thus represent the concept of the mystical vision. They consist of thirty-two threads, paralleling the Thirty-two Paths of Wisdom, which are the paths upon which the initiate ascends. They are called the "watchers of the paths," since their purpose, as spelled out in the Torah, is to prevent misleading thoughts — "that you not stray after your heart and after your eyes."

The blue thread in the Tzitzit-fringes was colored with a special dye made from a mollusk called the *Chilazon,* most probably related to the Murex and Purpura. The blue thread is spoken of as an object of mystical contemplation, "The blue is like the sea, the sea is like the sky, and the sky is like the Throne of Glory" (*see* **96**). Through it, one climbs from the terrestrial to the astral, and then to the transcendental.

There are four Tzitzit-fringes in the Tallit, each having eight threads, making a total of thirty-two threads.

The four Tzitzit-fringes are said to represent the four basic concepts in each of the four universes. These are the four "elements" (or stages of matter) in the physical universe of Asiyah-Making; the four archangels, Michael, Gabriel, Uriel and Raphael, in Yetzirah-Formation, the universe of angels; the four legs of the Throne in Beriyah-Creation, which is the Universe of the Throne, and finally, the four letters of the Tetragrammaton in Atzilut-Nearness, the Universe of Sefirot.

The four Tzitzit-fringes are attached to the Tallit, a shawl-like garment that covers the body. This Tallit is said to represent the Chashmal (Electrum) mentioned in Ezekiel 1:4. In Kabbalistic teachings, the Chashmal is the garment that protects from the Klipot (Husks) of Evil, also mentioned in the same verse: "A storm wind . . . a gread cloud, and flashing fire." As is evident from the context, Ezekiel had to pass through these three Klipot before he could experience his vision, which begins with the Chashmal. It is therefore through the Tzittzit fringes that this inner Chashmal can be reached.

93. The blue thread is a sign of Malkhut-Kingship, indicating that God is King over all the paths.

The example is a "king who travels abroad." This is the Divine Essence when it is lowered so as to be the subject of a vision. The slaves are terrified of the king, lest they err, and he therefore gives them a sign, namely, the Tzitzit.

The seven white threads in the Tzitzit correspond to the seven elements of Zer Anpin, as discussed earlier in **82.** The blue thread has the connotation of Malkhut-Kingship, the daughter, and at the same time, also indicates Binah-Understanding (*see* **96**).

94. The Thirty-two Paths consist of the Ten Numbers, and the Twenty-two Letters. The Ten Numbers correspond to the Ten Sefirot. The Twenty-two Letters are divided into Three Mothers, Seven Pairs, and Twelve Elementals. The Three Mothers are the three horizontal base lines of the Tree, while the Seven Pairs are the seven vertical lines. The Twelve Elementals are the diagonals. (*see* Fig. 10).

THE THIRTY-TWO PATHS

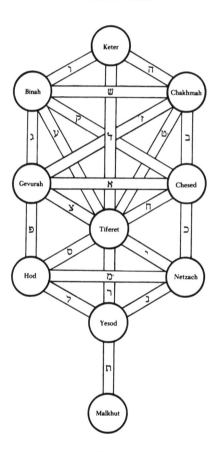

Fig. 10.

The Three Mothers and Seven Pairs also parallel the Ten Sefirot. The Three Mothers are the three highest Sefirot, while the Seven Pairs are the seven lower ones. Each of the Seven Pairs thus reaches upward from one of the lower seven Sefirot.

Left over are the Twelve Elementals, corresponding to the twelve diagonals.

The first statement is that each of these Twelve Elementals consists of six "names." The six names parallel the six directions of a three-dimensional continuum. Each of the Twelve is thus a complete spatial continuum. in its own right.

The twelve diagonal paths themselves are in the world of Sefirot, which is the Universe of Atzilut-Nearness. These are reflected in the Twelve Directors, which are the archangels in the world of the Throne, which is the Universe of Beriyah-Creation. It is with regard to these archangels that Isaiah said, "I saw God sitting on a high and exalted Throne . . . above Him stood the Seraphim (archangels), each one had six wings" (Isaiah 6:1,2). He is speaking of the archangels that are in the world of the Throne.

Each of these Director Archangels has six wings, and these correspond to the Six Powers that it has in the world below the throne, the world of angels, which is the Universe of Yetzirah-Formation. This makes a total of Seventy-two Powers.

Each of these Power-Angels is the guardian angel of one of the Seventy-two nations, corresponding to the seventy-two languages. These are the reflection of the Powers in the physical world.

As mentioned above, even though Asiyah-Making includes the physical world, it is primarily its conceptual aspect. The level of Asiyah-Making is therefore spoken of as the seventy-two languages, rather than as the nations. Language is a conceptual, rather than a physical, entity, and the languages represent the seventy-two ways of expressing worldly concepts.

On a deeper level, each of the seventy-two languages has a root in God's name of seventy-two elements, and therefore, any one of these languages can be used to enter the realm of the mysteries. This reflects the Midrashic teaching, where Elijah said, "I bring heaven and earth to bear witness, that any human, Jew or Gentile, man or woman, freeman or slave, according to his deeds he can be worthy of *Ruach HaKodesh* (the "Holy Spirit," the transcendental experience)" *(Tana DeBei Eliahu Rabba 9)*.

These seventy-two elements exist in all four universes, making a total of 288. This is the significance of the 288 sparks of Holiness that exist in creation (see *Etz Chaim, Shaar RaPaCh Netzutzin*).

95. The Tree is the array of the Sefirot, connected by the Thirty-two Paths, as in the Diagram. This diagram contains twelve diagonal paths, corresponding to the twelve diagonal directions.

As outlined in *Sefer Yetzirah* (chapter 5), these twelve paths also correspond to the twelve signs of the zodiac, the twelve months of the year, and the twelve primary functions of the body. They also correspond to the twelve tribes, and the twelve ways in which the four letters of the Tetragrammaton, YHVH, can be permuted.

These directions are said to spread to infinity. By trying to penetrate this infinity, one can approach the Tree, thus reaching its paths. The quotation from *Sefer Yetzirah* therefore says, "Inside them is the Tree."

They are called the "Arms of the world," a term borrowed from the verse, "His pride is in the skies *(Shechakim); a dwelling is the God of Eternity (Kedem), and underneath are the arms of the world*" (Deuteronomy 34:26, 27). As mentioned in a number of places (*see* 1), the term *Shechakim* always refers to Netzach-Victory and Hod-Splendor, the two Sefirot involved in prophecy and inspiration.

The verse then says that a "dwelling is the God of eternity," indicating that God is eternal, beyond space and time. The word for "Eternity" here is *Kedem,* a term that generally applies to Keter-Crown. God is called "a dwelling," since He also encompasses space and time. Therefore, underneath this concept are the "arms of the world," the infinities of the diagonal boundaries that define space.

As discussed earlier (in 30), creation consists of five dimensions, consisting of space, time, which is the fourth dimension, and a fifth spiritual dimension *(Sefer Yetzirah 1:5)*. In the *Sefer Yetzirah,* these are divided into three major concepts, the Universe, which is the three dimensions of space, the Year, which is the time dimension, and the Soul, which is the spiritual dimension. All twenty-two concepts, paralleling the twenty-two letters of the Hebrew Alphabet, are reflected in each of these three categories.

The *Sefer Yetzirah* states that the Axis *(Teli)* is the king over the Universe, the Sphere or Cycle *(Galgal)* is the king over the year, and the Heart *(Lev)* is king over the Soul.

The *Sefer Yetzirah* also states that each of these twelve have parallels in the Soul, namely the twelve main functions of the body, under the rule of the Heart. There are also twelve signs of the zodiac in the Universe, and twelve months in the Year, under the rule of the Axis and Sphere respectively.

All three domains thus yield a total of thirty-six. Since each of these has a counterpart "above," there are a total of seventy-two.

The source of all spiritual elevation, however, is the Heart, which is the king over the Soul. Of the five dimensions, the one through which the initiate travels into the mystical realms is that of the Soul. The author therefore states that they all are included in the Soul. It is in the Heart that the Thirty-two Paths exist (**63**).

The sixty-four Forms mentioned here are those seen by Ezekiel. Each of the four legs of the Throne has four angels, and each of these angels has four "faces," making a total of sixty-four "faces" or Forms (see *Pirkey Rabbi Eliezer 4*).

The Heart ultimately contains the sixty-four. These are the Thirty-two Paths with "motivation from below," and these same paths with "motivation from above."

These sixty-four can be realized only through the Heart, which is the dimension of Soul. The next seven are completed through the cycle of the week, which is Time, the domain of the Sphere. These parallel the seven lower Sefirot.

The last one involves space — the single point in space through which the Divine can shine. This is the concept of the Divine Presence *(Shekhinah)*, which is the Sefirah of Malkhut-Kingship manifest in the physical spatial world. This is the "advantage" of the world, the extra dimension perceived only by the initiate.

The great Kabbalist, Rabbi Judah Low (The Maharal of Prague), who is credited with having made the Golem, explains it in this manner. The world consists of six directions, two for each of its three dimensions, and it was for this reason that it was created in six days. The Sabbath, the seventh day, is the central point, unifying the six directions and the six days. The number seven is therefore the perfection of creation, and this is the reason why it occurs in so many contexts in the Torah. This is the point of Malkhut-Kingship.

The level that transcends the physical is eight. This is the reason, for example, why circumcision is on the eighth day, since this allows one to draw down a soul from the transcendental plane. This is also the eight strings in the Tzitzit-fringes, and the eight days of Chanukah. This is the "advantage" of the land.

The seven days represent the seven lower Sefirot, while the eighth is the Sefirah of Binah-Understanding, the gateway to the upper three Sefirot. It is therefore called an "advantage."

96. Even though "Earth" is usually identified with Malkhut-Kingship, there is a higher "Earth," identified with Binah-Understanding. While the lower earth is called the "Lower Shekhinah," the upper earth is called the "Higher Shekhinah." These two levels correspond to the two letters Heh in the Tetragrammaton, where Binah-Understanding is the first Heh, and Malkhut-Kingship is the final Heh. It is from the upper Earth that the lower Earth was graven.

This Upper Earth is identified with the Throne, which is in the Universe of Beriyah-Creation. According to the correspondence between Sefirot and Universes, Beriyah-Creation corresponds to Binah-Understanding.

This is also the "Sea of Wisdom." The "sea" always is a female element, and usually this is Malkhut-Kingship. But the "Sea of Wisdom" is the female element associated with Chakhmah-Wisdom, and this is Binah-Understanding. This is said to be the blue in the Tzitzit-fringes.

The Throne is Binah-Understanding. This is the "high and exalted Throne," seen by Isaiah. The "Throne of Glory," however, is associated with Malkhut-Kingship, since "Glory" always refers to this Sefirah. The Universe of the Throne, which is Beriyah-Creation, is derived from Binah-Understanding. But at the same time, it is the degree immediately below the lowest Sefirah of Azilut-Nearness, which is Malkhut-Kingship. It is therefore called a "Throne" for Glory, which is Malkhut-Kingship.

The blue thread in the Tzitzit-fringes therefore contains the concepts of both Binah-Understanding and Malkhut-

Kingship. The main concept of the blue is Malkhut-Kingship, since blue is the color of royalty (**93**). But it also expresses the eighth level, the one above the mundane, which is Binah-Understanding. When these concepts are brought together, the eighth level is called the "Throne of Glory," since it is through the level above the mundane that Malkhut-Kingship, which is the Divine Presence (Shekhinah) is revealed in the world.

Malkhut-Kingship is called a precious stone, since it receives and reflects all the other Sefirot. Similarly, a diamond reflects white light as all colors (*see* **146**).

97. The *Terumah,* the Lifted Offering, was specified for the building of the Tabernacle in the desert after the Exodus from Egypt.

Prayer is the "service of the heart." It is therefore one of the primary ways of enhancing the Heart on high, opening up the Thirty-Two Paths. (*see* **103**).

98. Of the seventy-two , seventy refer to the seventy nations, while the other two are Israel and the Satan (*see* **167**).

The fruit mentioned here is the Etrog (Citron), which together with the Lulav (Palm Frond), myrtle and willow, are taken in hand on the festival of Succot (Tabernacles). This is discussed below (**176**).

If all the bullocks offered during the festival of Succot (mentioned in Numbers 29:12-34) are counted, the total number is seventy. The Talmud states that these were to expiate for the seventy nations *(Succot 56b).*

But the commandment that Israel observes on this festival involves things taken from trees, notably the Etrog or citron, the Lulav or palm frond, the myrtle and the willow twigs. Israel thus takes the Tree itself.

In the right hand, one holds the Lulav, together with the myrtle and willow, and these represent the Tree itself. The "heart" of this Tree is the Etrog, held in the left hand, opposite the heart.

It was primarily on the feast of Succot that people were able to grasp onto this Tree. They therefore had a festival of "Drawing" when water was drawn for a special "Water Sacrifice" on the altar during Succot. The Talmud says that it was called a celebration of Drawing because the people drew *Ruach HaKodesh* (Holy Spirit, the transcendental experience; *Yerushalmi, Succot 5:1).*

Over each of these Paths is a Watchman, mentioned above (**92**). The Tree of Life is the Tree of the Sefirot, where these Thirty-Two Paths are defined.

99. The forms are the Cherubim. These are identical with the Chayot (Life Angels), as defined by the prophet (Ezekiel 10:15). These Chayot were therefore the first things that Ezekiel saw in his vision (Ezekiel 1:5).

100. The "Blessed Holy One" is the name that refers to Zer Anpin. This consists of the six Sefirot which are called "Heaven" (*see* **30**.)

101. This can also be read, "the thirty-six given over to the heart" (alluding to **97**). These are the thirty-six (Lamed Vav) righteous men who sustain the world. These are the thirty-six individuals who walk the Thirty-Two Paths of Wisdom.

102. Here again, "heaven" refers to Zer Anpin, while "earth" is Malkhut-Kingship. But in a more general sense, "earth" is the physical world, while "heaven" is the transcendental. In either case, one who wishes to ascend on high must always travel along the path from Malkhut-Kingship to Yesod-Foundation. Looking at the diagram of paths, it is evident that, while there are many paths interconnecting the other Sefirot, there is only one path leading from Malkhut-Kingship, the lowest Sefirah, upward, and this is the path leading to Yesod-Foundation. This path is called Tzadik, the Pillar of Righteousness, represented by the letter Tav.

Just as it is the only path upward, it is also the only path downward, bringing all blessing and spiritual sustenance. This is strong when there are righteous people in the world; otherwise it is weak. Since the universe only exists through God's creative force flowing through this path, the world cannot endure it if it is weak.

Only the righteous can offer the Heart, and it is thus written "from every man who would offer his heart" (Exodus 25:2). It is from the others that mundane offerings are taken.

103. Although the Yud represents the Sefirah of Chakhmah-Wisdom, it is also paralleled in human wisdom. The Thirty-Two Paths are primarily paths of wisdom.

As discussed earlier, these Thirty-Two Paths are in the Heart, which is where the revelation of Binah-Understanding ends, and Chakhmah-Wisdom begins to be revealed (63). The concept of the Lifted Offering (Terumah) is that the individual lifts himself through Wisdom, to travel on the Thirty-Two paths.

The Hebrew word for "wisdom " is Chakhmah, and as the Zohar states, this has the same letters as *Ko'ach Mah,* the "power" or "potential" of What. *(Zohar 3:28a, 235b).* Alternatively, *Ko'ach Mah* means "a certain potential." In the first sense, it is the power to question, to go beyond what is grasped with Understanding. In the alternate sense, it is an undefined potential, a potential that cannot be grasped with Understanding, which is a lower level, but which must be experienced in its own right. As such, it is man's power to experience, since Wisdom is built out of experience. When one travels on the Paths of Wisdom, one begins with the Heart, which is Understanding. But then, one goes beyond this, to the Experience of Wisdom, which cannot be understood.

104. There is a commandment in the Torah that states that when one finds a nest with eggs or chicks, one must send away the mother bird before taking anything from the nest. The explanation given here is reiterated a number of times in the Zohar.

Binah-Understanding is the Sefirah that immediately precedes the seven lower Sefirot, which parallel the seven days of creation. Binah-Understanding is the future, the end point of the time continuum, and hence, it represents the completion of the concept of time. It is only from a juxtaposition of Chakhmah-Wisdom and Binah-Understanding, past and future, that existence as we know it can come into being *(see* **30**). Creation can only exist in the context of time, and is therefore expressed in terms of days.

Binah-Understanding is therefore the Mother Womb from which all creation emerged. It is also the Mother from which all the lower seven Sefirot emanated.

105. Here it is said that the lower seven Sefirot can be taken, but that Binah-Understanding must be sent away. This means that one may not delve any higher than the lower seven Sefirot, but that it is forbidden to even try to penetrate the upper three *(Radbaz, Metzudot David 206).*

There might appear to be a contradiction here, since in this statement it appears that it is forbidden to probe

Binah-Understanding, while in other places it appears that Binah-Understanding is the highest level that can be reached, and that even Chakhmah-Wisdom is accessible. But the meaning is this:

Even though Zer Anpin is built out of six of the lower seven Sefirot, it is a complete structure, and therefore has Ten Sefirot in its own right. When the Tikyney Zohar states that "Understanding is the Heart," it is speaking of Binah-Understanding as it is expressed in Zer Anpin *(Tikuney Zohar 17a, Etz Chaim, Shaar Partzufey Zachar U'Nekevah 4)*. Thus, when Binah-Understanding enters into the lower seven Sefirot of Zer Anpin as the Heart, then it is approachable. But when it is in its own place, as the Mother of Zer An, then it is impossible, and must be "sent away." (See Introduction to *Shaar HaHakdamot*).

The "children" are the Seven Sefirot, corresponding to the seven days of the week. They are also said to correspond to the seven days of Succot, since it is during this festival that people "draw the Holy Spirit," and experience these seven Sefirot. (**98**).

Besides the Four Species discussed earlier, the primary commandment of the festival of Succot is the Succah itself. The Succah is a hut, having four walls, and covered with a roof made of nonedible vegetable matter. This roof is called the *S'chach*. The words Succah and *S'chach* both have the connotation of seeing and covering (*see* **88**). The festival was therefore one of visions.

The house itself is Chakhmah-Wisdom, since "with Wisdom a house is built." It is with our Wisdom that we reach up to the higher spheres (**103**).

The roof of the Succah contains small openings through which the sky can be seen. This is the concept of a vision, it is mostly covered and concealed, and we can only see through the narrowest cracks.

When we enter into our Wisdom, the potential to experience that which cannot be understood, it is like entering a Succah. The roof above is covered, but it has small cracks through which the light can be seen.

106. Of the five dimensions alluded to in Sefer Yetzirah, the three spatial dimensions are the World, the time dimension is the Year, and the spiritual dimension is the Soul. The

Axis (Teli) is the ruler of the World, the Sphere or Cycle (Galgal) rules the Year, and the Heart rules the Soul.

The Axis represents Zer Anpin, and in the Kabbalah, this is what the verse in Song of Songs is referring to *(Etz Chaim, Shaar Arikh Anpin 5:3)*. Zer Anpin consists of the six Sefirot that parallel the six directions of the three-dimensional world.

The entire verse is, "His head is fine gold, his locks are curled, black as a raven."

The seven lower Sefirot parallel the seven astrological planets: Mercury, Venus, Mars, Jupiter, Saturn, the Sun, and the Moon. (The outer planets are not considered to affect the earth.) The "head" of Zer Anpin parallels the "first swirlings," which correspond to the spiral nebulae. This is called the "Encompassing Serpent," or the "Milky Way" by many of the ancients. The verse therefore states, "His locks are curled."

This is also the meditation on space. Seeking to penetrate the infiniteness of the galaxies, one can make the mental jump to the head and Mentalities of Zer Anpin.

The Sphere is king of the Year, this being the time dimension. It is the womb of the present, out of which the future is born.

The word *Galgal,* sphere, can also be translated as "cycle." The cycle of life runs from the womb to the grave. In Talmudic language, the same work, *Kever,* is used for both the womb and the grave (see *Ohalot 7:4*).

Finally, the Heart is king over the Soul, the spiritual dimension. This is the dimension paralleling the line from Keter-Crown to Malkhut-Kingship (**30**). As discussed earlier, the Heart is Yesod-Foundation of Chakhmah-Wisdom and Binah-Understanding extending into the "chest" of Zer Anpin. But Yesod-Foundation of Chakhmah-Wisdom is also a "garment" concealing Yesod-Foundation of Keter-Crown. Furthermore, the "chest" of Zer Anpin is on the same level as the "head" of Malkhut-Kingship, the Female, and therefore, the "heart" of Zer Anpin radiates into the "head" of the Female. Just like in general, Keter-Crown is outside the head, so the "heart" of Zer Anpin is the force outside the head of Malkhut-Kingship, and therefore is the "crown" of the Female.

It is therefore evident that the Heart is actually the primary point of the spiritual dimension that connects Keter-Crown to Malkhut-Kingship.

The word "Heaven" always refers to Zer Anpin. Therefore, "the heart of heaven" is the heart of Zer Anpin.

The verse quoted here is speaking of the revelation at Sinai, where the people saw the voices mentioned in **47,** and indeed, this verse (Deuteronomy 4:11) precedes the verse quoted there. The people saw the "Seven Voices," which are the Sefirot of Zer Anpin and the Female.

The path through which these Voices are "seen" is through the "heart of heaven." That is, by ascending through the "head" of Malkhut-Kingship to the "heart" of Zer Anpin that forms Her crown. As mentioned earlier (in **82**), the seven are taken together when Zer Anpin and the Female are united. The Thirty-Two Paths connect the Sefirot of Zer Anpin.

In another sense, the Axis represents the longitudinal angle, the Sphere represents the Azimuthal angle or latitude, and the Heart is the radius. These three elements thus represent a three dimensional continuum in sphereical coordinates.

107. This is the Priestly Blessing. It is said with the hands raised and the ten fingers spread, the ten fingers alluding to the Ten Sefirot (**124**).

The three blessings represent Universe, Year and Soul. These are the three levels of spiritual projection, from space, to time, to the spiritual dimension.

The end points of these three dimensions are Zer Anpin, Binah-Understanding, and Malkhut-Kingship. These are the three names, YHVH, in the Priestly Blessing. As discussed earlier, the name YHVH can be filled in in four different ways, corresponding to the four levels of creation (**70**). The three lowest of these levels correspond to the three end points, and these are the three Names in the Priestly Blessing.

If the two letters Heh in the Tetragrammaton YHVH are taken as different letters, then the four letters of this Name can be permuted in twenty-four ways. It is because of this that some Kabbalists write these two Heh's somewhat different from each other. If the two Heh's are not differentiated, then the four letters only have twelve permutations. Thus, there are twelve in each domain, but the twelve must be doubled (as in **95**). The twelve usual permutations of the Name correspond to the twelve diagonal directions.

Each verse in Exodus 14:19-21 contains seventy-two let-

ters, and these three verses also correspond to the three levels.
(*See* **110.**)

The "leaders," or more literally "heads" mentioned here
are the archangels of the Universe of Beriyah-Creation. The
"officers" are the angels of Yetzirah-Formation. The "army"
itself is the domain of Asiyah-Making.

108. Beside the three horizontal levels, there are also
three vertical "pillars." These pillars are called Love *(Chesed)*,
Severity *(Din)*, and Harmony *(Mishpat)*. The right pillar,
headed by Chesed-Love, is represented in the world of angels
by Michael. The left pillar is headed by Gevurah-Strength, and
is represented by Gabriel. The middle pillar is headed by
Tiferet-Beauty, and is represented by Uriel.

This being so, there are seventy-two Forms in Yetzirah-
Formation, mentioned here, and seventy-two Powers in
Beriyah-Creation. The ones in Beriyah-Creation correspond to
the souls of Israel, Since Beriyah-Creation is the level of
Neshamah-Souls. But the answer is that the Forms and Powers
are united through the sacrifice.

109. The concept of an animal sacrifice is to unify the
animal in man with his spiritual essence. Just as the animal is
"brought close" to God, so is the person bringing the sacrifice.

As discussed earlier, (5), the concept of Nose parallels Zer
Anpin and Yetzirah-Formation. Breath, on the other hand,
emanates from the Mouth, which is Malkhut-Kingship, the
lowest level of Atzilut-Nearness, and therefore, Breath is the
level of Beriyah-Creation. The concept of the "pleasant fragrance" therefore represents the link between Beriyah-Creation
and Yetzirah-Formation. When this takes place, Yetzirah-
Formation, which is the world of angels, and the level of Ruach
in the soul, is strengthened, and it can then affect man in the
physical world. For one thing, this is the level of *Ruach
HaKodesh*, (Divine Spirit), where man actually experiences
the level of Ruach. This experience can also consist of communion with an angel, which is also on the level of Ruach. In such
cases, the Breath, which is *Re'ach* (from the same root as
Ruach), is said to "descend."

110. The three verses are:

"And there traveled the angel of God, who went before the
camp of Israel, and it went behind them, and the pillar of cloud
moved from before them, and it stood behind them.

"And it came between the camp of Egypt and the camp of Israel, and there was cloud and darkness there, but it gave light, and one did not come near the other all the night.

"And stretched Moses his hand over the sea, and God caused the sea to recede by a strong east wind all the night, and He made the sea into dry land, and the waters were divided."

By tradition, it was with the Name emanating from these verses that Moses split the Red Sea. (See p. 184.)

The pillar of cloud mentioned in the first verse refers to the cloud that conceals the mysteries from our eyes. Through this Name, the cloud is brought "behind" us, separating us from the Husks of evil, personified by the "camp of Egypt." The same is true of the angel that guards the path of enlightenment.

The physical world is likened to night. Through this Name, man and evil "do not come together all the night." Even though this is a world of "cloud and darkness," it gives light.

The sea refers to Malkhut-Kingship, the Sefirah that must be penetrated before one can enter the mysteries. Wind (Ruach, also meaning Spirit) is the level of Zer Anpin, and the east is Tiferet, the source of "seed" (**73**). The force of Tiferet-Beauty in Zer Anpin opens Malkhut-Kingship so that it can be entered, and we can then pass over on dry land.

The actual splitting of the Red Sea was the primary preparation of the Israelites for the greatest of all visions, the revelation at Sinai. In making use of this Name, the individual can follow the same path. The methods of using this Name are discussed in Rabbi Abraham Abulafia's *Chayay Olam HaBa* and *Sefer HaCheshek,* as well as in the fourth (unpublished) part of *Shaarey Kedushah* by Rabbi Chaim Vital.

112. The total number of letters in these names, when written correctly and not counting suffixes, is seventy two. It is therefore the name of seventy-two, used to reach the "heart of heaven."

These names are not found in any other Kabbalistic texts, nor is there any instruction regarding their use. The suffix *"on"* or *"ron"* is also found in angelic names, such as Metatron and Sandelfon.

113. Of the twenty-two Paths corresponding to the letters of the alphabet, twelve are diagonals, and these correspond to the twelve tribes of Israel. It is to these paths that one is given access through the above-mentioned names.

Through these channels all force flows from the higher Sefirot to the lower ones. When the Sefirot are thus fortified, they can in turn influence events in the lower worlds. But when people are not worthy, the Sefirot are still granted blessing, but only on the condition that they do not bestow any of it to those below.

This is a lesson related to the above names. The channels through which they can be used are only open when the generation is worthy. We therefore find many cases where people themselves were worthy of attaining particular mysteries, but they could not attain them because the generation was not worthy.

The "rods" in this case are the channels.

The King here is Keter-Crown, and his "brothers" are the other Sefirot.

114. There are four basic levels of creation, represented by Chakhmah-Wisdom, Binah-Understanding, the six Sefirot of Zer Anpin, and Malkhut-Kingship. When these can be differentiated, they are said to comprise a "square." When they cannot be differentiated, they are called a "circle."

These concepts are not differentiated in the true spiritual sense. It is only when they are reflected in the physical that they can be seen as being different.

The square is therefore Malkhut-Kingship, which is the level in which all can be seen. It is the level that parallels Asiyah-Making, which also encompasses the physical world. The circle, on the other hand, is Binah-Understanding.

The square also denotes that which is made by man, as discussed in the Talmud *(Yerushalmi, Nedarim 3:2)*. It is in the physical world, the domain of Malkhut-Kingship, that man works. But it is within the works of man that the circle, representing the spiritual, can move.

The square represents Asiyah-Making, the domain of the physical world, while the circle is Beriyah-Creation, the universe of souls.

115. The letters represent the body, which is in Asiyah-Making. The vowel points are the Neshamah-Soul, which is in Beriyah-Creation.

It is through the proper combination of letters and vowels that one can enter into the spiritual domain (see *Chayay Olam HaBah*).

117. Alef is usually said to represent Keter-Crown (**70**). Actually, the "Holy Palace" is the confluence of the four basic concepts, Keter-Crown, Chakhmah-Wisdom, Binah-Understanding, and Malkhut-Kingship, and it is seen as the center point of the six Sefirot of Zer Anpin. The four concepts are denoted by the four corners of the Alef. Furthermore, in the diagram of the Thirty-Two Paths, Alef is the channel between Chakhmah-Wisdom and Binah-Understanding.

118. These Ten Sayings parallel the Ten Sefirot, and are their reflection in the physical world. The Ten Sayings are:

1. "Let there be light" *(Genesis 1:3)*, Chakhmah-Wisdom.
2. "Let there be a firmament" *(1:16)*, Binah-Understanding.
3. "Let the waters be gathered" *(1:9)*, Chesed-Love.
4. "Let the earth put forth grass" *(1:11)*, Gevurah-Strength.
5, "Let there be luminaries in the firmament" *(1:14)*, *Tiferet-Beauty.*
6. *"Let the waters swarm with living creatures" (1:20)*, Netzach-Victory.
7. "Let the earth bring forth living creatures" *(1:24)* Hod-Splendor.
8. "Let us make man in our image" *(1:26)*, Yesod-Foundation.
9. "Behold I have given you every herb" *(1:24)*, Malkhut-Kingship.

There is a question as to what is the tenth saying. Some say that it is implied in the first verse, "In the beginning God created the heaven and the earth" *(Rosh HaShanah 32a)*. This is the saying that parallels Keter-Crown, which is also implied but not expressed.

Others say that the tenth verse is, "It is not good for man to be alone" (Genesis 2:18), and that this corresponds to Malkhut-Kingship, which is man's mate *(Bereshit Rabbah 17:1)*. This is actually not a dispute, since "the beginning is imbedded in the end," and therefore, Keter-Crown and Malkhut-Kingship are one. This is the "head" mentioned above (**82**).

According to some opinions, the Ten Sayings parallel the Ten Sefirot in their usual order, as above. Others say that the three Sayings involving man represent the three Mentalities, while the others are the seven lower Sefirot.

The Torah is the counterpart of Zer Anpin, and it is called the Torah of Truth *(Emet)*. This is because it emanates from the first three Sefirot, which are represented by the three letters of *EMeT*.

Yud therefore represents the Ten Sefirot of Zer Anpin. Shin represents the confluence of the three lowest Sefirot, Netzach-Victory, Hod-Splendor and Yesod-Foundation, into Malkhut-Kingship. In the diagram of Thirty-Two Paths, Shin is the channel between Hod-Splendor and Netzach-Victory, but actually, it connects the lower triplet to Malkhut-Kingship.

Malkhut-Kingship, the lowest Sefirah of Atzilut-Nearness, is the root of the Universe of Beriyah-Creation. (*See* **128**).

124. The Ten Commandments parallel the Ten Sefirot of Zer Anpin. But Zer Anpin also parallels both man and the Torah. Man's body has 613 parts, 248 limbs, and 365 vessels. The Torah likewise has 613 commandments, 248 imperatives and 365 prohibitions. This indicates that besides consisting of Ten Sefirot, Zer Anpin is a Personification *(Partzuf)*, containing elements that parallel all parts of the human body. As such, Zer Anpin is the macrocosmic Man.

125. Although the word *Saper* is nominally translated as "declare," the root actually has three basic connotations:

1. To declare or express.
2. To record or decree. A book is a *Sepher*.
3. To delineate or count. A number is a *Mi-Spar*.

The first function of the Sefirot is to express God's greatness. Through them we can meditate on God and speak of Him.

Secondly, it is through the Sefirot that God expresses His providence over creation, issuing decrees and recording events. It is in this context that the Sefirot are God's "Book." This is the significance of the three "books" open on the New Year, one for the righteous, one for the wicked, and one for those in between

Finally, the Sefirot delineate God's glory, bringing it into the finite realm of number. Although God is infinite, and in potential encompasses an infinite number of basic concepts, the Sefirot limit these to ten. This is the concept of the Tzimtzum-Constriction, where the infinite is constricted into the finite (see *KaLaCh Pitchey Chakhmah 24, Pardes Rimonim 2:6*).

These three concepts are the *Saper* (Number), *Sepher* (Book), and *Sippur* (Telling), mentioned in *Sefer Yetzirah* (1:1).

These parallel the three basic dimensions, Soul, Year, and Universe. The first connotation relates to the dimension of Soul, since it is to the soul that God's glory is expressed. The second is that of time, since God's decrees function within the framework of time. Finally, it is the universe that delineates God's glory into the realm of number.

"Heaven" here refers to Zer Anpin, while "Glory" is Malkhut-Kingship. Through the Sefirot, Zer Anpin is expressed in Malkhut-Kingship.

126. The Kedushah consists of the verse, "Holy, holy, holy, is the Lord of Hosts, the whole earth is filled with His glory" (Isaiah 6:3). The three "holy's" in this verse are the three dominions (see *Targum* ad loc.).

127. The question here is, if there are four basic levels of creation, why are there three holy's and not four? The answer is that the four concepts are arranged in a three by three array in the Ten Sefirot.

Furthermore, the Sefirot are expressed in three concepts: Soul, Year and Universe. In the Targum on the Kedushah, it is translated, "Holy in the highest heaven . . . Holy in earth . . . and Holy for ever and ever." "Heaven" is the dimension of Soul, "Earth" is Universe, and "for ever and ever" is Time.

These three concepts also parallel the three stages of time, past, present, and future. We remember the past, and therefore, the past is in the Soul. The Universe is the present. But the future is pure Time, and does not affect the Soul or Universe.

The two names YHVH represent mercy "before the sin, and after the sin" *(Rosh HaShanah 17b)*. Hence they represent the past and future. The Thirteen Attributes of Mercy are for the present.

The fact that there are Thirteen Attributes also attests to the triplet nature of the Sefirot, and to the fact that they are arranged in three columns. The top members of each column are doubled, each one drawing from the level above it. Thus,

Thirteen Attributes are derived from the Ten Sefirot (*see* Hai Gaon, quoted in *Pardes Rimonim 11:1*).

In general, the triplet structure is derived from the basic dialectic (1).

128. The first "Holy" parallels the spiritual dimension, as mentioned above. This is the dimension from Keter-Crown to Malkhut-Kingship.

The second "Holy" is the time dimension. This is the dimension defined by Chakhmah-Wisdom and Binah-Understanding, as well as Daat-Knowledge, which is their confluence. It is from these upper Sefirot that the lower ones emanate, and hence, they are the "root" of the Tree.

The third "Holy" is Zer Anpin, which defines the concept of space, and is also the concept of connection (30). It is this concept that unites all the Sefirot.

129. The six Sefirot of Zer Anpin consist of two triplets, Chesed-Love, Gevurah-Strength and Tiferet-Beauty, and Netzach-Victory, Hod-Splendor and Yesod-Foundation. The higher triplet receives from the three Mentalities, while the lower triplet functions to bestow to Malkhut-Kingship, and hence to the rest of creation.

The upper triplet is called the "children" (of Abba-Father and Imma-Mother), while the lower triplet is called "grandchildren." If the lower are not worthy, the upper are only given enough for themselves, but not enough to give to others (*see* **113**).

130. The concept of "the whole earth is *filled* with His Glory," refers to Chakhmah-Wisdom, the "Filling" mentioned above (in **3**). The concept of Chakhmah-Wisdom is sameness and homogeneity, and it therefore indicates that God's glory is universally present (*see* **30**).

134. The concept of Heart includes Chakhmah-Wisdom, Binah-Understanding, and Malkhut-Kingship (as in **106**).

135. This can be understood in the light of the fact that the following individuals are usually identified with particular Sefirot:

Abraham	Chesed-Love
Isaac	Gevurah-Strength

Jacob	Tiferet-Beauty
Moses	Netzach-Victory
Aaron	Hod-Splendor
Joseph	Yesod-Foundation
David	Malkhut-Kingship

143. Binah-Understanding is called the "Treasury of Wisdom," since without understanding, wisdom cannot be grasped.

When the Torah speaks of the "Spirit of God," the name Elohim is used, this being the name associated with Binah-Understanding. It is from the level of Elohim that the Ruach-Spirit emanates, since Ruach is on the level of Zer Anpin which emanates from Binah-Understanding.

While Chakhmah-Wisdom is the concept of similarity and undifferentiated homogeneity, Binah-Understanding is the concept of difference and differentiation. All letters, forms and concepts therefore stem from Binah-Understanding.

144. This is Chesed-Love, which parallels the right hand.

145. This is Gevurah-Strength, which parallels both fire and the left hand.

146. The Throne of Glory is Tiferet-Beauty.**152.** Zer Anpin is constructed out of six Sefirot, Chesed-Love, Gevurah-Strength, Tiferet-Beauty, Netzach-Victory, Hod-Splendor, and Yesod-Foundation. Still, once it exists as a Personification *(Partzuf),* it becomes a complete structure, and it then consists of a full Ten Sefirot. It is for this reason that even though creation took place in six days, it consisted of Ten Sayings.

In the "growth" of Zer Anpin from six Sefirot to ten, the three upper Sefirot, Chesed-Love, Gevurah-Strength, and Tiferet-Beauty, are doubled. Chesed-Love then becomes Chakhmah-Wisdom, Gevurah-Strength becomes Binah-Understanding, and Tiferet-Beauty becomes Keter-Crown. These are the caps of the three columns of Zer Anpin, and are the three Crowns of Israel.

Since Tiferet-Beauty in Zer Anpin becomes an aspect of Keter-Crown, the question then arises, why is it called the Throne of Glory?

The Tefillin allude to the purpose of creation. Usually,

purpose and will are represented by Keter-Crown, since this is
even higher than the intellect. But will and purpose must also
be carried out in terms of action, which is represented by the
arm. When this takes place, it must first be channeled through
the Heart.

The concept of a throne is that of lowering, since when one
sits on a throne, his body is lowered. When God acts, thereby
placing the Tefillin on His "Arm,", the Tefillin are called a
"throne," since their concept is lowered into the realm of action.

153. Aravot is the feminine plural of Arav, which means
"west." This name of heaven is only mentioned one place in the
Bible: "Praise the Rider of Aravot" (Psalms 68:5). Since God is
the "Rider" of Aravot, the latter is considered to be His vehicle
or "chariot" *(Merkava).* It is through Aravot that God lowers
Himself and oversees the world, as the Psalm continues,
"Father of orphans, judges of widows . . ." *(Pardes Rimonim
68:6).*

The vehicle of God's providence is Malkhut-Kingship. Of
the seven heavens, the Talmud states that Aravot is the highest *(Chagigah 12b).* Hence, it is actually the head of
Malkhut-Kingship, and as mentioned earlier, the head of the
Female is opposite the heart of Zer Anpin, which is the Sefirah
of Tiferet-Beauty. It is for this reason that it is mentioned after
Tiferet-Beauty, rather than as the tenth Sefirah. In this sense,
it is also to the "West" of Zer Anpin, opposite Yesod-
Foundation, and this is the derivation of its name.

The head of Malkhut-Kingship is located in the precise
center of the Sefirot of Zer Anpin. The author therefore states
that "water is at its right, and fire at its left." Furthermore,
when the Sefirot of Zer Anpin are conceived of as being in a
three-dimensional array, Malkhut-Kingship, the Holy Palace,
is in the center *(Sefer Yetzirah 4:3).*

All the Sefirot act through Malkhut-Kingship, whether
those on the right side, which pertain to water and love, or
those on the left side, which represent fire and judgment.
Therefore, both fire and water find their attributes in
Malkhut-Kingship.

154. The question then arises, if Aravot is in the place of
Tiferet-Beauty, then how are the two differentiated.

As mentioned earlier, however, the Heart, which is called
the Holy Palace, is actually the confluence of the four Sefirot,

Keter-Crown, Malkhut-Kingship, Chakhmah-Wisdom, and Binah-Understanding. When the Sefirot of Zer Anpin are in a three-dimensional array, this is the precise center. Since in this mode it is definitely different than Tiferet-Beauty, it is always counted separately.

In the Soul dimension, Malkhut-Kingship is precisely opposite Keter-Crown, and therefore it supports all the others. Malkhut-Kingship also supports the others through "motivation from below." Such motivation is the entire purpose of creation, and since Keter-Crown represents purpose, in this mode, Malkhut-Kingship becomes Keter-Crown.

Since Malkhut-Kingship is the visible end of the Soul dimension, it is said to be the dimension of thought. It reaches toward Keter-Crown, and therefore the interface with the Infinite Being (Ain Sof) is along this dimension, so that it does not have any boundary.

155. When we speak of the Personification of Zer Anpin, it is usually pictured facing downward with its head to the east and its feet to the west, bestowing spiritual sustenance to the world. The Female, Malkhut-Kingship, which is opposite Tiferet-Beauty, is therefore also to the east.

The "seed of Israel" travels down the spinal cord from the brain, and therefore comes from the east.

156. Malkhut-Kingship, the Bride, is also seen as lying with her head to the east. Therefore, her womb is to the west, and it is in this womb that all seed is "mixed together." Makhut-Kingship is therefore called Aravot, which has the double connotation of "west" and "mixture."

157. This is the Sefirah of Yesod-Foundation. The reason why it is eighth, rather than ninth as in the verse, is discussed below.

Souls are born through the union of Yesod-Foundation and Malkhut-Kingship. Therefore, Yesod-Foundation is called the "foundation of all souls."

The question then arises, how can we say that Yesod-Foundation, the eighth Sefirah, sustains all souls, when we have already said that the seventh Sefirah, represented by the Sabbath, is the sustainer of all souls (**56**). The reply is that all souls indeed do come from the seventh, Malkhut-Kingship, the womb of souls.

Malkhut-Kingship is called the seventh rather than the tenth, since it is represented as being in the center of the six Sefirot of Zer Anpin. The six Sefirot represent the six directions, while Malkhut-Kingship is their center point. In this aspect, the Sabbath is seen as the middle of the week, preceded and followed by three days.

158. Yesod-Foundation only functions to create souls when it is in conjunction with Malkhut-Kingship. Therefore, the main day in which it functions is the Sabbath.

Yesod-Foundation corresponds to the sixth day, which is when Adam was created. He did not attain his main aspect of soul, however, until the first Sabbath and therefore, he would have been permitted to eat of the Tree of Knowledge on the Sabbath. His main sin was the fact that he did not wait, but ate of it on the sixth day.

159. Here we see Malkhut-Kingship as the source of all the other Sefirot. This may seem to contradict the usual concept of Malkhut-Kingship, as drawing from all the other Sefirot. But as mentioned earlier, with respect to "motivation from above," Malkhut-Kingship draws from the other Sefirot, but with respect to "motivation from below," it bestows to the others.

The concept of Keter-Crown is that of purpose, while that of Malkhut-Kingship is fulfillment. These two define the spiritual dimension, which is called Soul. The ultimate purpose of creation involves "motivation from below," and in this respect, Malkhut-Kingship is dominant.

This is the concept of Heart, where Keter-Crown (through Chakhmah-Wisdom and Binah-Understanding) shines into Malkhut-Kingship. This is the prime point of the soul dimension. Heart is thus the "King" of the Soul dimension, that is, its aspect of Kingship. Heart is thus the motivating force for the lower seven Sefirot.

161. The date palm is the Lulav, discussed earlier (**98,101**). It is the spinal cord that acts as the channel from the three Mentalities, Chakhmah-Wisdom, Binah-Understanding and Keter-Crown, to Yesod-Foundation (**166**).

As discussed earlier, the splitting of the Red Sea was the initiation into the mysteries of the Sefirot, which is the Tree of Life. After the Israelites crossed the Red Sea, they came to

Mara and were in a state of preparation for the Tree of Life, but the Satan had removed it.

165. The Torah was created and "written" two thousand years before the creation of the universe, as above. This is difficult to understand, however, since the Torah contains accounts regarding people, and these people have free will. But actually, when the Torah was first writtten, it did not contain the accounts themselves, but only a system that stated how accounts would be written with regard to various types of actions. Rather than a book, the Torah was very much like a computer program, set to produce a specific book from specific events. It was only after the Torah was actually written down by Moses that its form was fixed for all eternity.

In its first stage, the Torah is likened to water, which is fluid and changes shape to fill its vessel. Ultimately, however, it became firm and permanent like stone.

168. The discussion now returns to Yesod-Foundation. In the usual representation, Yesod-Foundation is the ninth Sefirah, following Netzach-Victory and Hod-Splendor, while Malkhut-Kingship is the tenth. In the representation of the Bahir, presented here, however, Malkhut-Kingship is the seventh Sefirah, while Yesod-Foundation is the eighth.

Since Malkhut-Kingship pertains to the Sabbath, it was counted as the seventh, just like the Sabbath is the seventh day **(158)**. Yesod-Foundation, however, only functions through Malkhut-Kingship. Yesod-Foundation parallels the male organ, and, since the male organ cannot function without the female, is secondary to the female. Therefore, Yesod-Foundation follows Malkhut-Kingship, and is the eighth Sefirah.

One reason why circumcision is on the eighth day is so that a Sabbath should pass before the child is circumcised, thus giving him the strength of the Sabbath *(Zohar 3:44a)*.

Another reason for circumcision being on the eighth day is because it initiates the child into the eighth level. Seven represents the perfection of physical creation, exemplified by the Sabbath, while eight is the level above the physical, namely, the transcendental. In the Sefirot, this corresponds to the level of Binah-Understanding.

When a man is circumcised, he thus possesses all eight

directions. Since his sexual organ has been rectified through circumcision, he can "cling to his wife." As mentioned earlier, through his wife, a man becomes worthy of the concept of "head," but this is only true when he is circumcised. He then is worthy of Binah-Understanding, the eighth level.

169. These refer to Netzach-Victory and Hod-Splendor, which are here considered to be the last two Sefirot. Usually, these are the seventh and eighth Sefirot, but here they are interchanged with Malkhut-Kingship and Yesod-Foundation to become the ninth and tenth. The reason for this is because the usual order refers to the Ten Sefirot taken as absolutes, before they are rectified into Partzufim. Here, however, they are presented as paralleling the Ten Sayings of creation, which pertain to the six days of creation, and hence to the six Sefirot of Zer Anpin. Netzach-Victory and Hod-Splendor correspond to the feet of Zer Anpin, and the feet are the lowest part of the body, even below the sexual organ.

The usual picture of Zer Anpin presents this Personification in a lying down position with his head to the east. The right foot, corresponding to Netzach-Victory is raised upward, while the left foot, corresponding to Hod-Splendor, is lowered downward. Hence, Netzach-Victory and Hod-Splendor, are said to represent the up-down directions.

In his vision, Ezekiel saw the Ophanim below the Chayot *(Ezekiel 1:15-21)*. This teaches that the Ophanim (Wheels) are the angels of Asiyah-Making, below the Chayot (Living Creatures) of the Universe of Yetzirah-Formation. The ground upon which "feet" stand is considered the next lower level or universe. Hence, the Ophanim represent the "feet" of the Chayot, and in general are "feet."

Since the head of Zer Anpin is to the east, his feet are to the west. Hod-Splendor, however, the left foot, inclines to the north, the sides of Gevurah-Strength, which is the source of judgment and evil (**163**). As mentioned earlier, it is from Hod-Splendor that Evil is nourished (**30**).

The Divine Presence *(Shekinah)* is Malkhut-Kingship, the Bride. Although her head is near the heart of Zer Anpin, her feet are under his, and this is the "end of the Divine Presence." Her seven Sefirot are called "seven earths," and Netzach-Victory and Hod-Splendor parallel the lowest of them.

Netzach-Victory and Hod-Splendor are the lowest Sefirot, touching the "ground." Therefore, when one ascends on high, they are the first Sefirot that can be reached, and hence, they serve as the source of prophecy.

170. The two "victories" refer to Netzach-Victory and Hod-Splendor. The third is Yesod-Foundation.

171. Up until here, the discussion has been of the downward sequence of the Sefirot, as they emanate from God. There is, however, also an upward sequence, emanating from man when he influences the Sefirot through "awakening from below."

In a meditative sense, this is speaking of meditating on the Sefirot, where one climbs the ladder upward. Whereas one can "run" downward after he has reached the highest level, the ascent upward is a difficult process, requiring much training and discipline, and one cannot "run" upwards.

When the verse says, "the whole earth is filled with His glory," it implies that wherever one is, one has access to the Infinite Being.

The lowest of the Sefirot is Malkhut-Kingship, and hence, this is the furthest from the Infinite Being. Malkhut-Kingship is therefore also the closest to the forces of evil, and must be protected from Evil by the Chashmal, which is an emanation of Chakhmah-Wisdom and Binah-Understanding. When one grasps the lowest level, he also has access to the higher levels through the concept of the Chashmal. The Zohar thus teaches, "One who grasps any one of them, grasps them all" *(Tikuney Zohar 17a)*.

172. The seven "Holy Forms" are the seven inferior Sefirot. When the Torah says that man is created in the "form of God," it means that his body is a counterpart of the structure of the Sefirot.

The structure of the Sefirot which is Zer Anpin was originally androgynous, as was Adam at the time of his creation. Thus, when the Torah says that Adam was "in the image of God, male and female" (Genesis 1:27), it means that the androgynous Adam was in the form of the androgynous Zer Anpin.

The Hebrew word Tzela, usually translated as "rib," actually should be translated as "side," as affirmed by the Targum, the standard Aramaic translation of the Bible. When the Bible states, "He took one of his ribs," it actually means "one of his sides," that is, the feminine side. Since it originated in the structure of the Sefirot, the female is considered to be one of the Sefirot.

The concept of the Male is that of giving, while the Female is that of receiving, holding, and giving birth. Thus, without the Female, creation could neither take place nor endure.

The Etrog is the citron fruit, while the Lulav is the palm frond, and they are both taken in hand on the festival of Succot. The Etrog represents Malkhut-Kingship, the feminine essence, while the Lulav is Yesod-Foundation, the masculine essence.

173. The feminine principle is the seventh Sefirah, Malkhut-Kingship. This Sefirah is also identified with the Divine Presence *(Shekhinah),* the Essence of God that pervades all creation. It is this Essence that is the true beauty of all things. Thus, whenever one contemplates any beauty, he must realize that this is the Divine Essence, and can thus make use of it to begin the ascent on the Ladder.

Although the word *Nekevah* alludes to the orifices of a woman in the physical sense, it also refers to the spiritual orifices of Malkhut-Kingship. It is through these orifices that one can ascend into the spiritual realm. This is represented by the opening on the bottom of the letter Heh.

174. While outwardly the Song of Songs is simply a beautiful love song, it actually is the most profound song of unification of Zer Anpin and his Bride. It thus contains a hidden holiness, just like this mundane world contains the hidden holiness of the Shekhinah. Thus, when one recites the Song of Songs and meditates on its inner meaning, one can gain accesss to its inner essence, as well as to the inner hidden essence of the mundane world, which is the Shekhinah.

The Song of Songs is thus said to be the Holy of Holies. The "Holies" are the six male Sefirot of Zer Anpin, while the "Holy of Holies" is the "Holy" that pertains to these "Holies," namely Malkhut-Kingship. The word "holy" in general indicates separation from the mundane world, and it is insofar as they are transcendental that the Sefirot are called holy. Similarly, when a person enters into a mystical state, he is said to enter the realm of the "Holies," that is, of the Sefirot. But the one

Sefirah through which one must first pass is Malkhut-Kingship, and it is therefore the "Holy of Holies."

One reason why one must enter through Malkhut-Kingship is because it is the lowest of the Sefirot. Another reason is because, as the feminine element, it pertains to the concept of receiving. Thus, when a person sanctifies himself and makes himself a receptical for the Divine, he is a receptical just like Malkhut-Kingship. But in a spiritual sense, when two things resemble each other, they are said to be bound together. Hence, when a person resembles Malkhut- Kingship, he is also bound to it.

175. As mentioned above, the beauty of the world is a reflection of the Divine Essence, the Shekhinah, which dwells in the world. The very work Shekhinah comes from the root *Shakhan,* meaning "to dwell."

The four species taken on Succot consist of the Etrog, the Lulav, the myrtle and the willow. The last three are bound together to form a single bunch, which is held in the right hand while the Etrog is held in the left. Thus, the right hand grasps the male Sefirot, while the left grasps the female, Malkhut-Kingship. In order to fulfill the commandment, the Lulav and Etrog, male and female, must be brought together.

176. Of the four species, the Etrog is Malkhut-Kingship, the Lulav is Yesod-Foundation, the three myrtle branches are Chesed-Love, Gevurah-Strength, and Tiferet-Beauty, while the two willow twigs are Netzach-Victory and Hod-Splendor.

Even though Yesod-Foundation is usually said to parallel the male organ, here the Lulav is the spinal cord. Actually, however, the Kabbalah teaches that the sexual impulse travels from the brain through the spinal cord, and then to the male sex organ. Hence, the sexual organ is merely the external manifestation of Yesod-Foundation, while its inner manifestation is actually the spinal cord. The sexual impulse, and hence the inner essence of Yesod-Foundation, is expressed at the time of union and copulation, and at that time Yesod-Foundation is in its mode of Chai-Life. The number of vertebrae in the spine is thus eighteen, the numerical value of *Chai.*

177. The willow twigs correspond to the Sefirot of Netzach-Victory and Hod-Splendor, which in turn parallel the two legs. They incline to the west and the north, as above (**169**).

The two legs normally function together, and similarly, Netzach-Victory and Hod-Splendor are usually represented as a pair, and not separately. Hence, they are said to be "mixed."

178. Besides representing the two legs, in an inner sense, Netzach-Victory and Hod-Splendor are said to represent the two kidneys as well as the two testicles *(Pardes Rimonim 5:24)*. In this sense, they always work as a pair, and the essence of the two is always mixed.

The "Brook" refers to the Sefirah of Yesod-Foundation, especially when it "flows" at the climax of the sex act. At this time, it is functioning in conjunction with Netzach-Victory and Hod-Splendor, the two testicles, and the latter two Sefirot are then called the "willows of the brook."

This copulation is represented by the Lulav and Etrog being brought together when they are taken in hand. The Etrog, which is Malkhut-Kingship, is then the "sea" into which the "brook" flows.

This flux actually is derived from the essence of all six male Sefirot. In this sense, they are all called "brooks."

179. Here there is a discussion of the two aspects of God's relationship to creation, how He "fills all worlds and surrounds all worlds" *(Zohar 3:225a)*.

In describing the Tzimtzum, the Ari states that God withdrew His light from a sphere, creating a Vacated Space and it was in this Space that all creation took place. However, creation could not take place without God's power, so into this Space, God drew a thread of light. From this thread of light were formed ten concentric spheres, which surround all creation.

The ten concentric spheres are the Ten Sefirot with which God surrounds all worlds. The thread of light contains the Ten Sefirot with which He fills all worlds, and these are the Ten Sayings with which the universe was created.

This world is therefore like a "mustard seed in a ring." The Spirit is that of the Ten Sefirot that are in the thread of light.

180. The three Spheres are the lowest Sefirot, Netzach-Victory, Hod-Splendor, and Yesod-Foundation. These are said to surround the physical world, that is, all influence and enlightenment in the physical world comes through these.

183. "Life of Worlds" represents the Sefirah of Yesod-Foundation (as in **180**). As mentioned earlier, it is called "Righteous" when passive, and "Life" when active (**74**).

186. The concepts of Truth and Knowledge have already been explained (**51**).

198. Here, there is an allusion to the lowest three universes, Beriyah-Creation Yetzirah-Formation, and Asiyah-Making. These three correspond to the levels of Binah-Understanding, Zer Anpin, and Malkhut-Kingship, which in turn are end points of the dimensions of Time, World, and Soul.

Therefore, when the soul is created, the scripture says, "let us *make* man in our image." This is directed along the Soul Dimension, from Keter-Crown to Malkhut-Kingship, the latter which parallels the Universe of Asiyah-Making. Since this line intersects all the other Sefirot, the verse is in the plural: "Let us make . . ."

The Time dimension stems from Chakhmah-Wisdom and Binah-Understanding, and these are the archtypes of male and female. Therefore, when male and female come into being, this is the fulfillment of the concept of time, which has its endpoint in Binah-Understanding, paralleling Beriyah-Creation. Therefore, the word "create" is used.

Finally man must be brought into the dimension of World. This is the concept of relationship and Zer Anpin, paralleling the Universe of Yetzirah-Formation, and hence, the word "formed" is used here.

THE THREE VERSES IN HEBREW

וַיִּסַּע מַלְאַךְ הָאֱלֹהִים הַהֹלֵךְ לִפְנֵי מַחֲנֵה יִשְׂרָאֵל וַיֵּלֶךְ מֵאַחֲרֵיהֶם וַיִּסַּע עַמּוּד
הֶעָנָן מִפְּנֵיהֶם וַיַּעֲמֹד מֵאַחֲרֵיהֶם:
וַיָּבֹא בֵּין ׀ מַחֲנֵה מִצְרַיִם וּבֵין מַחֲנֵה יִשְׂרָאֵל וַיְהִי הֶעָנָן וְהַחֹשֶׁךְ וַיָּאֶר אֶת־
הַלָּיְלָה וְלֹא־קָרַב זֶה אֶל־זֶה כָּל־הַלָּיְלָה:
וַיֵּט מֹשֶׁה אֶת־יָדוֹ עַל־הַיָּם וַיּוֹלֶךְ יְהוָה ׀ אֶת־הַיָּם בְּרוּחַ קָדִים עַזָּה כָּל־
הַלַּיְלָה וַיָּשֶׂם אֶת־הַיָּם לֶחָרָבָה וַיִּבָּקְעוּ הַמָּיִם:

THE SEVENTY-TWO TRIPLETS

כדת	אכא	ללה	מהש	עלם	סיט	ילי	והו
הקם	דרי	מבה	יזל	ההע	לאו	אלד	הזי
חרו	מלה	ייי	נלך	פהל	לוו	כלי	לאו
ושר	לכב	אום	ריי	שאה	ירת	האא	נתה
ייז	רהע	חעם	אני	מנד	כוק	להח	יחו
מיה	עשל	ערי	סאל	ילה	וול	מיכ	הדה
פוי	מבה	נית	ננא	עמם	החש	דני	והו
מחי	ענו	יהה	ומב	מצר	הרח	ייל	נמם
מום	היי	יבם	ראה	חבו	איע	מנק	דמב

Notes to the Introduction

1. Raavad on *Sefer Yetzirah* 1:5 (26b). Although Raavad is usually identified as Rabbi Avraham ben David of Posquieres (1120–1198), the accepted opinion is that it was a different Raavad who wrote this commentary. See Introduction to *Etz Chaim* (Ashlag, Tel Aviv, 5720) pp. 19, 21, *Shomer Emunim* (HaKadmon), Introduction 2#2, *Avodat HaKodesh* 2:13, *Shem HaGedolim, Alef* 11, *Sefarim, Resh, Kuntres Acharon.* See *Korey HaDorot 10b,* Zvi Benyamin Blaamau's introduction to *Sefer HaEshkol, p. xiv.*

2. See Ramban on *Genesis* 1:1, 2:7, 24:1, 28:29, 46:1, 49:24, *Exodus* 2:25, 15:27, 20:8, *Leviticus* 23:40, 26:16, *Numbers* 15:31, *Deuteronomy* 16:20, 22:6, 33:12, 33:23.

3. Particularly in the *Hashmatot* and *Tosefot.* See *Zohar* 1:253b, 1:262b, 1:263a, 1:263b, 1:265a ff., 2:270b, 2:271a, 3:300b.

4. See *Metzaref LeChakhmah 12 (31b), Yechusim* 10b, *Shalshelet HaKabbalah* p. 57, *Korey HaDorot* 30a, *Shem HaGedolim, Sefarim,* Bet 33.

5. *Shem HaGedolim loc cit.* Even though the *Bahir* cites many things found in *Sefer Yetzirah,* it might have actually been written earlier. According to a reliable tradition, it was Rabbi Akiba who actually wrote the *Sefer Yetzirah,* even though its teachings are attributed to Abraham. See *Pardes Rimonim* 1:1, *Korey HaDorot* 30a. Although the teachings of the *Sefer Yetzirah* may have been known from earlier sources, they were not redacted until after the *Bahir.*

6. *Metzaref LeChakhmah, Korey HaDorot,* loc. cit.

7. *Pardes Rimonim* 21:6

8. see the section on structure. In **17**, he begins the discussion of the letters. In **45** he initiates the discussion of the Seven Voices, and again in **123**, he begins the discussion of the ten fingers, which leads into the discourse on the Sefirot. He is also the author of the closing section of the text (**197-200**), which discusses the mystery of masculinity and femininity.

9. See **26** where Rabbi Rahumai calls him Berabi, a title meaning "master of the generation." *Cf.* Rashi on *Kiddushin* 80b. In **51** we also find that the disciples ask Rabbi Berachia to explain one of

Rabbi Amorai's sayings. Use of such an anonym is not unusual, and we thus find that Rabbi Meir's real name was actually Nehemiah (Eruvin 13b). Another name used by Rabbi Meir was Nahorai, which has the same type ending as Rahumai and Amorai. Similarly, Rav's actual name was Rav Abba, and he was also known as Abba Arikhta *(Chullin* 137b, Rashi, *Betza* 9a, *Arukh, "Abba").*

10. *Bava Batra* 10b. From the fact that Rabbi Yochanan calls him "Rabbi" we see that he was already ordained. See *Seder HaDorot, Seder Tanaim VeAmaraim, "Nehuniah."*

11. See *Midrash Tanaim* on *Deuteronomy* 26:13 (p. 175).

12. *Megillah* 28a. *Seder HaDorot* identifies Rabbi Nehuniah the Great with ben HaKana.

13. *Megillah* 28a.

14. *Shavuot* 26a. *See* **32.**

15. Introduction to *Sifra.* Rabbi Nehuniah's statement **(1)** contains one of these Thirteen Rules.

16. *Eduyyot* 6:3, *Chullin* 129b, *Tosefta Bava Kama* 7:5, *Pesachim* 29a.

17. *Pirkey DeRabbi Eliezer* 43 (103a).

18. *Berakhot* 4:2 (28b). See *Bahir* **150.**

19. *Avot* 3:5.

20. *Berakhot* 7a. See *Kuzari* 3:65.

21. *Hekhalot Rabatai* 17:1, 22:4, 5. Also see *Zohar Chadash,* Ruth 80a, 82d.

22. *Hekhalot Rabatai* 16:3. Rabbi Yonatan ben Uziel was actually senior to Rabbi Yochanan ben Zakkai. See *Sukkah* 28a.

23. *Hekhalot Rabatai* 2:8, 15:1.

24. *Pardes Rimonim* 21:12. See *Kiddushin* 71a, Radal *ad loc.*

25. *Chagigah* 14b.

26. *Pirkey DeRabbi Eliezer* 15. See *Bava Metzia* 59b.

27. There is some question as to how Rabbi Akiba could have been a disciple of Rabbi Nehuniah. We find, however, that he was even together with Rabbi Yochanan ben Zakkai, see *Pirkey DeRabbi Eliezer* 7, Radal *ad loc.* 7:1. This is not difficult, however, since Rabbi Akiba died at the age of one hundred and twenty *(Sifri, Zot HaBerakhah* 357). His death occurred during the Hadrianic persecutions around 135 c.e., and since the destruction of the Temple occurred in the year 70, he was around 55 years old at the time. It was around the time of the destruction that both Rabbi Nehuniah and Rabbi Yochanan ben Zakkai flourished.

28. *Zohar* 1:11a. Cf. *Shabbat* 33b.

29. *Zohar Chadash,* Ruth 79a. Also see *Zohar Chadash* 75d, 76b, 76d, 79d, 81a, 84b.

30. *Pirkey DeRabbi Eliezer* 31 (71b). Cf. *Zohar Chadash* 62b, 80c. In the Talmud we find an Amora by this name.

31. *Pirkey DeRabbi Eliezer* 21 (49a), 29 (65b), 51 (125a).
32. *Hekhalot Rabotai* 16:3.
33. *Nedarim* 20a. Another candidate may be Rabbi Yochanan ben Yehoshua mentioned in *Yadayim* 3:5, who was Rabbi Akiba's brother-in-law, and who supports his statement regarding the Song of Songs. See *Bahir* **174**, where this statement is attributed to Rabbi Yochanan. Another possibility is that this may be Rabbi Yochanan ben Zakkai.
34. In **21**. In a similar quotation in *Bereshit Rabbah* 1:3, 3:9, the speaker is Lulayni ben Tavri, cf. *Midrash Tehillim* 24:4. In *Midrash Tehillim* 18:29 we find a Rabbi Lulyani who is apparently a disciple of Rabbi Ishmael and a contemporary of Ben Azzai. See, however, Buber on *Tanchuma B, Bereshit,* note 22.
35. *Avot* 4:4, *Pirkey DeRabbi Eliezer* 23 (54b), 52 (125a), 54 (128a).
36. 36. *Zohar* 2:103b. From the context, he was senior to Rabbi Shimon. The town Ono is found in *Shir HaShirim Rabba to* 2:25, *Eichah Rabbah to* 1:17, *Zohar Chadash* 81b.
37. Tavrus would then be identified, not as his father, but as a place name. This would be Tavvros Umanos (Taurus Amanus), which is Har HaHor on the northern boundary of the Holy Land. See *Targum J.* on Numbers 34:7, 20:22, 20:25, Deuteronomy 32:50.
38. *Megillah* 7b, *Sanhedrin* 65b. See Rabbi Yehudah Barceloni on *Sefer Yetzirah* p. 102.
39. *Avodat KaKodesh* 3:17 (80a).
40. See Rabbi Yehudah Barceloni *loc. cit.* pp. 102, 103.
41. Ramban on Genesis 5:2. See *Shomer Emunim* 1:11.
42. *See* Shem Tov on *Moreh Nevuchim* 1:62 (93a), *Shomer Emunim* 1:13. In his commentary to Sanhedrin 10:1, Seventh Principle, Maimonides mentions the *Shiur Komah.* Also see *Yad, Yesodey HaTorah* 2:7.
43. *Raavad, Introduction to Sefer Yetzirah* 2c.
44. In **68, 88, 150**.
45. *Chagigah* 2:1 (11b).
46. *Ibid.* 13a. Cf. *Kiddushin* 71a.
47. *Gittin* 60b.
48. Rashi, *Shabbat* 6b, *Bava Metzia* 92a. See *Tshuvot Rashbash* 189 where the publication of Kabbalah is questioned because of this.
49. See Hai Gaon, in *Otzer HaGaonim, Chagigah, Chelek HaTsuvot* p. 21.
50. Rabbi Shem Tov, *Sefer HaEmunot* 3:2 (Ferera, 5316) 19b, quoted in *Shalshelet HaKabbalah* p. 59, and in *Or HaBahir* 80:1. See *Tshuvot R.M. Alshakir* 117.
51. *Shem HaGedolim, Alef* 10.
52. Commentary to *Yad, Lulav* 8:5, *Bet HaBechirah* 6:14,

Introduction to Commentary on *Eduyyot*. *Cf.* Introduction to *Etz Chaim* p. 18. Also see Introduction to *Sefer HaEshkol* p. xv.

53. See *Advodat HaKodesh* 2:13 (33d), 3:18 (81b), *Shomer Emunim*, Introduction 2, 2.

54. *Metzaref LeChakhmah* 13. Cf. *Rekanti, VaYeshev, Minchas Yehudah* 14. Also see *Pardes*.

55. Bachya on *Genesis 32:10*.

56. Cf. *Iggeret Temon*, p. 30. Also see Rabbi Yehudah ben Barzilai, Commentary on *Sefer Yetzirah* (Berlin, 1885), p. 239; *Shoshan Yesod Olam* (Sasoon, ms. 290), end of p. 220.

57. See note 161 in text. The *Zohar* derives its name from *Daniel* 12:3, see *Tikuney Zohar* 1a.

58. It is interesting to note that it is only in this section that concepts found in the *Sefer Yetzirah* are discussed. See **58, 63, 70, 84, 95, 110.** Two other less obvious allusions are in the next section, **124** and **185.**

59. *Shomer Emunim*, Introduction 2, 2. See *Sichot HaRan* 199, Introduction to *Likutey Halachot, Kokhavey Or, Sichot VeSippurim* 13 (p. 88). Cf. *Chagigah* 13a.

60. *Shomer Emunim* 2:46.

61. *Emunot VeDeyot* 6:8. Cf. *Or HaShem* 4:7, *Tshuvot Ralbach* 8.

62. *See* **95, 98, 100, 108, 172.**

63. *Kiddushin* 71a.

64. *Avot Rabbi Natan* 13:3, *Bereshit Rabbah* 44:22, *VaYikra Rabba* 23:2, *Devarim Rabbah* 1:9.

65. Rashi on *Sukkah* 45a "Ani." The *Midrash Lekach Tov, BaShalach* 20 states this in the name of an identified *Sefer HaYashar*. An interesting hypothesis would be that this *Sefer HaYashar* is actually an older name for the *Bahir,* or, alternatively, a text derived from it. In *Lekach Tov, VeEtChanan* 7b, it is stated that this *Sefer HaYashar* is quoted in the *Hekhalot,* which was written by Rabbi Nehuniah's disciple, Rabbi Ishmael. The subject matter brought from *Sefer HaYashar* there also closely resembles **45-47** in *Bahir.* See *Taam Zekenim* 56a, Buber's introduction to *Lekach Tov* 9:20, 21, *Torah Shlemah, BaShalach, Miluyim* 3 (p. 284). Also *see* Ibn Ezra on Exodus 14:19, Rambam on *Sukkah* 4:5, *Zohar* 2:51b, 2:270a, *Metzaref LeChakhmah* 16 (40a).

66. *Etz Chaim, Shaar Egolim VeYashar* 2.

67. *Shomer Emunim* 2:43, *KaLaCh Pitchey Chakhmah* 24.

68. Rabbi Schneur Zalman, *Torah Or, MiKetz* 39a. See *Pelach Rimon* 4:3, *Shomer Emunim* 2:36. Also see *Etz Chaim, Shaar Drushey ABYA* 1, *Zohar HaRakia* on *Zohar* 1:15a.

69. *Zohar* 1:15a. This is the opening statement in *Bereshit.* Also see *Tikuney Zohar* 5 (19a).

70. *Shefa Tal* 3:5, *Shaarey Gan Eden* 2:3 (2b), *Zohar HaRakia* loc cit., *Kisey Melech* on *Tikuney Zohar* loc. cit. Also see *Mavo Shaarim* 1:1:2. Cf. *Elemah Rabatai, Eyin Kall* 4:1 (25a).

71. *Tikuney Zohar* 56 (91b). Cf. *Berakhot* 10a. This might be the concept of "Filling" discussed in **3, 5**.

72. *Shomer Emunim* 2:37, *Likutey Moharan* 64. *See* my article "Paradoxes" in *Jewish Life* 41:3 (February, 1974) p. 38.

73. See *Likutey Amarim (Tanya), Shaar HaYichud VeHeEmunah* 6.

74. Cf. *Pardes Rimonim* 2:6.

75. *Zohar* 3:127b. Cf. *Shaarey Gan Eden* 2:1 (2b). Also see *Pardes Rimonim* 1:9.

Notes to The Bahir

1. As a prefix, the letter *Bet* means "in." This can indicate a "filling." The "filling" may allude to *(Isaiah 6:3)*, "The whole earth is *filled* with His glory." See **130, 134.** Counting the word itself, the numberical value of *Maley* is seventy-two, see **94, 110, 167.**

2. This verse is not found anywhere in the Bible, but see I Kings 2:45. Cf. *Tikuney Zohar Chadash* 116d.

3. When God changed his name from Abram to Abraham. *See* Genesis 17:5. Cf. *Nedarim* 32b.

4. The first verse refers to the creation of the firmament, which took place on the second day of creation. See *Bereshit Rabbah* 3:9.

5. Alluding to the Sefirah of Foundation, as in I Chronicles 29:11. *See* Introduction.

6. The word "founded" is also an allusion to the *Sefirah* of Foundation. *See* Index under *Sefirot.*

7. Referring to the upper "earth," *see* **169.** Also see Rekanti, *BeHar* (31c).

8. As in the case of all the other sayings in the first chapter of Genesis.

9. When the *Gimel* is elongated "at its head," it becomes a *Dalet.* Left over is its tail, which converts the *Dalet* into a *Heh.* According to the reading of the Vilna Gaon (HaGra), however, the *Gimel* and *Dalet* are in place of *Vav Heh.* The tail of the *Gimel* is removed, making a Vav, and this tail converts the *Dalet* into a *Heh.*

11. The reference is to the two *Heh*'s in the Tetragrammaton. These are separated by the letter *Vav.*

12. The numerical value of *Vav* is six. Each of the three dimensions in our physical universe implies two directions, making a total of six. The six directions are north, south, east, west, up, down. See *Sefer Yetzirah* 4:3.

13. *Bereshit Rabbah* 1:14, cf. *Chagigah* 12a, b. According to Rabbi Akiba, the word *Et* always comes to add something. From here it is apparent that he maintains that the Garden of Eden is on earth, as above.

14. Referring again to the Garden of Eden. According to this, it would have originally been in heaven.

15. The apparent reference is to the word *Ruach* (spirit or wind) in Genesis 1:2. The relationship between the *Chet* and the *Patach* is unique, since at the end of a word, the vowel is read before its consonant, and this is the only case where this occurs.

16. *See* **162, 163, 199**.

17. It is thickened, and not written as a thin line as in the *Resh*.

18. *Patach* and *Segol* are vowel points. The meaning is somewhat ambiguous, but might refer to the shape of the letter, which looks like a *Patach* and *Segol*. Alternatively, it might refer to the fact that in the word *Dalet*, the first vowel is a *Patach*, while the second is a *Segol*. *Dalet* means "door," while *Patach* means "opening." Regarding *Segol*, see **89, 90, 178**.

19. This is an allusion to *Tefillin*, see **152**. According to the order of the *Sefirot*, *Patach* is Wisdom, while *Segol* is Love, the Right Hand. See **142, 144**. See *Tikuney Zohar* 70 (129a,b).

20. *See* **84, 85, 86**. This is alluded to by the word "from" in the verse, which is indicated by the letter *Mem*.

21. *See* **37**.

22. *Cf.* Psalm 118.19.

23. According to the order of the *Sefirot*, this is Beauty. See note 19.

24. *See* **115, 116**.

25. The *Targum* renders this as *Ein Igla*, meaning "Calf's Eye." Bachya *a.l.* identifies this with "crystal." This stone is related to dreams. *See* Ibn Ezra *ad loc.*, Radak, *Sefer Sherashim* (p. 211).

26. In Hebrew, *Charach* means to burn. *Sefirah* is Victory.

27. This alludes to the *Tallit* in which God wrapped Himself at Sinai. See *Rosh HaShanah* 17b. *Cf.* Psalm 104:2, Daniel 7:9. *See* **92, 96**.

28. Referring to either the Commandments or the *Sefirot*. See *Or HaGanuz* ad loc.

29. Cf. *Tanchuma, Yitro* 11.

30. *Chagigah* 13a. This alludes to *Keter* (Crown), the highest *Sefirah*. See **141**.

31. *See* **169, 170, 178**.

32. *Bereshit Rabbah* 14:9. *See* Chapter 3, note 6 in my translation of *Derekh HaShem*.

33. *See* **14**.

34. *See* **5**. The numerical value of *Bet* is two, alluding here to the two thousand years.

35. Up until now, the first five *Sefirot* have been discussed, Crown, Wisdom, Understanding, Love or Kindness (silver), and Strength (gold). Strength is the attribute of Justice.
36. See **195**.
37. *Sefer Yetzirah* 6:4.
38. Truth is thus identical with peace. See **17, 190, 11**.
39. The reference is to a regular *Tzadi* and a final *Tzadi*. Its form is that of a *Yud* attached to a *Nun*. see *Zohar* 1:2b.
40. Ben Zoma lost his mind when he entered Paradise, *Chagigah* 15a.
41. Mentioned in *Sefer Yetzirah 1:1*.
42. The illusion is to the *Sefirah of Malkhut* (Kingship), which is feminine.
43. *Shavuot* 35b. The exception is *Song of Songs* 8:12.
44. The "Congregation of Israel" is Kingship. See *Or HaGanuz* ad loc. Cf. *Zohar* 3:197a.
45. The Seven *Sefirot,* corresponding to the seven days of the week. See **160**.
46. Mentioned in Ezekiel 1. See *Chagigah* 2:1 (11b). This refers to the deepest mysteries.
47. See **150**.
48. From *Sefer Yetzirah* 4:3, we see that the "Holy Palace" is the center of the Six Directions, and this is usually assumed to be the Sefirah of Kingship. See **154, 175, 117**. Cf. *Tikuney Zohar* 18 (32a).
49. See **49** that "Kings" refer to the *Sefirot. Tzioni, Chayay Sarah* (17a), however, reads *Malachim* or "Angels."
50. See **185**.
51. The reference is to the *Sefirah* of Foundation, which is opposite the body. See **156**.
52. *See* end of **71**. Holiness means separation.
53. The *Sefirah* of Kingship. *See* end of **75**.
54. The Talmud says that the name of Abraham's daughter was Bakol. *Bava Batra* 16b. Regarding the significance of "All," *see* **22**.
55. The reference is to Kingship, and its older brother, directly above it, is Foundation.
56. Alluding to Ecclesiastes 2:8.
57. See **69**.
58. See **70**.
59. The first word in the Ten Commandments is *Anochi,* which begins with an *Alef.* See *Bereshit Rabbah* 1:10.
60. See **6, 118**.
61. See **130**.
62. Circumcision is the *Sefirah* of Foundation, while "his mate" is Kingship. When these are counted separately, there are seven lower

Sefirot, but when they are considered as one, there are only six.

63. The two arms are Love and Strength, the body is Beauty, while the two legs are Victory and Glory. See *Tikuney Zohar* 17a. To this Foundation and the Head [of its mate] are added, yielding a total of seven. The *Sefirot* are enumerated below, **142 ff.**

64. The letter *Nun* assumes two shapes, bent in the middle of a word, and straight at the end. See *Shabbat* 104a.

65. *See* **124.**

66. *See* **16.** Cf. *Berakhot* 61a, *Menachot* 29b.

67. *Hekhelot Rabatai* 1:1.

68. See *Targum* to Lamentations 4:17. Also see *Targum* to Isaiah 21:5, Radak *ad loc.*

69. One looks down from a watchtower, and the fact that this shares the same root indicates that the word means "looking down."

70. The reference here is to the accent mark. As they are generally ordered, *Zarka* and *Segol* are the first two accent marks. See *Pardes Rimonim* 29.

71. See *Chagigah* 13b.

72. Zarka is the first of the accents.

73. *See* **187, 193.**

74. The ritual fringes, *see* Numbers 15:38.

75. Each of the four fringes contains eight threads, making a total of 32.

76. *See* **63.**

77. The white threads are the sign of the king, while the blue is that of his daughter, which is the Sefirah of Kingship *(Malkhut)*. This follows Maimonides' opinion that only one of the eight threads is blue. See *Yad, Tzitzit* 1:6. Raavad *ibid.,* however, maintains that six threads are white and two are blue. This clearly refutes the opinion of those historians who attribute the *Bahir* to the Raavad or his school.

78. Psalm 120:7.

79. *See* **100, 107.** Cf. *Otiot DeRabbi Akiba* (first version) in *Batey Midrashot* (Jerusalem, 5728), p. 350. "Heaven" and "Heaven of heaven" indicate three levels, these being the Axis, Sphere and Heart. See *Pardes Rimonim* 21:6. Each of these three includes 24 names. *See* **95.** The method of deriving the names is found in **110.**

80. These are the seventy nations mentioned in Genesis 10. Each of these has its own Overseer. See *Targum J.* on Genesis 11:7, 8, Deuteronomy 32:8. For the significance of the extra two, *see* **167.**

81. Like the twelve edges of a cube. Regarding the tree, *see* **119.**

82. *Sefer Yetzirah* 5:1. The expression "Arms of the World," appears in Deuteronomy 33:27. *See* **189.**

83. *See* **106.**

84. The Three Kings mentioned in *Sefer Yetzirah* 6:1,2. The Axis is king over the universe, the Sphere, over the year, and the Heart, over the soul. These are defined in **106**.

85. *See* **63, 106**.

86. *Menachot* 43b.

87. This is the *Etrog*. *See* end of **172**.

88. *See* **83**. The *Lulav* parallels the spinal cord in man. *See* **176**.

89. *See* note **85**:

90. The word *Shamayim* comes from fire and water. *See* **59**.

91. *See* **94**.

92. *Lu* has a numerical value of 36, while *Lav* has a numerical value of 32. *See* **98**.

93. *See* note **84**.

94. These are the 36 Righteous Ones who maintain the world, *Sukkah* 45b. The *Sefirah, Yesod* (Foundation) is also called Righteous, and is alluded to by the *Lulav*. The *Lulav* parallels the spinal cord (note **88**), and this is connected to the sexual organ, which is *Yesod.See* **155**.

95. *Chagigah* 12b.

96. The numerical value of *Yud* is ten.

97. This teaches us that the *Yud* refers to Wisdom, and this is indeed the significance usually given to the first letter of the Tetragrammaton. *Also see* **118**.

98. That is, the *Sefirah* of Wisdom. *See* **142**. Here again, *Li* can be read as "to the *Yud*."

99. When one finds a nest with chicks or eggs.

100. "Mother" therefore refers to the *Sefirah* of Understanding *(Binah)*. Regarding variant readings of this verse, see *Minchat Shai* ad loc.,*Berakhot* 57a,*BaMidbar Rabbah* 10:4,*Zohar* 3:290b, *Tikuney Zohar* 69 (106b).

101. *See* **72**. The festival of *Succot* enters the discussion, since it is on this festival that the Lulav and Etrog are taken.

102. This verse speaks of Passover. Other editions, however, substitute "the eighth day," and the reading is then from Leviticus 23:35, 36.

103. *See* **14, 15**. A *Succah* must have a minimum of three walls, like the letter *Bet*.

104. The axis, Sphere and Heart are here defined. *See* note **84**.

105. The *Teli* mentioned in *Sefer Yetzirah* 6:1,2. The meaning of this word is obscure, the only similar word occurring in Genesis 27:3, meaning "quiver." The author of the *Bahir* associates it with the word *Taltalim*, which itself is somewhat ambiguous. According to Rashi, it is derived from the root *Talah* (to hang), while according to others, it comes from the root *Talal*, meaning "heaps." *See* Ibn Ezra *ad loc.*,

Radak, *Sefer Sherashim* "*Talal*," *Zohar* 1:125a. According to many
authorities, the *Teli* is the imaginary line, the axis around which all
heavenly bodies rotate. See *Pardes Rimonim* 21:8, Rabbi Moshe
Chaim Luzzatto, *Choker U'Mekubal* 13, also Rabbi Avraham ben
Chiyah, *Tzurat HaAretz* 13 (17b), *Sheveiley Emunah* 2 (19a). A
similar opinion seems to indicate that it is the force of gravity. *See*
Rabbi Yosef Giketalia, *Ginas Egoz* 32b. Many authorities, however,
associate the Teli with the *Nachash Bariach* (Encompassing
Serpent), mentioned in Isaiah and Job. *See* Ibn Ezra, Ralbag on Job
26:13, Radak on Isaiah 27:1 (quoting *Pirkey DeRabbi Eliezer*, not in
our editions), *Sefer Sherashim*, "*Nachash*," *Bareita* of *Shmuel HaKa-
tan* 1. Also see *Otzar HaShem, Chakmuni*, HaGra on *Sefer Yetzirah*
6:1, commentaries on *Avodah Zarah* 3:3, *Mordecai*, Ibid. 840, *Derekh
Emet* on *Zohar* 1:125a. Cf. *Bereshit Rabbah* 2:4. Although some associate this with the constellation Draco, others clearly state that it is
the Milky Way. *See* Ralbag on Job 26:13, *Netzutzey Orot* on *Zohar*
1:25a. The *Kol Yehudah* on *Kuzari* 4:25 (54b) states that the word *Teli*
is phono-semantically related to *Tanin*, meaning "serpent." Another
possibility presented there is that it is derived from the word *"to
spread."* Thus, the *Targum* on Isaiah 44:25, translates "He spread the
heaven," as *Talit Shamaya*. Also see *Zohar* 1:44a, *Or HaGanuz* on
Bahir 95, HaGra on *Sifra Detzniuta* 11c. The *Sefer Yetzirah* states
that the *Teli* is King over the universe. It is therefore the source of the
six directions of the universe, which in turn are the counterparts of
Man the Macrocosm. *See* **82**. In later Kabbalistic texts, this is called
the *Partzuf* (Personification) of *Zer Anpin*. Here, the author calls it
the "likeness that is before the Blessed Holy One." See *Zohar* 3:132a,
3:136a, 3:140a, *Etz Chaim, Shaar Arih Anpin* 5 (p. 186).

    106. *See* Rabbi Moshe Butril on *Sefer Yetzirah*, who states that
this should be translated Cycle rather than Sphere. The *Sefer Yetzirah* 6:2 states that this is King over the year. The present is the
womb in which the future is born. Wisdom is the past, while Understanding is the future. See *Sefer Yetzirah* 1:5, HaGra *ad loc*. This is
therefore identified with Understanding, the Mother, discussed at
the end of **104**.

    107. *See* **63**. The Heart, Sphere and Axis respectively are Wis-
dom, Understanding, and the Seven lower Sefirot. *See* Raavad on
Sefer Yetzirah 6:1, *Or HaGanuz*, on *Bahir* 95, *Pardes Rimonim* 21:8.

    108. This is the Priestly Blessing.

    109. This is the Name used in the Priestly Blessing in the Tem-
ple. *Kiddushin* 71a.

    110. *See* **10**.

    111. Alluding to the *Sefirot* of Strength, Love and Beauty. *See*
11, 22.

112. The 72 among the angels, and the 72 of Israel, mentioned in **94**.

113. *See* **5**.

114. See *Pesikta Zutrata* on Exodus 14:21, Rashi, *Sukkah* 45a "Ani," Ibn Ezra on Exodus 33:21, *Zohar* 2:270. It is vocalized in *Pardes Rimonim* 21:5. For an explanation of this Name, see *Raziel HaMalach* (Margolies edition) p. 54ff.

115. *Sefer Yetzirah* 5:4, 1:1.

116. This is not a verse in the Bible, but it is found in the Prayer Book in *Yehi Kavod*. See *Siddur Rav Amram Gaon* (Rav Kook, Jerusalem, 1971). p. 9. Also see *Hekhalot Rabotai* 31:4, *Rokeach* 320.

117. For the variants, see *Or HaGanuz* ad loc., *Tikuney Zohar* 70 (134b), *Pardes Rimonim* 21:9.

118. Referring to the plate *(Tzitz)* placed on the High Priest's forehead, mentioned in Exodus 28:36-38.

119. *See* 2 Kings 2:11, 1 Kings 18:20.

120. A variation of these is vocalized in *Pardes Rimonim* 21:9. For variants, see *Or HaBahir* and *Or HaGanuz ad loc.* In one manuscript they are cited as AH-TzYTzaH-RON, ABROThY-HON, VeSheBaBYOMT-RON, DMaGDE-RON, BaNaThYaH-RON, EdaShYHaG-AON, KiSAY-DaMaN-HaNaN, YHVH YHHYV YHAH AHVHY DaMHaD-ROS, DaMHaRy-RON. In another, they are AH-TZYTzY-RON, ABROChYH-RON, VeShaBOBThMak-RON, DMORTRON, TzaPhTzaPhShYT-RON, YHODMY-RON, BRaKhYHV-AON, ERSYH GAON, KSAYMaNGwM-HON, HVYV YHHV YVYH YHAH AHVH, DaMHaRY-RON, TmaK-ThON, RMUHaT-RON, VeTzaPhTzaPhShiTh-RON, YHVuRMa-RON, BaRChYH GAON, EdShGaDRa-AON, KSAUTh, HVHVYHVH, VYHAHAHYH, VHaDMaThThY-HON. See *Otiot DeRabbi Akiba* 350, 343. (See p. 203)

121. *See* **106**.

122. *See* **196**.

123. *See* **109**.

124. One cannot "hear" letters without vowels, so they can only be heard as a result of sacrifice, which is the *unification. See* **108**.

125. *See* **26**.

126. *See* **70, 154**.

127. See *Avot Avot* 5:1. The numerical value of *Yud* is ten. *See* note 96.

128. *See* **81**.

129. *See* **185, 74**.

130. *See* **75**.

131. Alluding to reincarnation. *See* **122, 155, 184, 185**.

132. *See* **109**.

133. *Sefer Yetzirah* 1:3. *See* **138, 188, 1932**.

134. There are 613 commandments in the Torah. See   *Makkot* 23b. Also see *BaMidbar Rabbah* 13:16, 18:21. Actually, the Ten Commandments contain 620 letters, but the last seven letters in *Asher LeReyekha* are not counted, this being the essence of the Torah, as in *Yerushalmi, Nedarim* 9:4. *See* Saadia Gaon on *Sefer Yetzirah* (Translated from the Arabic by Yosef Kapach, Jerusalem, 5732) p. 48, Rabbi Yehudah Barceloni on *Sefer Yetzirah* p. 278.

134a. *See* **84**.

135. Indicating that the *Sefirot* are expressions of God's action. For further discussion of the etymology of this word, see *Shiur Komah* 2.

136. *Kedushah* is the verse, "Holy, holy, holy," cited in **128**.

137. *See* **111**.

138. *See* **107**.

139. See *Rosh HaShanah* 17b. This appears to support the opinion of the Ari, that the Thirteen Attributes are *(Exodus 34:6),* "God (1), merciful (2), and gracious (3), slow (4) to anger (5), and abundant in love (6) and truth (7). Keeping mercy (8) to the thousandth generation (9), forgiving sin (10), rebellion (11) and error (12), and cleansing (13)." See *Etz Chaim, Shaar Arich Anpin* 9, *Shaar HaKavanot, Inyan VaYaavor* 3 (p. 286), *Zohar* 2:4b, 3:13b. Others, however, count the two Tetragrammatons at the beginning among the Attributes.

140. The *Sefirah,* Crown. *See* **141**.

141. The *Sefirah* of Wisdom, *see* **142**. Regarding the Tree, *see* **118, 119, 176**.

142. The *Sefirah* of Understanding, which restricts and is the root of Judgment. *See* **113**.

143. *See* **63, 92, 106, 147**.

144. *See* **106**.

145. In the priestly blessing. *See* **107, 124**.

146. *See* **2, 10, 12, 163**. We thus see that Chaos is associated with the *Sefirah* of Strength, the attribute of Isaac. It is also fire, as in the next paragraph. *See* **44, 145**.

147. *See* **51, 52**.

148. Since Strength is lower than Love.

149. *See* **75, 190**.

150. *Avot* 5:1. *See* **118, 179**. We see here that the Ten Sayings continuously sustain creation, see *Likutey Amarim (Tanya), Shaar HaYachid VeHeEmunah* 1.

151. *See* note 133.

152. *See* **111**.

153. The *Yud* and the *Shin,* see **26, 117**. The *Alef* is Crown, while the other two are Wisdom and Understanding. *See* Esther 1:14.

154. *See* **3, 6, 103, 105.**
155. In Genesis 1:2. This is the Sefirah of Understanding. *See* **100.**
156. The *Sefirah* of Strength, also called Terror.
157. *See* Psalm 16:6, 11; II Samuel 1:23.
158. These refer to the "seven days of the week," namely the *Sefirot. See* **95.**
159. Alluding to I Kings 18:39.
160. This is the *Sefirah* of Beauty.
161. *Maz'hir Bahir* (Shining, brilliant). This is an allusion to both the *Zohar* and the *Bahir.*
162. The part of the Torah that was transmitted orally and finally included in the Talmud. *See* **149.**
163. Exodus 24:12. See *Berakhot* 5a that "commandment" here refers to the Oral Torah.
164. Psalm 119:137.
165. *Berakhot* 60b.
166. Cf. *Avot* 4:13, 6:5.
167. This is an allusion to God's *Tefillin, Berakhot* 6a. God's *Tefillin* represent the Crown of *Zer Anpin* (Beauty), as we find in *Tikuney Zohar* 17a. This is discussed at length in my booklet, *God, Man and Tefillin,* p. 37ff. Even though there is a Crown associated with the lower Sefirot, it is only "lent to his son." *See* note 105.
168. Mentioned in Psalm 68:5. This is the highest of the seven heavens, *Chagigah* 12b. The reference is to the Sefirah of *Malkhut* (Kingship). It also has the connotation of west *(Ma-arev),* which is Foundation, leading to the question in **154.**
169. *Shamayim* (heaven) is therefore the plural of "there" *(sham),* indicating that every direction is "there." *See* **114, 115.**
170. *See* **11, 59.**
171. Since it was stated that "man and his mate are as one." *See* **172, 82, 168.**
172. *See* note 48. Since it supports all the *Sefirot* when we speak of "awakening from below," it is counted separately. *See* **171.**
173. *See* **121, 122.**
174. According to traditional Kabbalah, east is *Tiferet,* while west is *Yesod. Cf.* HaGra on *Sefer Yetzirah* 1:5. Since *Malkhut* is attached to *Yesod* (**82**), it is also to the west. *Malkhut* is therefore called Sea *(Yam),* which also has the connotation of west. *See* **169, 170, 177.**
175. The *Sefirah* of *Yesod* (Foundation). *See* **61, 82, 83, 168, 180, 193.**
176 *See* **57, 180.**
177. *See* **168.** This explains why *Malkhut* and *Yesod* are seventh and eighth in the *Sefirot,* rather than ninth and tenth, as in

traditional Kabbalah. *Malkhut* is the Sabbath, which is seven, while *Yesod* is the eighth, which is the covenant of circumcision. As the seventh *Sefirah, Malkhut* is central among the six "days."

178. *See* 82.

179. *See* 147, 148, 190.

180. *Cf.* Proverbs 20:14. *See* 145.

182. *See* 2, 11, 12, 135.

183. This can also be translated as "What is my God," or "My God, what?" Regarding the significance of "what," see *Zohar* 1:3b.

184. *See* 8, 94, 110.

185. That is, the twelve simple letters mentioned in *Sefer Yetzirah* 5:1. These parallel the twelve tribes. *See* 114.

186. Referring back to 158.

187. This refers to *Netzach* and *Hod.* They are always together, as we find in *Zohar* 3:236a. These parallel the two feet in man. *See* 180; *Tikuney Zohar* 17a.

188. In the Talmud, *Chagigah* 13a, this is the distance between two spiritual levels.

189. Regarding the seven earths, see *Sefer Yetzirah* 4:12, *Avot Rabbi Natan* 37:9, *VaYikra Rabbah* 29:9, *Shir HaShirim Rabbah* 6:19, *Midrash Tehillim 8, Zohar* 1:39b, 1:157a, 3:10a. Ibn Ezra on Genesis 1:2 writes that they are the seven continents, but HaGra on *Sefer Yetzirah* 4:15 contends that they are spiritual worlds. See *Pardes Rimonim* 6:3.

190. Usually translated as "eternity of eternities." The root of this word *(Netzach)* means strength, and that which is strong is victorious and endures forever. Radak, *Sefer Sherashim, "Netzach."*

191. *Netzach* is "behind," to the west, while *Hod* is to the left, the north. The third one is *Yesod.*

192. See *Pardes Rimonim* 15:4. Up until now the discussion centered on the *Sefirot* in a downward sequence, emanating from God. Besides this, there is an influence from man, that ascends on high.

193. The upper *Shekhinah* (Divine Presence) is *Binah,* while the lower one is *Malkhut.* These are the two letters *Heh* in the Tetragrammaton. *See* note 11.

194. *See* 95, 98, 101, 108. *Also see* 8, 82, 168.

195. The *Etrog* alludes to the *Sefirah* of *Malkhut,* which is "man's wife," and is therefore feminine. *See* 98.

196. In *Yadayim* 3:5, this is cited in the name of Rabbi Akiba. It is also cited, however, by his brother-in-law, Rabbi Yochanan ben Yehoshua, and this may be the Rabbi Yochanan mentioned here. Alternatively, it might be that Rabbi Yochanan ben Zakkai, who was the mentor of Rabbi Akiba, is referred to here. *See* introduction note 33.

197. *See* **30, 172.**

198. Cf. *Sukkah* 35a, Rashi ad loc. *"Hadar."* The word *Dar* means to dwell. The *Etrog* is *Malkhut,* the Divine Presence, since the word *Shekhinah* comes from the root *Shokhen,* meaning to dwell. *See* **190, 193.**

199. The *Lulav* parallels the *Sefirah* of *Yesod. See* **83, 98, 155.**

200. The three myrtle branches associated with the *Lulav* therefore parallel the *Sefirot of Chesed, Gevurah,* and *Tiferet. See* **144, 145.**

201. *See* **128.**

202. The *Sefirot* of *Netzach* and *Hod. See* **169.**

203. *See* **156.**

204. *See* **20, 113, 119.**

205. In the cantellation notes. *See* **36, 89, 90.** *See* Bachya on Numbers 21:19, that it is therefore above the word.

206. *See* Bachya, *Tzioni,* on Numbers 21:19.

207. Lebanon comes from the root *Laban,* meaning "white." It thus refers to the *white* matter of the brain. See *Zohar* 3:235b. Lebanon also consists of the letters spelling out *Lev Nun. Lev* (heart) alludes to the 32 paths of wisdom, while *Nun* is 50, alluding to the fifty gates of Understanding. See *Etz Chaim, Shaar Leah VeRachel* 3 *in Hagah, Shaar HaIburim 5.*

208. This is again *Netzach* and *Hod. See* **50, 169, 170.**

209. The Ten Sayings refer to the ten times that the expression "And God said," appears in the first chapter of Genesis. See *Avot* 5:1. Regarding the Ten Spheres, see *Yad, Yesodey HaTorah* 3:1. The Ten *Sefirot* also are said to be concentric circles. See *Etz Chaim, Shaar Egolim VeYashar* 2.

210. The reference is to *Netzach, Hod* and *Yesod,* which are the two legs and Foundation. *See* **157, 169, 170.**

211. *See* **57, 82, 157, 158.**

212. The Sabbath therefore includes both *Yesod* and *Malkhut.*

213. The expression is found in Exodus 31:13. *Cf.* Leviticus 20:8, 21:8, 22:32. *See* **171.**

214. *Yebamot* 62a, 63b, *Avodah Zarah* 5a, *Niddah* 13b.

215. *Avot* 2:5. This saying is attributed to Hillel.

215. *Cf.* Proverbs 18:23.

217. He must be reborn. *See* **121, 122, 155.**

218. The question is how can "counsel" be included in Understanding. Counsel is the *Sefirah* of *Chesed,* while Understanding is Justice, since it is the root of *Gevurah.* It is known that *Chesed* precedes *Gevurah. See* **144, 145, 74.** The answer is that "one is above the other." There is a lower Attribute of Justice, which is *Gevurah,* and a higher one, which is *Binah* (Understanding).

219. This is *Malkhut. See* **196.**

220. This has been defined earlier as *Tiferet. See* **108, 137.** The *Sefirah* of *Daat,* however, follows *Chakhmah* and *Binah,* and is directly above *Tiferet.* He therefore answers, "one is above the other." Just like *Binah* is the source of *Gevurah,* so *Daat* is the source of *Tiferet.* The saying of Rabbi Akiba is cited as proof that there are such parallels.

221. *See* **11, 82.**

222. *See* **147, 148.**

223. For the significance of the word "health," see **13.**

224. *See* **91, 193.**

225. Sometimes a word is read differently than it is written. In this case, the word is spelled *Yado,* without a *Yud,* and would normally be read as "his hand." Tradition, however, dictates that it be read *Yadav,* as if it had the *Yud,* and it is translated as "his hands," in the plural.

226. *See* **28.**

227. *Sefer Yetzirah* 1:12. Water is *Chesed,* while fire is *Gevurah. See* **11, 145.**

228. It was said earlier that water includes fire. Water is the right hand, while fire is the left. *See* **11, 145.** The right hand therefore includes the left, and this answers why it is in the singular. It also explains why the plural and singular are mixed when speaking of hands.

229. *See* note **82.** In *Seder Rabbah DeBereshit* (in *Batey Midrashot)* p. 30, this is attributed to Rabbi Ishmael.

230. *See* **25, 147.** Cf. *Pardes Rimonim* 22:4.

231. Mentioned in Esther 1:6, cf. *Megillah* 12a. *See* **193.**

232. *See* **135.**

233. *See* **75, 137.**

234. *See* end of **178.**

235. God said this with regard to the destruction of Sodom and Gemorah.

236. *Shabbat* 104a, *Yoma* 38a. This is cited as a saying of Resh Lakish, an *Amorah.*

237. *See* **38.** Cf. *Tosefot, Shabbat* 204a *"It DeGarsi."*

238. As in **190.**

239. "There" is a place name. *See* **187.**

240. *See* **61, 157, 102, 180.**

241. *See* **188.**

242. Cf. *Shabbat* 89b, *Yerushalmi Bikkurim* 2:1 (6b), *Yerushalmi Sanhedrin* 11:5 (56b), *BaMidbar Rabbah* 18:3.

243. Cf. *Chagigah* 13b. The Torah was given to the 26th generation after Adam. When this is subtracted from a thousand, the remainder is 974.

244. *Sanhedrin* 65b. *Yad Ramah* ad loc. writes that this is Rabba bar Nachmani. *Cf.* Rabbi Yehuda Barceloni on *Sefer Yetzirah,* pp. 102, 103. *See* note 38 in introduction.

245. *Pesachim* 50b.

246. Referring to Genesis 38:29, 30. Peretz was the ancestor of David, Ruth 4:12. Amnon and the second Tamar, mentioned in II Samuel 13, were therefore her descendants. Tamar also means "date palm", as below.

247. *See* **172.**

248. These refer to three levels of creation. *See* **13.**

249. Genesis 1:26, "Let us *make* man in our image."

250. Genesis 2:7, "And God *formed* man of the dust of the earth, and blew in his nostrils a soul of life."

251. *See* **34, 162, 163.** North (or left) is normally the feminine side.

252. These "flying things" can be taken to mean angels. *See* **21.**

253. Edom is associated with Esau, Genesis 36:43. The final exile preceding the Messianic era is said to be that of Edom, and when the Messiah comes, he will destroy Edom. *See* Obadiah 1:6-21.

254. *Sanhedrin* 29a.

THE TWELVE NAMES

Pardes	Other Version	Manuscript	Our Verson
אהציצהרון	אהציצירון	אהציצהרון	אהציצהרון
אכליחהרון	אברוחיהרון	אברוחיהון	אכליחהרון
סמקהון	ושכובכמקרון	ושכביומהרון	שמקהרון
רמוהטרון	דמורסרון	דמנדערון	דמושהרון
וצפצפשיהרון	צפצפשיטרון	צפצפשיחרון	וצפצפסיחרון
יהורמרון	יהודמירון	יהורמירון	הורמירון
כרחיה גאון	ברכיהיאון	חיימרון	כרחיהרון
עדשגדראון	ערשיה גאון	בנהיהרון	ערש גדראון
כסאות	כסאימנגמהון	עדשיהגאון	כסאוה מכאהון
הוהויהה	הוהו יההי יויה יהאה אהוה	כסאידמנהנן	חזהויה
ויהאאהאיה		יהוהו יההיו יהאה אהוהי	הוהירי האה אהיה
והדמהתיהון	דמהרירון	דמהרירון	והראיחהון

ספר

הבהיר

להתנא רבי נחוניה בן הקנה

והרמב״ן ז״ל בפירוש התורה ובשער הגמול וכן הציוני קוראים לו בשם

מדרש נחוניה בן הקנה

1

אמר ר' נחוניא בן הקנה כתוב אחד אומר
ועתהלא ראו אור בהיר הוא בשחקים
וכא״א ישת חשך סתרו ונם ענן וערפל סביביו
קשיא בא הכתוב השלישי ויכריע ביניהם גמחשד
לא יהשיך מטך ולילה כיום יאיר כחשיכה כאורה :

2

א״ר ברכיה מ״ד והארץ היתה תהו ובהו מאי
משמע היתה שכבר היתה ומאי תהו דבר
המתהא בני אדם ומאי בהו אלא תהו היתה וחזרה
לבהו ומאי בהו דבר שיש בו ממש דכתיב בהו הוא
הוא :

3

ומפני מה התחיל התורה בב' כמה
דאתחיל ברכה ומנלן דהתורה נקראת ברכה
שנאמר ומלא ברכת ח' ים ודרום ירשה ואין
ים אלא תורה שנאמר ורחבה מני ים ומאי ומלא
ברכת ה' אלא כל מקום שנאמר בי״ת הוא לשון
ברכה כדאמרין בראשית ואין ראשית אלא
חכמה שנאמר ראשית חכמה יראת ה' ואין
חכמה אלא ברכה שנאמר ויברך אלהים את שלמה
וכתיב וה' נתן חכמה לשלמה. משל למלך שהשיא
את בתו לבנו ונתנה לו בחתונה ואמר לו
עשה בה כרצונך

4

ומאי דההיא ברכה לישנא
דברוך הוא דלמא לישנא דברך הוא דכתיב כי
לי תברע כל ברך מקום שכל ברך כורע . מלה״ד
למבקשים לראות את פני המלך ואינם יודעים אנה
המלך אנה ביתו שואלים אנה בית המלך תחלה
ואח״כ שואלים אנה המלך לפיכך כי לי תכרע
כל ברך ואפילו עליונים תשבע כל לשון :

5

ישב ר' רחומאי ודרש מ״ד ומלא ברכת ה'
ים ודרום ירשה . אלא בכ״מ בי״ת מבורך הוא
כי הוא המלא המלא שנאמר ומלא ברכת ה' ומשם
משקה הצריכים ומאי מלא פי' מן המלא נטל
עצה תחלה למה״ד למלך שרצה לבנות פלטרין

6

ומאי ברכה אלא משל למלך שנטע
אילנות בגנו ואע״פ שירדו גשמים שואב תמיד
וגם הקרקע לחה ושואבת תמיד צריך הוא
להשקותה מן המעיין שנאמר ראשית חכמה
יראת ה' שכל טוב לכל עושיהם וא״ת שהיא
חסרה כלום הרי הוא אומר תהלתו עומדת לעד:

7

ישב רבי אמוראי ודרש מ״ד ומלא ברכת ה'
ים ודרום ירשה כך אמר משה אם תלך בחקותיו
תירש העוה״ז והעוה״ב והעוה״ב שהוא נמשל לים
שנא' ורחבה מני ים והעוה״ז נמשל לדרום שנא'
כי ארץ הנגב נתתני ומתרגמינן ארי ארעא
דדרומא :

8

ועוד למה הוסיף הקב״ה ה״א באברהם
יתר משאר אותיות אלא כדי שיזכו כל אבריו
של אדם להי עולם הבא שהוא נמשל לים
כביכול בו נשלם הבנין דכתיב כי בצלם אלהים
עשה את האדם ואברהם בגימטריא רמ״ח כמנין
אבריו של אדם:

9

מ״ד ירשה רש היה לו לומר
אלא רש״יה אף הקב״ה בכלל והיינו רש יה

שלו בסלעים חזקים קצץ צורים וחצב סלעים
ויצא לו מעין מים גדול מים חיים אמר המלך
הואיל ויש לי מים נובעים אטע גן ואשתעשע בו
אני וכל העולם הה״ד ואהיה אצלו אמון ואהיה
שעשועים יום יום משחקת לפניו בכל עת .
אמרה תורה אלפים שנה הייתי בחיקו שעשועים
שנא' יום יום ויומו של הקב״ה אלף שנה שנא'
כי אלף שנים בעיניך כיום אתמול כי יעבור מכאן
ואילך בכל עתים שנאמר בכל עת והשאר
לעולם שנאמר ותהלתי אחטם לך מאי ותהלתי
דכתיב תהלה לדוד ארוממך מאי תהלה משום
דארוממך ומאי רוממה משום דאברכה שמך
לעולם ועד .

למה"ד למלך שהיו לו ב' אוצרות והקצה לו א'
מהם לבנו לסוף ימים אמר לבנו טול מה שיש
בשני אוצרות הללו אמר הבן שמא לא יתן לי
מה שהקצה לי א"ל טול הבל והיינו דכתיב ים
ודרום ירשה וינתן לך הכל ויה רש ולמי שתשמור
דרכי :

14

למה ב' סתומה מכל צד ופתוחה מלפניה
ללמדך שהוא בית לעולם והיינו דקב"ה מקומו של
עולם ואין העולם מקומו ואל תקרא ב' אלא בית
הה"ד בחכמה יבנה בית ובתבונה:

10

אמר ר' בון מ"ד מעולם נסכתי מראש
מקדמי ארץ מאי מעולם שצריך להעלימו מכולי
עלמא דכתיב גם את העולם נתן בלבם א"ת העולם
אלא העלם אמרה תורה אני קדמתי לעולם
שנאמר מעולם נסכתי מראש וא"ת שמא הארץ
קדמה לה ת"ל מקדמי ארץ כדאמרי' בראשית
ברא ומאי ברא ברא כל צרכי הכל ואח"כ אלהים
ומאי כתיב בתריה את השמים ואת הארץ .

15

ולמה
ב' דומה לאדם שנוצר בחכמה שסתום מכל **צד**
ופתוח מלפניו והא' פתוח מלאחריו כזה **את** לומר
זה זנב הב' שפתוחה מלאחרי' שאלמלא כן לא
יתקיים האדם כך אלמלא בית בזנבה של א' לא
יתקיים העולם:

11

ומאי גם את זה לעומת זה עשה האלהים ברא
בהו ושם מקומו בשלום וברא תהו ושם
מקומו ברע בהו בשלום שנאמר עושה שלום
במרומיו מלמד שמיכאל שר הימיני של הקב"ה
מים וברד וגבריאל שר שמאלו של הקב"ה אש
ושר שלום ביניהם מכריע והיינו דכתיב עושה
שלום במרומיו

16

א"ר רהומאי האורה קדמה
לעולם שענן וערפל סביביו שנאמר ויאמר אלהים
יהי אור אמרו לו קודם יצירת ישראל בנך תעשה
לו עטרה א"ל הן מלה"ד למלך שמתאוה לבן
ומצא עטרה נאה קלוסה ומשובחת שמח שמחה
ואמר זה לבני לראשו כי לו נאה אמרו לו ויודע
הוא שבנו ראוי לזה אמר שתוקו כך עלה
במחשבה ונודע שנאמר והשב מחשבות וגו' :

12

ומנלן דתהו הוא ברע דכתיב
עושה שלום ובורא רע הא כיצד רע מתהו
ושלום מבהו ברא תהו ושם מקומו ברע (שנא'
עושה שלום ובורא רע ברא בהו ושם מקומו
בשלום שנאמר עושה שלום במרומיו) :

17

יך ישב ר' אמוראי ודרש למה אל"ף בראש
שהיא קודמת לכל ואפילו לתורה

13

וישב רבי בון ודרש מ"ד יוצר אור ובורא חושך
אלא אור שיש בו ממש כתיב בו יצירה חשך
שאין בו ממש כתיב ביה בריאה כד"א דיוצר
הרים ובורא רוח ואב"א אור שיש בו עשיה
דכתיב ויאמר אלהים יהי אור ואין הויה אלא
ע"י עשיה ויצירה חושך דלא הוי ביה עשיה
כלומר דלא כתיב ביה עשייה אלא הבדלה
והפרשה בלבד קרי ביה בריאה כמד"א הבריא
פלוני:

18

ולמה בי"ת
קרובה לה מפני שהיא היתה תהילה ולמה יש לה
זנב כזה **ב** להראות מאיזה מקום היתה וי"א
שמשם נתקיים העולם

19

ולמה ג' שלישית להודיע
שהוא גומל הסדים ר"ע אמר למה ג' שלישית
מפני שגומלת ומתקיימת ומתגדלת כד"א ויגדל
הילד ויגמל א"ל והוא דברייי כי הוא גודל וגומל
הסד לשכנו עמו ואמן אצלו

נטע האילן ועמד ועשה פרי והצליח בשרשיו
שהשקוהו תמיד ששאבו מן המעין :

24

א"ר
ינאי הארץ נבראת קודם לשמים שנאמר ארץ
ושמים א"ל והכתיב את השמים ואת הארץ אני
מלא אמר להם למה"ד למלך שקנה חפץ נאה
ולא היה שלם ולא קרא עליו שם אמר אשלימנו
ואתקן בנייני וחבורו ואז אקרא לו שם הה"ד
לפנים הארץ יסדת ואח"כ ומעשה ידיך השמים
ואח"כ עטה אור כשלמה נוטה שמים כיריעה
המקרה במים עליותיו וגו' ואומר עושה מלאכיו
רוחות משרתיו אש וגו' ואח"כ יסד ארץ על
מכוניה בל תמוט לעולם ועד כשתיקון לה מכון
אז תאמוין בה שנאמר בל תמוט . ומה שמה
ועד שמה   ומכונה עולם והיינו עולם ועד :

25

א"ר ברכיה מ"ד ויאמר אלהים יהי אור ויהי אור
ולא אמר   יהיה אור (ס"א ולא אמר והיה אור)
משל למלך שקנה חפץ נאה והקצהו עד שזימן
לו מקום ושמהו שם הה"ד יהי אור ויהי אור
שכבר היה :

26

א"ר אמוראי מ"ד   ה' איש
מלחמה א"ר רחומאי ב"ר לא תיבעי לך   מילתא
דפשיטא לך שמע לי ואמלכינך א"ל למה"ד למלך
שהיה לו דירות נאות ושם שם לכל אחד ואחד מהם
ושם כולן זו טובה מזו אמר המלך אתן לבני דירה זו
ששמה אלף גם זו טובה ששמה יו"ד גם זו טובה
ששמה שי"ן מה עשה אספן כל הג' ועשה מהם
שם אחד ובית אחד א"ל עד מתי תסתום
דבריך א"ל בני אל"ף ראש יו"ד שני לה שי"ן
כולל כל העולם ולמה שי"ן כולל כל העולם
מפני שכתוב   בה תשובה :

27

שאלו תלמידיו
מה דלי"ת א"ל מלה"ד לי' מלכים שהיו במקום א'
וכלם עשירים ואחד מהם עשיר אף לא כאחד
מהם אע"פ שעשירו גדול נקרא דל כנגד
העשירים :

20

ומפני מה יש לה
זנב למטה לגימ"ל א"ל ראש יש לו לג' מלמעלה
ודומה לצינור כזה ך מה צינור זה שואב מלמעלה
ומריק מלמטה אף ג' שואבת דרך הראש ומריקה
דרך הזנב וזהו ג' :

21

א"ר יוחנן בשני נבראו
המלאכים דכתיב המקרה במים עליותיו וכתיב
עושה מלאכיו רוחות משרתיו אש לוהט ואמר
רבי לויטס בן טברוס הכל   מודים ומודה ר"י
דמים כבר היו אבל בשני המקרה   במים עליותיו
ומאי השם עבים רכובו ומאי המהלך על כנפי רוח
אבל שלוהים לא נבראו עד יום ה'

22

ומודים הכל
שלא נבראו ביום ראשון שלא יאמרו מיכאל היה
מותח בדרומו של רקיע וגבריאל בצפונו והקב"ה
מודד באמצעו אלא אני 'ה' עושה כל נוטה
שמים לבדי רוקע הארץ מאתי מי אתי כתיב אני
הוא שנטעתי אילן זה להשתעשע בו אני וכל
העולם וקבעתי בו כל וקראתי שמו כל ופי' כך
הוא ממש כפשוטו אני ה' עושה כל רקע הארץ מי
אתי ולא היה אתי לא מלאך ולא שרף אלא אני
בעצמי וקראתי שמו כל שהבל תלוי בו והבל
יוצא ממנו והכל צריכים לו ובו צופים ולו מחכין
ומשם פורחים הנשמות לבדי הייתי כשעשיתי
אותו ולא יגדל עליו מלאך לאמר אני קדמתי לך
כי גם בעת שרקעתי ארצי שבה נטעתי ושרשתי
אילן זה ושמחתי ביחד (ושמחתי בהם מי אתי
שגליתי זה סודי)

23

אמר רבי רחומאי מדבריך
נלמד שצורך העולם הזה ברא הקב"ה קודם
השמים א"ל הן מלה"ד למלך שביקש ליטע
אילן בגנו השניח בכל הגן אם יש שם מעין נובע
מים (ס"א המעמיד אותו) ולא מצא אמר אחפור
מים ואוציא מעין כדי שיוכל להתקיים האילן
חפר והוציא מעין נובע ממעין מים חיים ואח"כ

אותם וימותו א״ל לא קשיא כאן בזמן שישראל
עושין רצונו של מקום כאןכשאיןישראל עושיןרצונו
בזמן שאין ישראל עושין רצונו אש קרובה ובזמן
שעושין רצונו מדת הרחמים מתגלגלת וסובבת
הה״ד נושא עון ועובר על פשע

35

משל למלך שרצה
לרדות את עבדיו וליסרם עמד הגמון אחד ושאל
על מה א״ל על כן א״ל לא עשו עבדיך דבר זה
מעולם ואני ערב לך בהם ואתה תבדוק אהריהם
בין כך ובין כך שככה חמת המלך:

36

שאלו
תלמידיו ואמרו מפני מה ד׳ עבה מן הצד כזה ך
אמר להם מפני הסגו״ל שהזא בפתח קטן שנאמר
פתחי עולם שם שם פתח למעלה וסגול למטה
ובאה עבה

37

מאי פַתַח ומאי פתח הוא רוח
צפונית שהוא פתח לכל באי עולם מן השער שיצא
הרע יוצא הטוב ומה טוב לגלג עליהם חלא
אמרתי לכם פתח קטן אמרו לו שבחנו שנה לנו
שנה להם למלך שהיה לו כסא לפעמים לוקח
אותו על זרועו ולפעמים על ראשו א״ל למה לפי
שהוא נאהוחם לישב עליו א״ל ואנא שמו עלדראשו
א״ל במ״ם פתוחה שנא׳ אמת מארץ תצמח
וצדק משמים נשקף:

38

ישב ר׳ אמוראי ודרש
מ״ד אוהב ה׳ שערי ציון מכל משכנות יעקב
שערי ציון הם פתחי עולם ואין שער אלא פתח
כמד״א פתחו לי שערי (צדק) רחמים כך אמר
הקב״ה אוהב אני שערי ציון כשהן פתוחין למה
שהן מצד הרעה וכשישראל טובים לפני המקום
וראוים להפתח לטוב הקב״ה אוהבם מכל
משכנות יעקב שהם כלם שלום שנאמר ויעקב
איש תם יושב אהלים

28

א״ל מהו ה״א כעס עליהם א״ל
אמרתי לכם לא תשאלו לי על דבר אהרון ואח״כ
על הראשון א״ל וה״א אהרונה כתיבה א״ל ראוי
לכתוב גימ״ל ה״א ועל מה נכתבג׳ דלי״ת מפני
שהיה לו לכתוב ד׳ ה׳ ומפני מה כתב גימ״ל ד׳
אמר להם נחלפים הג׳ במקום ד׳ בראשה במקום
ה׳ ד׳ בקוצה מקום ה׳

29

מאי ה׳ אמר להם ה׳ תחתונה וה׳ עליונה

30

א״ל מאי ו׳ וא״י א״ל בו׳ קצוות
נחתם העולם א״ל והלא ו׳ אחת אמר להם והלא
כתיב עושה אור כשלמה:

31

א״ר אמוראי נ״ע היכן הוא א״ל בארץ

32

דרש ר׳ ישמעאל לר״ע
מ״ד את השמים ואת הארץ אלמלא לא נאמר
את היינו אומרים שמים וארץ אלהות הן א״ל
העבודה נגעת (ולא פגעת) אבל לא ברדת כן
דברת אבל את לרבות חמה ולבנה כוכבים
ומזלות ואת לרבות אילנות ודשאים וגן עדן

33

א״ל
הכתיב יהשליך משמים ארץ תפארת ישראל וא״כ
נפלו א״ל אם קרו לא שנו ואם שנו לא שלשו
מלה״ד למלך שהיתה לו עטרה נאה על ראשו
מלת נאה בכתפיו ובא לו שמועה רעה השליך
העטרה מעל ראשו והמלת מלפניו:

34

שאלו
מפני מה צורת חי״ת פֶּתַח ונקודה בְּפֶּתַח קטן א״ל
מפני שכל הרוחות סתומות הוץ מרוח צפון שהיא
פתוחה לטוב ולרע א״ל לטובה והכתיב יהונה רוח
סערה בא מן הצפון ענן גדול ואש מתלקחת ואין
אש אלא חרון אףדכתיב ותצא אש מלפני ה׳ ותאכל

הקולות ואת הלפידים וכי נראים קולות אלא וכל
העם רואים את הקולות קולות שאמר דוד יקול
ה' על המים אל הכבוד הרעים ה' קול ה' בכח
ואומר בכח ידי עשיתם ואומר אף ידי יסדה
ארץ קול ה' בהדר ואמר קרא הוד והדר פעלו
וצדקתו וגו' קול ה' שובר ארזים זו קשת
שמשברת עצי ברושים ועצי ארוזים . קול ה'
חוצב להבות אש זה שעושה שלום בין המים
ובין האש שחוצב כח האש ומונע אותם מללחוך
המים וגם מונען מלכבותו . קול ה' יחיל מדבר
שנאמר ועושה חסד למשיחו לדוד ולזרעו עד
עולם . קול ה' יהולל אילות ויחשוף יערות
ובהיכלו כולו אומר כבוד · וכתיב השבעתי
אתכם בנות ירושלים בצבאות או באילות השדה
הא למדת שבשבע קולות נתנה תורה ובכלם
נגלה אדון העולם עליהם וראום והיינו דכתיב
וכל העם רואים את הקולות :

כתוב אחד

46

אומר יויט שמים וירד וערפל תחת רגליו וכתוב
אחד אומר וירד ה' על הר סיני וכתוב אחד אומר
כי מן השמים דברתי עמכם הא כיצד אשו
הגדולה היית בארץ שהוא קול אחד ושאר
הקולות היו בשמים שנאמר מן השמים השמיעך
את קולו ליסרך ועל הארץ הראך את אשו
הגדולה ודבריו שמעת מתוך האש . מאין היה
יוצא הדיבור מן האש שנאמר ודבריו שמעת
מתוך האש

47

ומאי ותמונה אינכם רואים זולתי קול
(כדאיתא בתוס') כדאמר להם משה לישראל
כי לא ראיתם כל תמונה תמונה ולא כל
תמונה משל למה"ד למלך שעומד על עבדיו
ועטף כסות לבנה לא די לאימת מלכות שיסתכלו
במלבושיו ועוד רחוק היה המלך ושמעו את קולו
יכולים לראות גרונו (נ"א גדלו) אמרת לא הא
למדת שראו תמונה ולא כל תמונה והיינו דכתיב
ותמונה אינכם רואים זולתי קול וכתיב קול
דברים אתם שומעים :

39

משל לשני בני אדם א'
מזומן לעשות רע ועשה טוב וא' מזומן לעשות
טוב ועשה טוב למי משבחין יותר למי שרגיל
לעשות רע ועשה טוב אולי יעשה פעם שניה
הה"ד אוהב ה' שערי ציון מכל משכנות יעקב
שהן כלם שלום שנאמר ויעקב איש תם יושב
אוהלים :

40

שאלו תלמידיו מהו הולם א"ל
נשמה ושמה חולם שאם תשמע תחלים גופך
לעתיד לבא ואם תמרוד בה ישובו חלאים
בראשך וחלים בראשה

41

ועוד אמרו שכל חלום
הוא בחולם וכל מרגלית לבנה היא בחלם כדכתיב
ואהלמה

42

אמר להם עולו ושמעו דקדוקי נקודה
דאורייתא דמשה ישב ודרש להם חירק שונא
את הרעים ומייסרם ובצדו הקנאה והשנאה
והתחרות דכתיב וחרק עליו שיניו אל תקרי
חרק אלא רחק אלא במדות אלו יתרחק ממך
הרע וכ"ש דהטוב דבק בך

43

חרק אל תקרי חרק
אלאקרחאלא כל מקום(שנאמר)(שדבק חרק נשאר
קרח שנאמר ונקה

44

ומאי משמע דהאי חרק לשון
שורף משום דהוא אש שורפת כלהאשות דכתיב
יותפול אש ה' ותאכל את העולה ואת העצים
ואת האבנים ואת העפר ואת המים אשר בתעלה
להכה :

45

אמר מר מ"ד וכל העם רואים את

48

כתוב אחד אומר

וכל העם רואים את הקולות וכתוב אחד אומר
קול דברים אתם שומעים הא כיצד בתחלה
רואים את הקולות מאי ראו ז' קולות שאמר
דוד ולבסוף שמעו הדיבור יוצא מבין כולם והא
אנן תנן עשרה כרבנן תנן דאמרי דכולהו אמרן
בחדא מילתא כן כולהו אמרן כחדא מילתא והוי
ז' אמירן מז' קולות ועל תלת נאמר קול דברים
אתם שומעים ותמונה אינכם רואים זולתי קול
הא למדת דכולהו בחדא מילתא אמירה ובעבור
שלא יטעו ישראל לומר אחרים עזרוהו מן
המלאכים אך קולו לבדו אינו חזק כ"כ בעבור כן
חזר וכללן .

49

ד"א שלא יאמרו העולם הואיל
והם י' מאמרות לי' מלאכים שמא לא יוכלו
לדבר על פה אחד כתב בי' אנכי וכלל כל הי'
ומאי י' מלאכים ז'קולות וג' מאמרות ומאי נינהו
מאמרות דכתיב וה' האמירך היום ומאי
נינהו ג' דכתיב ראשית חכמה קנה חכמה ובכל
קנינך קנה בינה כד"א יונשמת שדי תבינם
נשמתו של שדי היא תבינם שלישי מאי היא
כדאמר ליה ההוא סבא להההוא ינוקא במופלא
ממך בל תדרוש ובמכוסה ממך בל תחקור במה
שהורשית התבונן ואין לך עסק בנסתרות :

50

תנא דכבוד אלהים הסתר דבר מאי דבר כדאמר
ראש דברך אמת פי' כ"ע אמת וכבוד מלכים הקור
דבר מאי דבר דכתיב יהדבר דבור על אפניו א"ת
אופניו אלא אֲפָנָיו כמו ופני ילכו :

51

שאלו
תלמידיו את רבי ברכיה רצה דבריו לפניו לא נתן
להם רשות פעם אחד נתן להם רשות והוא דעביד
לבודקן (די"ה) [דין הוא] השתא כוונו לנפשייהו
יום א' בדק אותן אמר להם השמיעוני חכמתכם
פתחו ואמרו בראשית א' זורוח(ה') מלפני יעטוף
ונשמות אני עשיתי פלג אלהים מלא מים ועל

ידם אדם לומד תורה דכתיב יההוי כל צמא לכו
למים ואשר אין לו כסף לכו שברו ואכלו דא"ר
חמא בזכות גמילות החסד אדם לומד תורה
כדכתיב כל צמא לכו וגי' לכו שברו וינמול לכם
הסד ושברו ואכלו

52

ד"א ואשר אין לו כסף לכו
אליו כי יש אצלו כסף דכתיב סכי לי הכסף ולי
הזהב מאי לי הכסף ולי הזהב מלה"ד למלך שיש
לו ב' אוצרות אחד של כסף ואחד של זהב שם
של כסף בימינו ושל זהב בשמאלו אמר זה יהיה
מקומו וקל להוציאו ועושה דבריו בנחת והוא
יהיה דבוק עם העניים ומנהיגם בנחת הה"ד ימינך
ה' נאדרי בכח ואם שמח בהלקן טוב ואם לאו
ימינך ה' תרעין אויב (א"ל) מאי ימינך ה' תרעין
אויב א"ל זה הזהב (דכתיב לי הכסף ולי הזהב)

53

ולמה נקרא שמו זהב שבו כלולות שלש מדות זכר
והוא הזיי"ן נשטה והיא הה' וה' שמות לנשמה
רוח חיה יחידה נפש נשמה מאי עבידתיה בה"א
היא כסא לזיי"ן דכתיב כי גבוה מעל גבוה שומר
ובי"ת היא קיומם כדאמר בראשית ברא

54

ומאי
עבידתיה בה"א מלה"ד למלך שהיתה לו בת
טובה ונעימה ונאה ושלימה והשיאה לבן מלך
והלבישה ועטרה וקשטה ונתנה לו בממון רב
אפשר לו למלך זה לישב חוץ מבתו אמרת
לא אפשר לשבת עמה כל היום תמיד אמרת לא
הא כיצד שם חלון בינו לבינה וכל שעה שצריכה
הבת לאביה או האב לבתו מתחברים יחד דרך
החלון הה"ד כל כבודה בת מלך פנימה ממשבצות
זהב לבושה

55

ומאי היא בי"ת דכתיב בחכמה
יבנה בית נבנה לא נאמר אלא יבנה עתיד הקב"ה
לבנותה ולקשטה אלפים ברבבה על אשר היית"ה
כדאמרי' מה (הוה) [הוי'] דתהלת התורה בבי"ת
דכתיב יואהיה אצלו אמון ואהיה שעשועים יום

61

שאלו אותו מאי צדיק א"ל זה נו"ן יו"ד צדי"ק
אף זוגו נו"ן יו"ד הה"ד יוצדיק יסוד עולם .

62

שאלו לו מאי דכתיב יויקחהו שדה צופים דכתיב
לכה דודי נצא השדה א"ת השדה אלא השידה
ומאי שדה א"ל לכה דודי נצא השדה (פי' לכו
להקב"ה) לטייל ואל אשב תמיד במקום אחד

63

ומאי לב א"ל א"כ בן זומא מבחוץ ואתה עמו
ל"ב הוא שלשים ושתים והיו סתומים ובהם נברא
העולם מאי ל"ב א"ל ל"ב נתיבות משל למלך
שהיה יושב בחדרי חדרים ומנין החדרים ל"ב
ולכל חדר יש לו נתיב נאה למלך זה להכנס הכל
בחדרו ע"ד נתיבתו אמרת לא נאה לו (שלא)[אלא]
לגלות פניניו ומשבצותיו ומצפוניו וגנזיו והמודותיו
אמרת לא מה עשה נגע בבת וכללבהכל הנתיבות
ומלבושיה והרוצה להכנס בפנים יסתכל (ס"א
יכנוס) הנה ונשא למלך גם נתנה לו במתנה
לפעמים קורא אותה באהבתו אחותי כי ממקום
אחד באו ולפעמים קורא אותה בתי כי בתו היא
ולפעמים קורא אותה אמי

64

ועוד כי אין דין אם
אין חכמה שהרי נאמר וה' נתן חכמה לשלמה
ואחרי כך דן את הדין על מתכונתו שנאמר
וישמעו כל ישראל את המשפט אשר שפט
המלך שלמה ויראו מלפני המלך כי ראו כי חכמת
אלהים בקרבו לעשות משפט:

65

ומה חכמה נתן
הקב"ה לשלמה שלמה נושא שמו של הקב"ה
דא"ר יוחנן כל שלמה האמור בשה"ש קודש
לבד מאחד אמר הקב"ה הואיל ושמך כשם כבודי
אשיאלך בתי והא נשואה היא אימא במתנ הנגתנונה
לך דכתיב וה' נתן חכמה לשלמה ולא פירש והיכן
פירש להלן שנא' כי ראו כי חכמת אלהים בקרבו

יום תרי אלפין שנין שהוא ראשית תרי והכתוב
אומר שבע דכתיב וההיה אור הלבנה כאור החמה
ואור החמה יהיה שבעתים כאור שבעת ימי
בראשית דאמרינן מה המהלו' אף לבנה לו'(אלא)
[אנא]אלפים אמרי'

56

א"ל ע"כ חמשה מכאן ואילך
מאיא"לאני אפרש תחלה זהב מאי זהב שממנו יוצא
הדין ואם תטה דבריך ימינושמאל(נזהר)[תפרע]
ממך

57

מאי והיה אור הלבנה כאור החמה ואור החמה
יהיה שבעתים כאור שבעת הימים מיבעי ליה
אלא אותן ימים שבתוב בהן כי ששת ימים עשה
ה' וגו' אמרו לו חביריו וכן קבלתי מדכתיב כי
ששת ימים עשה ה' כד"א ששה כלים נאים
עשה הקב"ה והא ז' הן וכן כתוב וביום השביעי
שבת וינפש מאי וינפש מלמד שיום השבת
מקיים כל הנשמות שנאמר וינפש

58

ד"א שמשם
פורחין כל הנשמות שנאמר וינפש עד אלף דור
שנאמר דבר צוה לאלף דור וסמיך ליה אשר כרת
את אברהם ומאי כרת לי' ברית בין ו' אצבעות
ידיו וי' אצבעות רגליו נתבייש אברהם א"ל
הקב"ה אני בריתי אתך ובו תהיה לאב המון
גוים

59

ומאי שמים מלמד שגיבל הקב"ה אש ומים
וטפחן זה בזה ועשה מהן ראש לדבריו דכתיב
ראש דברך אמת והיינו דכתיב שמים שם מים
אש ומים וא"ל עד כאן עושה שלום במרומיו
יתן בינינו שלום ואהבה

60

ועוד אמרינן שבע ביום
הללתיך על משפטי צדקך א"ל מאי הם א"ל לא
דקדקתם בדברי צאו ודקדקו בהם ותמצאם :

ששומעים בו ומ"ט אמר שמעתי הבנתי מיבעי
ליה כד"א גוי אשר לא תשמע לשונו

70

ומ"ט יראתי
משום דאזן דמות אל"ף ואל"ף ראש לכל האותיות
ולא עוד אלא אל"ף גורמת לכל האותיות קיומם
ואל"ף דמות המוח מה אל"ף כשאתה זוכרה אתה
פותח פיך כך המחשבה כשאתה חושב תחשוב
לאין סוף ותכלית ומהאל"ף יצאו כל האותיות
הלא תראה שהיא בתחלתן ואמר וה' בראשם
וק"ל דכל שם הכתוב ביו"ד ה"א וי"ו ה"א מיוחד
הקב"ה ומקורש בקדש ומאי בקדש בהיכל הקדש
זאנה היכל הקדש הוי אומר במחשבה והיינו
אל"ף הה"ד ה' שמעתי שמעך יראתי

71

ובן
אמר חבקוק תפלתי ידעתי שנתקבלה בתענוג
(ס"א בהיכל הקדש) ואני גם התענגתי וכשהגעתי
לבקום פלוני והבנתי שמעך יראתי ע"כ ה'
פעלך בקרב שנים חייהו ביהודך מלה"ד למלך
אמון מופלא ומבוסה שנכנס לביתו וצוה הבל
שלא יבקשו עליו ע"כ המבקש יפחד פן ידע
המלך שהוא עובר על מצותיו ולכן אמר יראתי
ה' פעלך בקרב שנים חייהו . כך אמר חבקוק
הואיל ושמך בך ובך שמך פעלך בקרב שנים
חייהו פן יהיה לעד

72

ד"א מלה"ד למלך שהיה
לו מרגלית טובה והיא חמדת מלכות ובעת
שמחתו הובקה ומנשקה ושמה על ראשו ואוהב
אותה אמר חבקוק אע"פ שהמלאבים עמך אותה
המרגלית חמדה היא בעולמך על כן בקרב שנים
חייהו מאי משמע לישנא דשנים שנאמר ויואמר
אלהים יהי אור ואין אור אלא אלא יום דכתיב את
המאור הגדול לממשלת היום ואת המאור הקטן
לממשלתהלילהוהאותהשנניםהןהימיםהה"ד בקרב שנים
קרב אותה המרגלית החמודה (ס"א המולידה) את
השנים

לעשות משפטמאילעשות משפט הוי אומר אותה
חכמה שנתן לו האלהים ושהיא עמו בחדרו היא
בקרבולעשות משפט(ס"א מאי לעשות משפטאלא
כל זמן שאדם עושה משפט הבמת אלהים בקרבו)
ועוזרתו ומקרבתו ואם לאו מרחקתו ולא עוד אלא
מייסרתו דכתיב ויסרתי אתכם אף אני שבע על
חטאתיכם:

66

וא"ר רחומאי מ"ד אף אני אלא ה"ק
אמר(ויסרתי אתכם לכנסת ישראל)כנסת ישראלאל
תאמרו שאני מבקש רחמים עליכ אלא אף אני אייסר
אתכם לא די שאני אדון הדין אלא אף אני איסרכם

67

מאי שבע פי' כנגד ז' ספירות על חטאתיכם אלא
אמר ה' לכנסת ישראל ויסרתי אתכם אף אני
והם ענו בנו שנאמר שבע ביום הללתיך נתלו ו'
עליהםואמרו אף אנו שבע אע"פ שבבנו מי שממונה
על הזכות ועל הטובה אף אנו נתהפך וניוסר
למה מפני חטאתיכם ואם תשובו אלי ואשובה
אליכם דכתיב שובו אלי ואשובה אליכם
ואשוב לא נאמר אלא ואשובה אליכם פי' עמכם
ונבקש כלנו רחמים מן המלך למה אומר המלך
שובו בנים שובבים ארפא משובותיכם שובו
והשיבו מאי שובו והשיבו אלא שובו ובקשו
רחמים מאותן שבע שישובו עמכם הה"ד והשיבו
אותםשאמרו שבע עלחטאתיכם:

68

שאלו תלמידים
של רבי רחומאי מ"ד תפלה לחבקוק הנביא על
שגיונות תהלה מיבעי ליה אלא כל המפנה לבו
מעסקי עולם ומסתכל במעשה מרכבה מקובל
לפני הקב"ה כאלו מתפלל כל היום שנאמר
תפלה ומאי על שגיונות כדכתיב באהבתה תשגה
תמיד ומאי ניהו מעשה מרכבה

69

ד"א מ"ד
שמעתי שמעך יראתי וגו' מ"ט כשאמר שמע
אמר יראתי וכשאמר בקרב שנים לא אמר יראתי
אלא משמעך יראתי ומאי משמעך ממקום

73

והכתיב ממזרח אביא זרעך והשמש זורחת
ממזרח ואמר שהמרגלית היא יום אני לא אמרתי
אלא ויהי ערב ויהי בקר יום וכתיב ביום עשות
ה' אלהים ארץ ושמים

74

והכתיב ישת השך כתרו
סביבותיו סוכתו חשבת מים עבי שחקים א"ל
כתיב ביה ושחקים יזלו צדק וצדק זה מ"ה של
עולם שנאמר צדק צדק תרדוף וכתיב למען
תהיה וירשת את הארץ ואם תדין עצמך תהיה
ואם לאו הוא ידין עליך ותתקיים בע"כ :

75

ומאי
צדק צדק תרי זימני א"ל מדכתיב מנוגה נגדו
צדק ראשון צדק ממש והוא שכינה כדכתיב
צדק ילין בה ומאי צדק שני זה צדק שמפחיד
הצדיקים והאי צדק הוי צדקה או לא א"ל לא
ומה טעם כדכתיב וילבש צדקה כשריון וצדק הוי
קובע ישועה בראשו ואין ראשו אלא אמת שנאמר
ראש דברך אמת ואין אמת אלא שלום שנאמר
(כי) [הלא] אם שלום ואמת יהיה בימי אפשר
לאדם לומר כן אלא חזקיה אמר כך אותה המדה
שנתת לדוד אבי הוא ימי ושלום ואמת חצי ימי
וזהו שאמר חזקיה שלום ואמת יהיה בימי שהכל
אחד היינו הוא דכתיב שלום : ויהי ערב ויהי בקר
יום מה היום שלום אף הוא בקש שלום שנאמר
"שלום ואמת יהיה בימי באותה מדה שנתת לדוד
אבי דכתיב וכסאו כשמש נגדי

76

ומאי בקרב
שנים תודיע כך אמר ידעתי שאתה האל הקדוש
דכתיב מי כמוך נאדר בקדש וקדש בך ואתה
בקדש ואעפ"כ בקרב שנים תודיע ומאי תודיע
תרחם כד"א וירא אלהים את בני ישראל וידע
אלהים מאי וידע אלהים מלה"ד למלך שיש לו
אשה נאה והעמיד ממנה בנים וחבקן וגדלן ויצאו
לתרבות רעה שנאם ושנאה אמן חזרה אמם
אליהם ואמרה בני למה אתם עושים כך שאביכם

שונא אותי ואתכם עד שנכמרו רחמיהם ונתחממו
וחזרו לעשות רצון אביהם ראה אביהם כך
אהבם כבתחלה וזכר אמם הה"ד וירא אלהים וגו'
וידע וגו' וכתיב בקרב שנים תודיע

77

ומאי
ברוגז רחם תזכור אמר בעת שיחטאו לך בני
ותכעיס עליהם רחם תזכור ומאי רחם תזכור אותו
שא' ארחמך ה' חזקי ונתת לו המדה הזאת שהיא
שכינת' של ישראל זכות בנו שירש' ונתת לו
דכתיב וה' נתן חכמה לשלמה וזכור אביהם
אברהם דכתיב זרע אברהם אוהבי בקרב שנים
תודיע

78

ומהיכן היה לאברהם בת הן דכתיב
וה' ברך את אברהם בכל וכתיב כל הנקרא בשמי
ולכבודי בראתיו יצרתיו אף עשיתיו האי ברכה
בתו היתה או לא היתה אלא אמו הן בתו היתה
מלה"ד למלך שהיה לו עבד תמים ושלם לפניו
נסהו נסיונות ועמד בכלן אמר המלך מה אתן
לעבד זה או מה אעשה לו אמר אין לו אלא
אצונו לאחי הגדול ליעצו ולשמרו ולכבדו חזר
העבד אצל אחיו הגדול למד מדותיו אהבו ושמח
האח מאד וקראו אוהבי דכתיב זרע אברהם
אוהבי אמר מה אתן לך או מה אעשה לך הנה
כלי נאה עשיתי ובו מרגלית אחת אתן לו כמוהו
והן סגולות מלכים אתננה לו ויזכה במקומו הה"ד
וה' ברך את אברהם בכל :

79

ד"א שמעתי
שמעך יראתי הבנתי שמעך יראתי מאי הבין
שנתירא הבין מחשבתו של הקב"ה מה מחשבה
אין לה קץ דהא חשיב אינש ושפיל לסיפא
דעלמא אף האזן אין לה קץ ולא תשבע דכתיב
ולא תמלא אזן משמוע מ"ט מפני שהאזן דמות
אל"ף עיקר והן די בחצי הלא לא תמלא האזן
משמוע

80

ומאי זיי"ן דכתיב באזן דהא דהא אמרינן כל

מה שברא הקב"ה בעולמו שם שמו מעניינו דכתיב וכל אשר יקרא לו האדם נפש חיה הוא שמו כלומר הוא גופו ומנלן דשמו גופו היינו דכתיב זכר צדיק לברכה ושם רשעים ירקב אטו שמו מרקב אלא גופו ה"נ גופו

81

כגון מאי כגון שרש דשי"ן דומיא דשרש האילן ושורש כל האילן הוא מעיקרו ושי"ן בתרא מאי עבידתיה ללמדך שאם תקח ענף ותמעטהו שנעשה שרש זיי"ן מאי עבידתיה כמנין ימי השבוע ללמדך שכל יום יש לו כח ומאי עבידתיה הכא ללמדך שיש חפירה גדולה (בארץ) לאוזן לאין תכלית כך יש הכח בכל האיברים:

82

ומאי ז' כנגד איברים שבע שיש באדם כדכתיב 'כי בצלם אלהים עשה את האדם ברא אותו וכל איבריו וכל הלקיו והאמר ו' למה הוא דומה לעוטה אור כשלמה והא ו' אינו אלא בו"ק א"ל ברי' מילה וזוגו של אדם חשבונו א' וב' ידיו ג' ראשו וגופו ה' שתי שוקיו ז' וכנגדן כחותם בשמים דכתיב גם את זה לעומת זה עשה האלהים וחיינו 'כי ששת ימים עשה ה' את השמים ואת הארץ בששת לא נאמר כי כל יום ויום יש לו כח לבדו:

83

ומאי נו"ן ללמדך שהשמוה עיקר חוט השדרה הוא ומשם שואב הגוף תדיר ואלמלא חוט השדרה לא יתקיים המוח ובלי מוה לא יתקיים הגוף כי כל הגוף הוא לצורך ואם לא יתקיים כל הגוף לא יתקיים המוה ע"כ חוט השדרה מריק לכל הגוף מן המוח והיה נו"ן בתוכו והא נו"ן זאת ארוכה לעולם בתשלומי המלה ללמדך שנו"ן ארוכה כוללת הכפופה וארוכה אבל כפופה יסוד ללמדך שנו"ן ארוכה כלולה מזכר ונקבה:

84

מ"ם פתוחה מאי פתוחה

כלולה מזכר ונקבה מ"ם סתומה למאי היא עשויה כמין בטן מלמעלה והא אמר רבי חייא הבטן כמין טי"ת ההיא דאמר כמין ט' פנים כזה אנא דאמרי כמין ב' בחין

85

ומאי מ"ם א"ת מ"ם אלא מים מה המים להים אף הבטן לה לעולם ולמה מ"ם פתוחה כלולת זכר ונקבה וסתומה זכר ללמדך שעיקר הוא הזכר והוא הוסיף פתוחה לשם נקבה ומה הזכר הזה אינו מוליד אלא בפתיחה אף מ"ם סתומה אינה מולדת אלא בפתוחה ומה נקבה יולדת פתוחה וסתומה אף מ"ם סתומה ופתוחה:

86

ומה ראית לרבות מ"ם בפתיהה וסתימה משום דאמרינן א"ל מ"ם אלא מים והא אשה קרה ע"כ צריכה להתהמם בזכר ומה ראית לרבות נו"ן נקבה דכתיב לפני שמש ינון שמו בשני נוני נו"ן כפופה וארוכה וצריך להיות ע"י הזכר והנקבה

87

כתיב ולא תמלא אזן משמוע וכתיב ולא תשבע עין לראות מלמד ששניהם שואבים מןהמחשבה ומאי מחשבה מלך שצריכין לו כל מה שנגבר בעליונים ובתהתונים

88

ומאי הוה הא דאמרינן עלה במחשבה ולא אמרינן ירד דהא אמרינן המסתכל בצפיית המרכבה ירד ואח"כ יעלה התם משום דאמרינן ויקרא ארי' על מצפה ה' הכא במחשבה לית בצפיית כלל ולית ליה תכלית כלל וכל דלית ליה תכלית וסוף לית ליה ירידה כדאמרי אינשי ירד פלוני לסוף דעתו של חבירו ולא לסוף מחשבתו:

89

ישב רבי אמוראי ודרש מאי דכתיב סגו"ל א"ל סגולה שמה כדאיתא לעיל בתר זרקא זרקא מ"ט כשמו כן הוא דהוא נזרק

כגון דבר הנזרק ובתריה אתיא סגולת מלכים
והמדינות

90

מ"ט דכתיב ברוך כבוד ה' ממקומו
מכלל דליכא דידע את מקומו ואמרי' שם אתגא
אזלא ואתיה על ראש קונה דכתיב קונה שמים
וארץ וכדו אזלא הוי בזרקא וסגול אבתריה והוי
בראש כל אותיות

91

ומ"ט היא בסוף תיבה ואינה
בראש ללמדך שאותה תגא עולה עד למעלה
למעלה ומאי משמע דהאי תגא לישנא אבן
יקרה היא מכלילת מעוטרת דכתיב אבן מאסו
הבונים היתה לראש פנה ועולה עד המקום
אשר נחצבה ממנו דכתיב משם רועה אבן
ישראל :

92

והא דאמר מ"ט אנו מטילין תכלת
בציצית ומ"ט שלשים ושתים מלה"ד למלך
שהיה לו גן נאה ולו ל"ב נתיבות ושם שומר
עליהם והודיע לו לבדו אותן הנתיבות א"ל
שומרם ולך עליהם בכל יום ובכל זמן שתדרכם
שלום לך ומה עשה אותו השומר שם שומרים
אחרים עליהם אמר אם אני לבדי באלה הנתיבות
אי אפשר לשומר אחד לקיים כל אלה הנתיבות
ועוד כי יאמרו העולם כי לי הוא מלך זה ושומר
ה לכך שם שומר זה שומרים אחרים לכל
הנתיבות אלה הם ל"ב נתיבות

93

ומ"ט דתכלת
אמר השומר שמא יאמרו השומרים האלה הגן
שלנו הוא נתן להם סימן ואמר להם ראו זה
סימן של מלך שהוא שלו הגן הזה ואלה
הנתיבות הוא תיקנם ואינם שלי והנה חותמו
מלה"ד למלך ובתו שהיו להם עבדים ובקשו
יילך למרחוק פחדו מאימת המלך נתן להם
המלך סימנו פחדו מן הבת נתנה להם סימן
אמרו מעתה משני סימנים אלה ישמרך
מכל רע [והוא] ישמור את נפשך :

94

ישב ר'
אמוראי ודרש מ"ד הנה השמים ושמי השמים
לא יכלכלוך מלמד שע"ב שמות יש לו
להקב"ה וכולם קבעום בשבטים דכתיב
ששה משמותם על האבן האחת ואת שמות הששה
הנותרים על האבן השנית כתולדותם וכתי' שתים
עשרה האבנים האלה הקים וגו' [הקיש] מה אלה
אבני זכרון אף אלה אבני זכרון לי"ב שבטים
ושתים עשרה אבנים הם ע"ב כנגד ע"ב שמות
של הקב"ה ומ"ט התחיל בשתים עשרה ללמדך
שי"ב מנהיגים יש לו להקב"ה ובכל אחד ואחד
ו' כוחות ומאי הם ע"ב שמות כנגד ע"ב
לשונות

95

ואילן אחד יש לו להקב"ה ובו י"ב
[גבולי] אלכסון גבול מזרחית דרומית גבול
מזרחית צפונית גבול מזרחית רומית גבול
מזרחית תחתית גבול מערב צפונית גבול מערב
דרומית גבול מערב רומית גבול מערב תחתית
גבול צפונית רומית גבול צפונית תחתית גבול
דרומית רומית גבול דרומית תחתית ומרחיבין
והולכין עד עדי עד והם זרועות עולם ובהם בפנים
הוא אילן ובכל אלו האלכסונין יש כנגדם
פקידים והם י"ב וגם בפנים בגלגל יש י"ב
פקידים וכן בלב י"ב פקידים אלה שלשים ושתים
פקידים עם האלכסוניים ולכל אחד יש שר אחד
כדכתיב כי גבוה מעל גבוה שומר נמצא
לרוח מזרחית ט' לרוח מערבית ט' לרוח דרומית
ט' לרוח צפונית ט' והיינו י"ב וי"ב וי"ב שהם
פקידים בתלי וגלגל ולב והם ל"ו וכלם ל"ו ול"ו
שכה א' יש להם וכח כל א' וא' בחבירו ואע"פ
שי"ב בכל א' וא' מן הג' כלם אדוקים זה בזה
וכל הל"ו כחות הנמצאות בראשונה שהוא תלי
ואם תדרוש בלב תמצא אותם עצמ' לכ"א י"ב
נמצא לג' ל"ו והוזרת הלילה נמצא כח כ"א בחבירו
הלכך כל א' ל"ו וכלם אינם יותר מל"ו צורות
וכלם נשלמו [בל"ב] נתיבות מסור ללב ונשארו
ד' והם ס"ד צורות ומנין דמסור לב ללב דכתיב

99

ומאי ניהו צורות דכתיב וישכן מקדם לג״ע את
הכרובים ואת להט החרב המתהפכת לשמור את
דרך עץ החיים ומאי וישכן מקדם לג״ע וישכן
באותן הנתיבות שקדמו לאותו מקום הנקרא ג״ע
ושקדם לכרובים דכתיב ואת הכרובים ושקדם
ללהט דכתיב ואת להט החרב המתהפכת
שקדם והכתיב שמים ואש קדמו דכתיב יהי
רקיע בתוך המים ויהי מבדיל בין מים למים
וכתיב ויקרא אלהים לרקיע שמים ומנלן דשמים
הוי אש דכתיב כי ה׳ אלהיך אש אוכלה הוא אל
קנא

100

ומנלן דשמים הקב״ה דכתיב ואתה תשמע
השמים אטו שלמה התפלל אל השמים שישמע
תפלתם אלא אותו שנקרא שמו על השמים
דכתיב השמים ושמי השמים לא יכלכלוך הוי
שמו של הקב״ה והוי אש ואמרת קדם אלא
אימא כחם קדם של אותם צורות של המקום
ההוא ואח״כ הצורות הקדושים ההם ומאי ניהו
כחם כד״א אין קדוש כה׳ כי אין בלתך ואין צור
כאלהינו:

101

ישב רבי ברכיה ודרש מאי לולב
דאטרינן אלא ל׳ו מסור ללב והיאך א״ל ג׳ שרים
הם תלי וגלגל ולב וכל אחד י״ב חזרו בשלשה
כמנין ל״ו ובהם שתקיים העולם דכתיב וצדיק
יסוד עולם.

102

תנא עמוד (פי׳ יסוד מן העץ) עד
ת״פ) אחד יש מן הארץ עד לרקיע וצדיק שמו
על שם הצדיקים וכשיש צדיקים בעולם העמוד
מתגבר ואם לאו מתחלש והוא סובל העולם
דכתיב צדיק יסוד עולם ואם חלש לא יוכל
להתקיים העולם הלכך אפילו אין בעולם אלא
צדיק א׳ מעמיד העולם שנאמר וצדיק יסוד
עולם לפיכך קחו תרומתי ממנו תחלה ואח״כ
וזאת התרומה אשר תקחו מאתם מאת השאר
ותהו זהב וגו׳

כי גבוה מעל גבוה שומר א״כ היינו ס״ד חסר
ח׳ לע״ב שמותיו של הקב״ה והיינו דכתיב
וגבוהים עליהם והם ז׳ימי השבוע והסר א׳ והיינו
דכתיב ויתרון ארץ בכל היא ומאי יתרון מקום
יתרון שממש נחצב הארץ והוא יתרון ממה
שהיה ומאי ניהו יתרון כל דבר שבעולם כשאנשי
העולם ראוים לקחת ממנו מזונם אז הוא יתרון

96

ומאי ניהו ארץ שנחצב ממנה הכל ונחצב ממנו
שמים והוא כסאו של הקב״ה והוא אבן יקרה
והוא ים החכמה וכנגדה תכלת בציצית דא״ר
מאיר מה נשתנה תכלת מכל מיני צבעים מפני
שהתכלת דומה לים וים דומה לרקיע ורקיע
דומה לכסא הכבוד שנאמר ויראו את אלהי
ישראל ותחת רגליו כמעשה לבנת הספיר וכעצם
השמים לטהר ואומר כמראה אבן הספיר דמות
כסא:

97

ישב ר׳ ברכיה ודרש מ״ד ויקחו
לי תרומה כך אמר הקב״ה (אותי תרומה) הרימו
אותי בתפלותיכם ומי הוא אותו שנדבו לבו
להמשך מן העוה״ז כי בו אני שמה שידוע לי
שמי וממנו ראוי לקחת את תרומתי שנאמר וזאת
התרומה וכתיב מאת כל איש אשר ידבנו לבו
תקחו את תרומתי מאותו המתנדב דא״ר רהומאי
אלמלא הצדיקים והחסידים שבישראל שמרימין
אותי על כל העולם בזכותיהן ומהן מתפרנס הלב
והלב מפרנסן

98

וכל הצורות הקדושות ממונות
על כל האומות וישראל קדושים נוטלין גוף
האילן ולבו ולבו מה לב שהוא הדר פרי הגוף אף
ישראל פרי עץ הדר מה אילן תמר ענפיו סביביו
ולולבו באמצע אף ישראל נטלו גוף האילן זה
שהוא לבן וכנגד הגוף חוט השדרה באדם
שהוא עיקר הגוף ומה לולב לו לב כתיב מסורת
כי לולב הם ל׳ו ל״ב ומה לב זה שלשים ושתים
נתיבות פלאים חכמה בו אף בכל נתיב מהן
צורה שומרת דכתיב לשמור את דרך עץ החיים

103

ד"א ויקחו לי תרומה ויקחו לקדש
תרומה שהיא י' והוא עשירי ומנלן דעשירי קדש
דכתיב העשירי יהיה קדש ומאי ניהו קדש דכתיב
ראשית כל בכורי כל וכל תרומת כל וגו' וכתיב
ראשית חכמה יראתה' [אין חכמה אלא יראת ה']
אל תקרי יראת ה' אלא מראותה'(ס"א ויראת ה'):

104

שאלו תלמידיו את ר' אליעזר רבינו מ"ד
קדש לי כל בכור וכי הקב"ה בכור
א"ל אין קדש לי כל בכור אלא שני בקדש (ס"א
שנתקדש) ונקרא על שם ישראל דכתיב בני
בכורי ישראל כביכול עמהם היה בשעת השעבוד
והיינו דכתיב שלח תשלח את האם וגו' . ולא
אמר שלח תשלה את האב אלא (ס"א שלח)
תשלח את האם בכבוד אותם שנקראת העולם
שנאמר האם בכור (וי"א בכור בכורים והוא
הנקרא עצרת שנקרא אם שנאמר כי אם לבינה
תקרא

105

ומאי ואת הבנים תקח לך ר' רחומאי
אומר אותם בנים שגדלה ומאי ניהו ז' ימי
הסוכות והיינו ימי השבוע שהם ז' איכא ביניהו
שהם יותר בקדש דכתיב בהם מקראי קדש והיינו
א"כ עצרת דהוא מקרא קדש א"ל אין אבל זה
א' וזה ב' דכתיב ביום הראשון מקרא קדש
וביום השביעי מקרא קדש א"ל מ"ט הוי עצרת
אחד מפני שבו נתנה תורה לישראל וכשנבראת
התורה ראשית היה הקב"ה שליט בעולמו עמה
יחידי דכתיב ראשית חכמה אמר הואיל וכן
קדושתך יהיה לך לבדך ומאי ניהו סוכות א"ל
ב"ת דכתיב בחכמה יבנה בית ומנלן דסוכות
הוי בית דכתיב ויעקב נסע סכותה ויבן לו בית :

106

ישב ר' ברכיה ודרש מאי תלי דמות הוא
שיש לפני הקב"ה שבו כלולים הגלגלים
דכתיב קווצותיו תלתלים ומאי גלגל זה בטן ומאי
לב דכתיב עד לב השמים ובו כלולים ל"ב נתיבות
פליאות חכמה

107

מאי דכתיב יברכך ה' וישמרך.יאר
ה' פניו אליך ויחנך . ישא ה' פניו אליך וישם
לך שלום זה שמו של הקב"ה המפורש והוא שם
של י"ב דכתיב יהו"ה יהו"ה יהו"ה מלמד
ששמותיו של הקב"ה שלשה חיילים וכל חיל
וחיל אינו דומה להבירו ושמן כלם בשמו חתומים
ביהו"ה והאיך תצטרף כ"ד עם השם יהו"ה היינו
אחד יברכך ה' וגם השני יאר ה' עם כ"ד שמותיו
של הקב"ה והם השלישי ישא ה' עם כ"ד שמותיו
של הקב"ה . ועתה תצטרף (כ"ד וגם) עם כ"ד
שמותיו של הקב"ה ג"פ והיינו(ויהיו) ע"ב שמותיו
של הקב"ה היוצאים מאלה ויסע ויבא ויט

108

ומי הם
אלה השרים מלמד שג' הם שהגבורה שר כל
הצורות הקדושות וכך הוא מצד שמאל של הקב"ה
עומד גבריאל ומימינו שר כל הצורות הקדושות
מיכאל ובאמצע הוא האמת שר לכל הצורות
הקדושות וכל שר כ"ד צורות ואין הקר לנדודיו
דכתיב היש מספר לגדודיו א"ב הם(עוד)ע"ב וע"ב
א"ל לא (תימא)אלא בעת שישראל מקריבין קרבן
לפני אביהם שבשמים מתיחדים והיינו יחודו של
אלהינו

109

ואמאי אקרי קרבן אלא מפני שמקרב
הכהנות הקדושות כדכתיב וקרב אותם אחד אל
אחד לך לעץ אחד וגו' ואמר לריח ניחוח ואין ריח
אלא באף ואין נשימה שהיא הריח אלא באף ואין
ניחוח אלא ירידה שנאמר וירד ומתרגמין ונחת
יורד ומתייחד בצורות הקדושותההם ומתקרב ע"י
הקרבןוהיינו (כדכתיב)[דאקרי]קרבן(ס"א אותיות)

110

· השם היוצא מן השלשה פסוקים ויסע ויבא ויט
הפסוק הא' כסדר הפסוק נסדרות בשם ואותיות
הפסוק הב' בהפך הפסוק והפסוק הג' שהוא ויט
כסדר הפסוק נפרדות בשם וכל א' וא' מן
הפסוקים ע"ב אותיות נמצא שבכל שם ושם
מע"ב שמות היוצאים מאלו הג' פסוקים ויסע

ויבא ויט ג' אותיות אלה הם ויסע ויבא ויט זהו
שם המפורש היוצא ממנו וה"ו יל"י סי"ט על"ם
וכו' אסור להזכירם אלה הם ע"ב שמות היוצאים
ומתחלקים לג' חלקים כ"ד לכל חלק ועל כל חלק
מג' חלקים שר גבוה עליהם ועל כל חלק יש לו
ד'רוחות לשמור מזרח מערב צפון דרום ומתחלקים
ו' לכל רוח נמצא לד' רוחות כ"ד צורות וכן לב'
וכן לג' וכולם חתומים ביהו"ה אלהי ישראל אלהים
חיים שדי רם ונשא שוכן עד מרום וקדוש שמו
יהו"ה בשכמל"ו :

ואינן יכולין לסבול צמא מאי עשה למעין עשה
י"ב צנורות וקראם י"ב   שמות ואמר אם יהיו
הבנים טובים כאבותם יזכו ואלתלא הצנורות
ירוו אבותם וישתו הבנים אחריהם ואם לא יזכו
הבנים ולא עשו דברים הגונים לפני הרי צנורות
עומדות לפני ובענין אתן להם המים שלא יתנו
לבניהם הרבה אחר שאינם עושים רצוני

111

ישב ר' אהלהא ודרש מ"ד
ה' מלך ה' מלך ה' ימלוך לעילם ועד אלא זהו
השם המפורש שניתן בו רשות לצרף ולהזכיר
דכתיב ושמו את שמי על בני ישראל והוא שם
של י"ב בשם של ברכת בהנים יברכך ה' וגו'
שהם ג' והם י"ב   ונקדו בו יְפָעֵל יְפוֹעֵל וכל
השומרו ומזכירו ומטהרו בקדושה ובטהרה
מקבלין תפלתו ולא עוד אלא שהוא אהוב למטה
ולמעלה ונחמד למטה ולמעלה ונענה מיד ונעזור
זה השם המפורש הנכתב על מצח אהרן ושם
המפורש ע"ב ובשם המפורש של י"ב שמסר
הקב"ה   למטטרי"ה העומד לפני הפרגוד והוא
מכרם לאליהו בהר הכרמל ובזכותם נתעלה ולא
טעים טעם מיתה

114

והאי
ליישנא דשֶבֶט דבר פשוט הוא   ואינהו מרובע
מ"ט דלית אפשר מרובע בגו טרובע אחר אלא
עיגולא בגו ריבועא והטי ואי טרובע בגו
ריבועא לא רהטי

115

ומאי ניהו עיגולא הדין נקודה
דאורייתא דמשה דאינהו כולה עיגולה ודמיין
באתוותא לנשמתא דהי בגופא דאינשא דלית
אפשר למחיי כל היכא דלית קימא בגה ולא
למבנק מימרא זוטא ורבתא בלא נשמתא כוותיה
הדין נקודה דלית אפשר למלתא רבא או זוטא
לאתאמרא בלא נק'

112

ואלו הן השמות   הנקראות
ומפורשות והמפוארות שהם י"ב לי"ב שבטי
ישראל אהציצה"רון אכליתה"רון שמקת"ן
דמושהרו"ן וצפצפסיתרו"ן הורטירו"ן ברחיהגאו"ן
ער"ש גדראו"ן בסאו"ה מנאהו"ן הזהוי"ה הוהיוי"י
האי"ה אהי"ה והראתיהו"ן וכולם נכללים בל"ב
נתיבות השמים ומתחלקין לכ"ד שמות כמו
שאמרנו למעלה ובהם כלול זכר ונקבה פקודיו
בתלי וגלגל ולב והם מעיינות החכמה :

116

וכל נק' עיגולא וכל אתיא
(נ"ל לשון אות) רבועא ומתקיימא אתיא בנקודה
ואינהון חייהון והדין נקודה אתיא דרך הציגורות
הדין אתיא על ידי ריח הקרבן ומד יורד דכתיב
ריחניהוח לה' שיורד לה' היינו דכתיב 'שמע
ישראל וגו' והמשכיל יבין :

113

ישב ר' רחומאי ודרש מאי י"ב שבטי יה
ישראל אלא מלמד שי"ב שבטים יש לו
להקב"ה ומאי ניהו משל למלךשהיה לו מעין נאה
וכל א' (ס"א אחיו) אין לו מים אלא מאותו המעין

117

אמר רבי יוחנ
מאי דכתיב 'ה' איש מלחמה ה' שמו אלא איש
סימן כדמתרגמינן ה' מארי מלחמה ה' מארי נצח
קרבייא . ומאי ניהו מארי אל"ף ראשונה היכל
קדישא היכלא קדישא ס"ד   אלא אימא היכל
הקדש

118

ה' בעשרה מאמרות שנברא בה
העולם ומאי ניהו היינו תורת אמת שכוללת כ

העולמים ושי"ן מאי הוי א"ל שרש האילן דשי"ן
הוי כמו שרש האילן

119

ומאי ניהו שרש האילן
א"ל כחותיו של הקב"ה זה על גב זה והן דומין
לאילן זה מה אילן זה שעל ידי מים מרבה
כחות אלו נופות מן האילן אף הקב"ה על ידי
המים מרבה כחות האילן . ומאי ניהו מים
של הקב"ה חכמה והיינו (הכמה זה) נשמתן של
צדיקים שפורחין מן המעין אל הצנור הגדול
ועולה ודבק באילן ועל ידי מי פורח על ידי
ישראל כשהן צדיקים וטובים שכינה שרויה
ביניהם ושרוים במעשיהם בחיקו של הקב"ה
ומפרה ומרבה אותן

120

דשכינה אקרי צדק דכתיב
רוכב שמים בעזרך וכתיב ושחקים יזלו צדק
וצדק זו שכינה דכתיב יצדק ילין בה וצדק נתן
לדוד דכתיב ימלוך ה' לעולם אלהיך ציון וגו' .
וכתיב ציון עיר דוד.

121

אמר מ"ד י' ימלוך ה' לעולם אלהיך
ציון לדור ודור הללויה מאי דור ודור א"ר פנחס דור
הולך ודור בא . ואמר רבי עקיבא דור בא שכבר
בא

122

משל למלך שהיו לו עבדים והלבישן כפי
יכלתו בגדי משי ורקמה קלקלו השורה השליכן
ודחפן מעליו והפשיטן בגדיו והלכו להם לקח
הבגדים ורחצן היטב עד שלא נשאר בהן סיג
והניחן אצלו מזומנין והלך וקנה עבדים אחרים
והלבישן הבגדים ההם והוא לא ידע אם טובים
אותם העבדים אם לאו והרי זכו בבגדים שכבר
באו לעולם ולבשום אחרים לעיניהם אבל הארץ
לעולם עומדת והיינו דכתיב וישוב העפר על
הארץ כשהיה והרוח תשוב אל האלהים אשר
נתנה:

123

אמר רבי רחומאי מאי דכתיב וישא
אהרן את ידיו אל העם ויברכם וירד והרי כבר
ירד אלא וירד מעשות החטאת והעולה ואה"כ
וישא אהרן את ידיו אל העם נשיאות זו למה לפי
שהקריב קרבן ונתקרב לפני אביהם שבשמים
כדאמר ליה (צדק אותו צדק שמקרב הכהות)[צריך
אותו] ומקרבן לעליונים וליחדן ליחד בכללן אלו ·
ומאי (העם דכתיב) אל העם בעבור העם

124

ומ"ט
בנשיאות כפים וליברוך להון בברכה אלא משום
דאית בידים עשר אצבעות רמז לי' ספירות שבהם
נחתמו שמים וארץ ואותם י' כנגד י' דברות ובכלל
אותן י' נכללו תרי"ג מצות ומנה אותם אותיות של
יו"ד דברות ותשכח דאינן תרי"ג אותיות ובהם כל
כ"ב אותיות חוץ מט' דלית בהון מאי טעמא ללמדך
דט' היא בטן (נ"א היא הנו"ן)ואינה בכלל הספירה

125

ואמאי קרי ליה ספירה משום דכתיב השמים
כסאי והארץ הדום רגלי (ס"א השמים מספרים
כבוד אל)

126

ומאי ניהו תלתא אינון ובכללן שלשה
חיילות ושלשה ממשלות.הממשלה הראשונה אור
ואור היום של ימים . הממשלה השנית חיות
הקדש ואופנים וגלגלי המרכבה וכל גדודיו של
הקב"ה מברכים ומעריצין ומהדרים ומפארין
ומקדישין למלך נאדר בקדושה ונאדר בסוד
קדושים רבה מלך איום ונורא ומכתירין בשילוש
קדושה

127

ומאי ניהו שלש ולא ארבע מפני שקדושת
מעלה שלש דכתיב ה' מלך ה' מלך ה' ימלוך
וכתיב יברכך ה' יאר ה' ישא ה' והשאר של מדות
ה' שלישי מאי הוי 'ה' אל רחום וחנון וגו' שלש
עשרה מדות

128

ומאי הוי קדוש קדוש קדוש ה'
צבאות מלא כל הארץ כבודו אלא קדוש כתר
עליון קדוש שורת האילן קדוש דבוק מיוחד
בכולן ה' צבאות מלא כל הארץ כבודו

129

ומאי ניהו קדוש שהוא דבק ומיוחד אלא
למלך שהיו לו בנים ולאותן בנים בזמן
שבניהם עושים רצונו נכנס ביניהם מעמיד הכל
ומשביע הכל ומשפיע להם טובה כדי שישבעו
האבות והבנים . וכשאין עושים הבנים רצונו
משביע לאבות כדי צרכם לבד.

130

ומאי ניהו מלא כל
הארץ כבודו אלא כל אותה ארץ שנבראת ביום
ראשון תתהלה שהיא למעלה.הכנגדהארץישראלמליאה
מכבוד השם הנכבד ומאי ניהו חכמהדכתיב כבוד
חכמים ינחלו ואומר ברוך כבוד ה' ממקומו

131

[ומאי
הוי כבוד ה'] משל למלך שהיתה לו מטרוניתא
בחדריו שכל תיילותיו משתעשעין בה והיו לה
בנים ובאים בכל יום לראות פני המלך וטברכין
אותו א"ל אטנו אנה אמר להם לא תוכלו לראותה
עתה אמרו ברוכה תהא בכל מקום שהיא

132

ומאי
דכתיב ממקומו מכלל דליכא דידע מקומו . משל
לבת מלך שבאה מרחוק ולא ידעי מהיכן באה עד
שראו שהיא אשת חיל והגונה בכל מעשיה אמרו
ודאי זאת מצורת האור נלקחה כי מעשיה יאיר
העולם שאלו אותה מאין את אמרה ממקומי אמרו
א"כ גדולים אנשי מקומך ברוכה תהא ומבורך
אנשי מקומך.

133

וכי אין כבוד יי' זה אחד מצבאותיו
לא גרע אמאי מברכין ליה אלא משל לאיש שהיה

לו גן נאה והנין לגן בקרוב ממנו חתיכת שדה נאה
עשה בו נינה נאההשקה את הגן בתחלת שקיותא
והלכו להם המים על כל הגן אך אותה חתיכה של
שדה שהיא אינה דביקה אע"פ שהכל אחד הוא
לפיכך פתח לה מקום והשקה אותה לבדה :

134

אמר רבי רחומאי כבוד ולב הרי הם אחד
אלא שהכבוד נקרא עלשהפעולות
מעלה ולב נקרא על שם פעולותמטה והיינו כבוד
השמוהיינו לב השמים.

135

א"ריוחנןמאי דבתיב והיה
כאשר ירים משה ידו וגבר ישראל וכאשר יניח
ידו וגבר עמלק מלמד שהעולם מתקיים בשביל
נשיאות כפים מ"ט משום דאותו כח שנתן ליעקב
אבינו ישראל שמו דלאברהםוליצחקוליעקב ניתנו
כחות לכל אחד ואחד ובמדה אשר הלך כל אחד
ואחד דוגמתם ניתן לו לאברהם חסד בשביל שהיה
גומל חסד למלאכים ויצא לקראתם מפתח האהל
ועוד וישתחו זאת היתה גמילות חסד שלמה .
והקב"ה מדד לו כמדתו כדבתיב תתן אמת ליעקב
חסד לאברהם הרי שנתן לו מדת החסד.אשה,נשבעת
לאבותינו מימי קדם מלמד שאם לא היה אברהם
גומל חסד וזוכה למדת חסד לא היה יעקב זוכה
למדת אמת שבזכות שזוכה אברהם למדת חסד
זכה יצחק למדת פחד דכתיב וישבע יעקב בפחד
אביו יצחק (אטו כולם אין) יש איש שישבע כך
באמונה פחד אביו אלא עד כאןלא ניתן כחליעקב
ונשבע בכח שניתן לאביו . שנאמר וישבע יעקב
בפחד אביו יצחק . ומאי ניהו תהו שממנו יוצא
הרע המתהא את בניאדם ומאי ניהו דכתיב ותפל
אש ותאבל[את]העולה וגו' וכתיב 'כי יי' אלהיך
אש אוכלה הוא אל קנא

136

ומאי ניהו חסד· היינו
תורה דכתיב הוי כל צמא לכו למים ואשר אין
לו כסף זהו כסף דכתיב לכו אליו אלא בלא כסף
ובלא מחיר יאכילכםתורה וילמדכםכי כבר זכיתם
לכך בזכות אברהם אשר גמל חסד בלא כסף והיינו
מאכל ומשקה ובלא מחיר (חסד פחד) יין וחלב

137

מהו יין וחלב ומה ענין זה אצל זה אלא מלמד
שהיין הוא פחד והלב הוא חסד ומפני מה הזכיר
יין תחלה מפני שהוא קרוב אלינו תחלה יין וחלב
ס"ד אלא אימא דמות יין וחלב ובזכות אברהם
שזכה למדת חסד זכהיצהקלמדתפחד.והואיל וזכה
יצחק למדת פחד זכה יעקב למדת אמת שהיא מדת
שלום ומדד לו כמדתו . שנאמר ויעקב איש תם
יושב אהלים ואין תם אלא שלום דכתיב תמים
תהיה עם ה' אלהיך ומתרגמינן שלים תהא ואין
תם אלא תורה שנאמר תורת אמת וכתיב תורת
ה' תמימה . ואין אמת אלא שלום דכתיב שלום
ואמת יהיה בימי ואין אמת אלא תורה שנאמר
תורת אמת היתה בפיהו וגו' ומה כתיב בתריה
בשלום ובמישור הלך אתי ואין מישור אלא שלום
דכתיב תום ויושר היוכך כאשר ירים משה ידו
ונבר ישראל מלמד שהמדה שנקראת ישראל בתוכה
תורת אמת

138

ומאי ניהו תורת אמת דבר שמורה על
אמיתות העולם ופעולתו במחשבה והוא מעמיד
י' מאמרות שבהם עומד העולם והוא א' מהם ובורא
באדם כנגד אותם י' מאמרות י' אצבעות ידים
וכשהיה משה מרים ידו ומכוין כמעט בכוונת הלב
באותה המדה הנקראת ישראל ובתוכה תורת
אמת ורומזת לו בי' אצבעות ידיו שהוא מעמיד
את הי' ואם לא יעזור את ישראל לא יתקדשו י'
מאמרות בכל יום ויום הילכךגבר ישראל [וכאשר
יניח ידו וגבר עמלק וכי היה משה עושה שגבר
עמלק דכתיב וכאשר יניח ידו אלא אסור לו לאדם
לשהות ג' שעות בפיו פרושות השמים :

139

שאלו תלמידיו למי נושאין כפים א"ל לרום
השמים ומנלן דכתיב תהום נתן
קולו רום ידהו נשא הא למדת שאין נשיאות
כפים אלא לרום השמים וכשישראל משבילים
ויודעים את סוד השם הנכבד ונושאים כפיהם
מיד נענים שנאמר אז תקרא וה' יענה (אימתי)
[אם א'] תקרא וה' יענה מיד

140

מאי אז אלא
מלמד שאין רשות לקרוא לאלף לבדו אלא על ידי
שנים האותיות הדבקים בה היושבים ראשונה
במלכות ועם האל"ף הם שלשה ונשארו ז' מי'
מאמרות והיינו ז'דכתיב אזישירמשה ובני ישראל
נ"כ

141

מאי ניהו י' מאמרות אל"ף (כמו)[כתר] עליון
ברוך הואומבורך שמו ועמומתי עמוישראל דכתיב
כי ה' הוא האלהים הוא עשנו ולא אנהנו עמו
ולאל"ף אנהנו להכיר ולידע אהד האהדים ומיוהד
דכתיב ה' הוא האלהים הוא עשנו ולא אנהנו
ולפיכך נכתב לא באל"ף כי הוא א' ומיוהד בכל
שמותיו

142

שנית חכמה דכתיב ה' קנני ראשית
דרכו ואין ראשית אלא הכמה דכתיב ראשית
חכמה יראת ה'

143

שלישית מחצב התורה אוצר
החכמה רוח אלהים חיים מלמד שהיה הקב"ה
עושה כל האותיות של תורה והקן ברוח ועשה
בו צורותיו והיינו אין צור כאלהינו אין צורה דומה
לאלהינו ואין צייר כאלהינו

144

שלישית הוי רביעית
מאי רביעית הם צדקת השם זכיותיו והסדיו עם
כל העולם והיינו ימינו של הקב"ה

145

המישית מאי
חמישית אשו של הקב"ה שנאמר ואת האש
הגדולה הזאת וגו' : והוא שמאלו של הקב"ה הם
חיות הקודש ושרפים הקדושים מימינם ומשמאלם
הם הנעימים הגבוהים עד למעלה דכתיב וגבוהים
עליהם ועוד וגובה להם ויראה להם והבוגבותם מלאות
עינים וגו' וסביביו מלאכים גם סביבותיהם

משתחוים לפניהם וכורעים ומשתהוים ואומרים
ה' הוא האלהים

146

ששית כבא הכבוד המעוטר
ומוכלל המאושר ומהולל הוא בית העולם הבא
ומקומו חקוק בחכמה דכתיב ויאמר אלהים
יהי אור ויהי אור :

147

אמר ר' יוחנן שני אורים
גדולים היו שנאמר ויהי אור ועל שניהם נאמר
כי טוב ולקח הקב"ה האחד וגנזו לצדיקים לעתיד
לבא והיינו דכתיב מה רב טובך אשר צפנת
ליראיך מלמד שאור הראשון גנוז אין כל בריה
יכולה להסתכל בה שנאמר וירא אלהים את האור
כי טוב וכתיב וירא אלהים את כל אשר עשה
והנה טוב מאד ראה הקב"ה את כל אשר עשה
וראה טוב מזהיר בהיר ולקח מאותו טוב וכלל בו
ל"ב נתיבות החכמה ונתגו לעוה"ז והיינו דכתיב כי
לקח טוב נתתי לכם וגו' הוי אומר זו אוצרה של
תורה(שבע"פ)ואמר הקב"ה אם ישמרו זאת התורה
בעוה"ז שזאת המדה נהשבת בכלל העוה"ז והוא
תורה שבע"פ ואמר שבזאת המדה יזכו לעוה"ב
שהוא הטוב הגנוזומאי ניהו עוזו של הקב"הדכתיב
ונוגה כאור תהיה הנוגה שנלקח מן האור
הראשון להיות כאור אם יקיימו בנים התורה
והמצות אשר כתבתי להורותם דכתיב ישמע בני
מוסר אביך ואל תטוש תורת אמך

148

וכתיב קרנים
מידו לו ושם הביון עוזו מאי הביון עוזו אלא
אותו האור שגנו' והחביא שנאמר אשר צפנת
ליראיך ומה שנשאר פעולת לחוסים בך בעוה"ז
ושומרי תונתך ומקיימים מצותיך ומקדשים שמך
הגדול ומיחדים בסתר ובגלוי שנאמר נגד כל בני
אדם

149

אמר רבי רחומאי מלמד שהיא אורה של
ישראל ונרה אור והכתיב כי נר מצוה ותורה
אור ואמרינן נר זו מצוה ומצוה זו תורה שבעל

פה ואור זו תורה שבכתב אלא מתוך שמן שבנר
מתקיים האור קרי ליה אור משל לחדר צנוע
בסופי הבית אע"פ שיום הוא ואור גדול בעולם
אין אדם יכול לראות באותו חדר אא"כ הכניס בו
אור הנר כך תורה שבכתב שאף על פי שהיא נר
צריכה היא לתורה שבעל פה לפרק קושיותיה
ולבאר סודותיה :

150

ואמר רבי רחומאי מאי
דכתיב ודרך חיים תוכחת מוסר מלמד שכל הרגיל
במעשה בראשית ובמעשה מרכבה אי אפשר
שלא יכשל שנאמר והמכשלה הזאת תחת ידך
דברים שאין אדם יכול לעמוד בהן אלא אם כן
נכשל בהן והתורה אומרת תוכחת מוסר אבל
באמת זוכה לדרך חיים לפיכך מי שרוצה לזכות
בדרך חיים יסבול תוכחות מוסר

151

ד"א חיים זו תורה
שנאמר ובהרת בחיים וכתיב כי היא חייך ואורך
ימיך ומי שירצה לזכות בה יטמא בהנאת גוף
ויקבל עול מצות ואם באים עליו יסורים יקבל
מאהבה ואל יאמר הואיל ואני מקיים רצון הבורא
ואני לומד תורה בכל יום למה באים עלי יסורים
אלא יקבלם מאהבה ואז יזכה לדרך חיים שלימה
כי מי יודע דעת הקב"ה וחייב לומר על הכל צדיק
אתה ה' וישר משפטיך וכל דעבדין מן שמיא
לטב עבדי

152

אמרת כסאו והא אמרת זה כתרו של
הקב"ה דאמרינן בג' כתרים נכתרו ישראל כתר
כהונה וכתר מלכות וכתר תורה על גביהם .
משל למלך שהיה לו כתר גבוה ומכושם ואוהבו
מאד לפעמים משאילו לבנו לשבת עמו ולפעמים
נטלו בזרועו היינו תפילין שבזרועו . ולפעמים
שמו בראשו והיינו תפילין שבראש ולפעמים
נקרא כסאו כי בזרועו נושאו כקמיע כען כסאו

153

ומאי שביעית הוא ערנות ולמה נקרא שמים
אלא שהוא עגול כמו ראש האיש ומלמד שמים

סימנו ואש משמאלו והוא באמצע והוא שמ״ם
כלומר שם מים מאש ומים ומבנים שלום ביניהם
באהאשותמצאצדומדתאשי׳באוהטים טצדן ומיצאו
מדת המים והיינו עושה שלום במרוטיו

154

שביעי
ולא ששי אלא מלמד שכאן היכל הקודש והוא
נושא את כולם ונהשב לשנים והוי שביעי ומאי
ניהו המחשבה שאין לה סוף ותכלית וכך המקום
הזה אין לו סוף ותכלית

155

שביעי הוה מזרחו של
עולם ומשם בא זרעם של ישראל כי הוט השדרה
משוך מן המוח של אדם ובא לאמה . ומשם בא
הזרע דכתיב ממזרח אביא זרעך כשישראל טובים
אביא זרעך מזה המקום ויתהדש לך זרע חדש
וכשישראל רעים מן הזרע שכבר בא לעולם
שנאמר דור הולך ודור בא מלמד שכבר בא

156

ומאי
דכתיב ממערב אקבצך מאותה המדה (ענוטה
תמיד) שנתייהדה תמיד למערב . למה נקרא שמה
מערב מפני ששם מתערב כל הזרע . משל למלך
שהיה לו כלה נאה וצנועה בחדרו והיה לוקה
מבית אביו עושר ומביא לה והיא לוקחת הכל
ומצנעת אותו תמיד ומערבת ומעבבת הכל לסוף
הימים בקש לראות מה אסף ומה קיבץ והיינו
דכתיב וממערב אקבצך ומאי ניהו בית אביו
דכתיב מזוהר אביא זרעך מלמד שממזרח מביא
וזורע במערב ואחר כך הוא מקכין מה שיזורע

157

שמיני מאי הוי הוי יש לו להקב״ה צדיק אחד בעולמו
והוא חביב לו מפני שמקיים עולמו והוא יסודו
ומצ... ומגדלו ומשמרו אהוב וחביב למעלה
אהוב . וחביב למטה נורא ואדיר למעלה נורא
ואדיר למטה מתוקן ומקובל למעלה מתוקן ומקובל
למטה והוא יסוד הנפשות כולן אמרת יסוד הנפשות
כולן ואמרת שמיני והכתיב וביום השביעי שבת
וינפש אין הוי שביעי משום דמבריע ביניהו דשית

איגן ג' מלרע וג' מלעיל והוא דמבריע ביניהו

158

ומ״ט
אקרי שמיני (בלבוש מלאתי שביעי וכי היה ז' לא אלא)
וכי לא היה בשביעי אלא מפני שהקב״ה שבת
בשבת . באותה מדה כתיב כי ששת ימים עשה
ה' את השמים ואת הארץ וביום השביעי שהוא
וינפש . מלמד שכל יום ויום יש לו מאמר שהוא
אדון לו לא מפני שהוא נברא בו אלא שהוא פועל
בו פעולה המסורה בידו פיעלו כולם פעולתם
וקיימו מעשיהם . לכך בא יום השביעי ופעל
פעילתו ושמחו כולם אף הקב״ה ולא עוד אלא
שגדלה נשמתם דכתיב וביום השביעי שבת
וינפש .

159

ומה הוי בו שביתה זו דלית בה מלאכה
והוי הנחה דכתיב שבת מישל למלך שהיה לו ז'
גנות ובגן האמצעי מעין נובע ממקור חיים משקה
לג' לימינו ולג' לשמאלו . ומיד שפעל פעולה זו
ומתמלא שמחים כולם כי אמרו לצרכינו הוא
מתמלא והוא משקה אותם ומגדלם והם ממתינים
ושואבים והוא משקה את השבעה והכתיב
ממזרח אביא זרעך והוי חד מנהון ומשקה לי׳
אלא אימא הוא משקה הלב והלב משקה את
כולם (רחמים נצח הוא יסוד ע' הסד דין והסוד נעוין
סופה בתהלה ותהלה בסופה ואמצע בתהלה כו') :

160

ישב ר' ברכיה ודרש מאי האי דאמרינן
(כ״ע)[כל יומא] העול״ם הבא ולא ידעינן
מאי קאמרינן העוה״ב מתרגמינן עלמא דאתי.מאי
עלמא דאתי מלמד שקודם שנברא העולם עלה
במחשבה לבראות אור . ונברא אור גדול שאין
כל בריה יכולה לסובלו ולשלוט בו צפה הקב״ה
שאין כל בריה יכול לסובלו לקח שביעי ושם להם
במקומו והשאר גנז לצדיקים לעתיד לבא אמר אם
יזכו בני בזה השביעי וישמרוה ואתן להם זה העולם
אהרון והיינו עוה״ב שכבר בא מקודם שמי
בראשי׳ הה״ד מה רב טובך אשר צפנת ליראיך וגו' :

161

מאי דכתיב ויבואו אלימה ושם שתים עשרה
עינות מים ושבעים תמרים ויחנו שם
על המים . וכי מה שבח היה בשבעים תמרים
באחת מקטני המקומות יש אלף. אלא זכות [נ"א
זכו לדוגמתם] שי"ג להם משל בתמרים דכתיב
ויבואו מרתה ולא יכלו לשתות מים ממרתהכי מרים
הם מלמד שרוות צפונית היתה מעכבת שנאמר
ויצעק אל ה' ויורהו ה' עץ וישלך אל המים וימתקן
המים מיד נתן הקב"ה ידו בשטן ומיעטו ואלמלא
כן לא היו ישראל יכולין לעמוד מפני שנאמר
שם שם לו חק ומשפט ושם נסהו מלמד שבאותה
שעה דבק בהם וביקש לאבדם מן העולם שנאמר
וילונו העם על משה לאמר מה נשתה . ועוד
קטרג על משה עד כי צעק אל ה' ונענה ומאי
ויורהו ה' עץ מלמד שעץ החיים היה סביב המים
ובא השטן ונטלו משה כדי לקטרג על ישראל
ולהחטיאם לאביהם שבשמים והיה אומר עתה
תבכנס במדבר ועדין אלה המים שהם מרים
הם טובים כי תספיקן מהם אבל במדבר לא
תמצאו אפילו לרחוץ ידיכם ופניכם ואז תמותו
ברעב ובצמא ובחוסר כל באו אל משה ואמרו
כך וכך דחה אותם . ראה כי לא יכול להם התחזק
על ישראל ועל משה ובאו העם וילונו על משה
כאן חסר לנו המים ומה נשתה במדבר בא השטן
וזיף דבריהם אל משה להחטיאם ומיד כשראה
משה השטן ויצעק אל ה' ויורהו ה' עץ אותו עץ
החיים הוא שהסיר השטן וישלך אל המים וימתקו
המים. שם שם לו חק ומשפט הקב"ה לשטן .
ושם נסהו לישראל ובא הקב"ה והזהיר להם
לישראל שאם שמוע תשמעו לקול ה' וגו'

162

משל
למלך שהיתה לו בת נאה ואחרים מתאוים לה .
ידע המלך בדבר ולא היה יכול להתקוטט עם
המוציאים בתו לתרבות רעה והזהיר את בתו
אל תחושי לדברי אלה המזיקים כי לא יוכלו לך .
ואל תצאי לפתח הבית ועשי מלאכתך בביתך
ואל תשבי בטלה אפילו שעה אחת ולא יוכלו
לראותיך ולא להזיק לך כי יש בהם מדה אחת
מתרחקים מכל דרך טוב ובוחרים בכל דרך רע

וכשרואין איש מדריך עצמו בדרך טובה והולך
בה . שונאים אותו ומאן ניהו השטן מלמד שיש
להקב"ה מדה שישמח רעה **והיא לצפונו של**
הקב"ה דכתיב מצפון תפתח הרעה על כל יושבי
הארץ. כלומר כל רעה אשר היא באה לכל יושבי
הארץ מצפון בא .

163

ומאי ניהו מדה היא צורת יד
ורגל ולה שלוחים הרבה ושמם של כולם רע רע
אף יש בהם קטן וגדול והם מחריבים את העולם
כי תהו לצד צפון ואין תהו אלא רע שמתהא
בני אדם עד שיחטיאם וכל יצה"ר שיש בבני אדם
משם הוא ולמה ניתן (בישראל) בשמאל מפני
שאין לו רשות בכל העולם אלא בצפון ולא רצה
להיות אלא בצפון ולא הורגל אלא בצפון לפי
כשיהיה בדרום עד שילמד מהלך הדרום והיאך
הוא יכול להטעות . יתעכב אותן הימים שילמוד
ולא יהטיא . לפיכך הוא לעולם בצפון בשמאל
והיינו דכתיב כי יצר לב האדם רע מנעוריו . רע
הוא מנעוריו ולא יטה אלא לשמאל שבבר הורגל
בה . לפום הכי אמר הקב"ה לישראל אם שמוע
תשמע לקול ה' אלהיך והישר בעיניו תעשה
והאזנת למצותיו ולא למצות יצה"ר ושמרת כל
חוקיו ולא חק יצה"ר אני ה' רופאך :

164

ומאי מרויה יצה"ר משל למלך שהפקיד
פקידים על מלכותו ועל סחורתו .
ועל כל אחד ואחד ממונה על אוצרות מאכל
הטובים ואחד ממונה על אוצר האבנים באו על כל
העולם לקנות מאוצרו הטוב ממאכל בא מזה
שממונה על האבנים וראה מה שקונין ממנו קנא
בו.מה עשה.שלח שלוחיו להרוס הבתים החלשים
כי בחזקים אין לו יכולת אמר בין כך ובין
כך שייתגדל להרוס בית אחד מן החזקים
יהרסו כ' מן החלשים ויבאו כולם לקנות
אבנים ממני ולא אהיה אני פחות מחביירי . הה"ד
מצפון תפתח הרעה על כל יושבי הארץ ואח"כב
כי הנני קורא לכל משפחות ממלכות צפונה נאם
ה'. ובאו ונתנו איש כסאו פתח שערי ירושלימוגו'.
והרעה תהיה עסק וגם יצה"ר ישתדל תמיד ומאי
טשמע דשטן הוי(מטמ)מטה)משמה העולם שהוא מג **ה**

את כל העולם לכף חובה . דכתיב ויט אליה
ומתרגם וסטא לותה וכתיב סטה מעליו ועבור :

165

שבעים תמרים מה טעם אלא קבלו עליהם
המצות כדכתיב אם שמוע תשמע
מיד ויבואו אלימה מאי אלימה אלי מה וש י"ב
עינות מים הקב"ה מסרן להם בתחלה עינות מים
ואח"כ החזירן להם אבנים דכתיב שתים עשרה
מ"ט מפני שבתחלה היתה תורה בעולם שנמשלת
למים ואח"כ נקבעת במקום קבוע מה שאין
המים עושין שהיום כאן ולמחר להן

166

מאי שבעים
תמרים מלמד שיש לו להב"ה שבעים קומות
ושואבים מי"ב פשוטים מה המים האלה פשוטים
אף הם פשוטים ומנלן דתמר הוי קומה דכתיב
זאת קומתך דמתה לתמר ולא עוד אלא שיש
בתמרים שבעים מינים דכתיב שבעים תמרים
ולא היו דומים אלו לאלו ופעולתם זה לזה וטעם
זה אינו דומה לזה .

167

ואמרת ע' תמרים (בגים'
אמרת) ע' קומות והא אמרת ע"ב אלא ע"א
וישראל הם ע"ב ושתים אינם בכלל . והאמרת
ע' אלא האחד שר השטן משל למלך שהיה לו
בנים קנה עבדים ואמר הנה לכם בשוה לכולכם.
אמר אחד מהם אני רוצה עמהם כי אני יש לי
יכולת לגזור מכם וכל אמר המלך הואיל והוא
לא יהיה לך חלק בתוכם ועשה הרבה ואבנים
יקרות וחיילות ואמר להם סורו אלי . מה עשה
המלך סדר חיילותיו וחיילותיו בניו כולם והראה
לעבדים ואמר להם אל יטעה אתכם טועה לאמר
חיילויו רב מחיילי הנה וזיילותיו של אותו הבן רמאי
וחושב לגזול אתכם . ואתם לא תשמעו לו כי
בתחלה יחלוק דבריו כדי שילוכד אתכם במצודתו
ואחר כך ישחק . ואתם עבדי ואני אעשה מכם
נקמה ואם לא תשמעו לי ותסורו מאחריו כי הוא
שר על זותני שנאמר לאנתהו אחרילבבכם ולא
תסורו כי אחרי התהו אשר לא יועילו ולא יצילו אך

<hr>

יכולים הם להזיק אך אני מייעץ אתכם אם שמוע
תשמע לקול ה' וגו' שתשמור מצותי כל המחלה
אשר שמ י במצרים לא אשים עליך למה אמר
כל זה לסגור לו כל הדלתות שלא ימצאך פעם
אחד רך ופעם אחד קשה בשמרך כל חוקיו כל
המחלה אשר שמתי במצרים על ידו לא אשים
עליך מאי כי אני ה' רופאך ומתי הכהו אלא
כשיבא הוא ויכה אני ה' רופאך

168

ומאי ניהו דאמרת
שמיני שבו נתחלו השמנה ובו נשלמה השמונה
להשבון אך הוא בפעולתו הוי שביעי ומאי ניהו
יד ימין ויד שמאל רגל ימין ושמאל ראש וגוף
וברית מבריע וזוגתו שהיא אשתו דכתיב ימי
המילה באו כנגדן ואלו תמניא לא הוי אלא שבעה
שהרי גוף וברית חד הוא הרי שמנה

169

תשיעי מאי
הוי א"ל תשיעי ועשירי הם יחד זה כנגד זה
והאחד גבוה מחבירו ת"ק שנה והם כעין ב'
אופנים הא' נוטה לצד צפון והא' נוטה לצד
מערב והולכים עד הארץ התחתונה ומאי תהתונה
אחרונה מז' ארצות למטה וסוף שכינתו של
הקב"ה תתהרגליו שנאמר השמים כסאי והארץ
הדום רגלי ושם נצחונו של עולם למטה שנאמר
נצח נצחים

170

מאי לנצח נצחים אלא נצח חד הוי
ומאי נינהו זה הנוטה למערב ושני לו מאי הוי
זה הנוטה לצד צפון ושלישי זההוי מטה שלמטה
שלישי הא אמרת ב' אופני המרכבה אלא אימא
סוף השכינה הוי ג"כ נצח והיינו לנצח נצחים נצח
חד נצחים תרי הרי תלתא

171

א"ל תלמידיו
מלמעלה למטה ידעינן אבל מלמטה למעלה לא
ידעינן אמר להו ולאו חד הוי טלמטה למעלה
ומלמעלה למטה אמרו רבינו אינו דומה העולה

הספרים וכל התורה קודש ושיר השירים קודש
קדשים ומאי ניהו קודש קדשים אלא שקודש הוא
לקדשים ומה הם הקדשים אלו שהם כנגד שש
קצוות שבאדם וקודש הוי להם קודש לכולהו

175

ומאי ניהו קודש זה אתרוג שהוא הדר הכל ואמאי
נק' שמו הדר א״ת שמו הדר אלא הדר זה אתרוג
שהוא נפרד מאוד לולב ואין מצות לולב קיימא
אלא בו והוא ג״כ אגוד עם הכל שעם כל א' וא'
הוא ועם כולן יחד הוא .

176

לולב כנגד מאי כנגד
חוט השדרה וכן הוא אומר   וענף עץ עבות צריך
הוא להיות ענפיו חופין את רובו ואם אין ענפיו
חופין את רובו אינו שוה כלום מפני מה מלה״ד
לאדם שיש לו זרועותיו ובחם יגין על ראשי הרי
זרועותיו שנים וראשו שלשה והיינו וענף לשמאל
עבות לימין נמצא עין באמצע עץ ולמה נאמר בו
עץ מפני שהוא שורש האילן

177

מאי וערבי נחל
משום דערבי נחל כנגד שוקי אדם שהם שנים
ומאי האי לישנא דערבי נחל משום הגדול שבהם
למערב וממשא יונק כחו ושל צפון קטן ממנו
מהלך ת״ק שנה והוא ברוח צפונית מערבית ובו
פועל ונקרא על שמו והם שניהם ערבים :

178

ד״א ערבי נחל שלפעמים מערבים פעולותם
זה עם זה ומאי וערבי נחל הוי אומר ע״ש המקום
שהם קבועים בו שנקרא נחל שנאמר כל הנחלים
הולכין אל הים והם אינם מלא . ומאי ניהו הים
זה הוי אומר זה אתרוג ומנלן דכל מדה ומדה מכל
אלה הז' נקרא נחל דכתיב   וממתנה נחליאל א״ת
נחליאל אלא נחלי אל וכל הששה הולכין אל דרך
אחד אל הים ומאי ניהו אותו דרך א' מבריע
בינתיים דכתיב   לפניו ילך דבר ויצא רשף לרגליו
וכולם הולכים לאותו צינור ומאותו צינור ליב
והיינו דכתיב וממתנה נחליאל במות כדמתרגם
דהיינו המוח לנחליאל ובנחליאל במות

ליורד שהיורד יורד במרוצה והעולה אינו כן ולא
עוד אלא העולה אפשר לו לעלות על דרך
אחרת שלא ירד · אמר להם צאו וראו ישב ודרש
להם כשם שהשכינה למעלה כך היא למטה
ומאי שכינה זו הוי אומר זה האור הנאצל מן
האור הראשון שהוא חכמה גם הוא מסובב הכל
שנאמר   מלא כל הארץ כבודו מאי עבידתיה הכא.
משל למלך שהיה לו ז' בנים ושם לכל אחד ואחד
מקומו א״לשבו זה ע״ג זה ואמר התתחתן אני לא אשב
למטה ולא אתרחק ממך א״ל אני מסובב וראה אתכם
כל היום והיינו מבה״כ ולמה הוא ביניהם כדי
להעמידם ולקיימן

172

ומה הם הבנים כבר אמרתי לכם
שז' צורות קדושה יש להקב״ה וכולם כנגדן באדם
שנאמר כי בצלם אלהים עשה את האדם ואלו הן
שוק ימין ושמאל יד ימין ושמאל והגוף וברית הרי
שש והא אמרת שבע שבעה הוי באשתו דכתיב
והיו לבשר אחד והא מצלעותיו נלקחה דכתיב ויקח
אחת מצלעותיו ואית ליה צלעאין כדאמרת ולצלע
המשכן ומתרגמין ולסטר משכנא ומאי סטר
אית ביה משל   למלך שעלה בלבו ליטע בגנו ט'
אילנות זכרים והיו כולם דקלים אמר כשיהיו כולם
ממין א' לא יתקיימו מה עשה נטע אתרוג
ביניהם והוא אחד מאותו הט' שעלה במחשבתו
להיות זכרים ואתרוג מאי חוה נקבה והיינו דכתיב
פרי עץ הדר   ומתרגמין פרי אילנא אתרוגין
ולולבין

173

מאי הדר היינו הדר הכל והיינו הדר
דש״ה דאמר ביה מי זאת הנשקפה כמו שחר יפה
כלבנה ברה כחמה איומה כנדגלות והיינו ע״ש
נקבה ועל שמה נלקחה נקבה מאדם שאי אפשר
שיתקיים העולם התחתון בלא נקבה ומ״ט
אקרי נקבה על שם דנקבי' רחבים ויש לה נקבים
יתרים על האיש ומאי ניהו שדים ורחם ובית
קיבול

174

ומאי ניהו שיר השירים דאמרת דהוא הדר
אין הדר הכל על כל ספרי הקודש דא״ר יוחנן כל

ומקדשי תיראו מאי ניהו זה מדה עשירית . זה
מדת טובו של· הקב"ה

181

ומ"ט אמר הכתוב את
שבתותי תשמורו ולא אמר שבתי משל למלך
שהיתה לו כלה נאה וכל שבוע ושבוע מזמנה
יום אחד להיות עמו והמלך יש לו בנים נאים
ואהובים אמר להם הואיל וכן הוא שמהו ג"כ
ביום שמחתי כי כן בשבילכם אני משתדל ואתם
ג"כ הדרו אותי

182

ומ"ט זכור את יום השבת ושמור
זכור לו· לזכור ושמור לנו"ן לכלה . ומ"ט ומקדשי
תיראו שמרו עצמיכם מהרהור מ"ט כי מקדשי
קדוש הוא למה כי אני ה'מקדשכם וע"כ כי אני ה'
(רופאך) מכל צד .

183

ומ"ט אמרינן על כל מה
שברא וכו' הי העולמים ולא אמרינן מה שבראתה
אלא אנו מברכין להקב"ה שמשפיע חכמתו כן
להי העולמים זה והוא נותן הכל .

184

ומ"ט אמרינן
אשר קדשנו במצותיו וצונו ולא אמרינן אשר
קדשתנו וצויתנו מלמד שהי העולמים כלולים
בו כל המצות כולן וברהמיו עלינו נתנם לנו כדי
לקדשנו בהם ואולי נזכה . ומ"ט כי בשעה שנזכר
בעוה"ז לעשותם ג"כ נזכה לעוה"ב הגדול ובידו
אוצרות הנשמות ובשעה שישראל טובים אוצרות
הנשמות זוכין לצאת ולבא בעוה"ז ואם אין טובים
לא יצאו. והיינו דארז"ל אין בן דוד בא עד שיכלו
כל הנשמות שבגוף ומאי כל הנשמות שבגוף הוי
אומר כל הנשמות שבגוף האדם ויזכו החדשות
לצאת ואז בן דוד בא זוכה להוליד כי נשמתו יצא
בכלל האחרים . משל למלך שהיה לו חיל ושלח
להם פת לאכול לרוב ונתעצלו ולא אכלו מה
ששלח להם ולא שימרוהו ונתעפשו ונפסד הפת
בא לדרוש ולפקוד אם יש להם מה לאכול ואם
אכלו מה ששלח להם . מצא להם פת מעופש

רמתה מאי רמתה אותה סגולת' שאהרי הזרקא .
ומבמית הגיא אשר בשדי מואב ראש הפסגה
ונשקפה על·פני·הישימון (ומיכאל בגיא) אי·שר·הוא
מזומן ומאי הוא אותו שבשדה מואב אל תקרי
מואב אלא מיאב·אותו·האב·שנאמר·עליו עקב·אשר
שמע אברהם בקולי וישמור משמרתי מצותי
הוקותי וגו' ומאי ניהו אותו השדה. אותו שהוא
בראש הפסגה וגם נשקפה על פני הישימון
ומתרגמינן שמיא ועל אותו הצינור נאמר מעין
גנים באר מים חיים ונוזלים מן לבנון ומאי ניהו
לבנון הוי אומר זה חכמה · ומאי ערבי נהל הוי
אומר אותו שנתן נחלה לישראל והיינו שני אופני
המרכבה :

179

תנא י' גלגלים וי' מאמרות הן
וכל גלגל וגלגל יש לו מאמר לא שהוא סיבבו
אלא שהוא מסבבו · העוה"ז כחרדלא בעיגולתא
מ"ט משום רוחא דמנשבא והאי מהני ואלמלא
כליא רוחא הדא שעתא או רגעא איתחרב עלמא.

180

שלשה גלגלים יש לו לעוה"ז והאיך העולם ניטה
לצפון ולדרום . היא צפונית מערבית הוא גלגל
ראשון הסובב עלינו(ס"א עליו). צפונית מערבית ס"ד
אלא כהו צפונית מערבית דהיינו שוקא דשמאל
ועליו גלגל שני והוא מערבית מערבית ס"ד אלא
אימא כהו הוי מערב . אלו הן נצחונו של עולם
ועליו גלגל שלישי וכהו מערבית דרומית ומאי
ניהו (כהו קמאה) דקא אמרת שני הוי אומר
שוקא של ימין והא כהו דמערבית דרומית הוא
יסודו של עולם שנאמר בו וצדיק יסוד עולם
וכח שני עומד מאהורי המרכבה וכהו הראשון
עומד מלפניו וצדיק יסוד עולם באמצע הוא יוצא
מרומו פי' א"ת מרומו אלא מדרומו של עולם
והוא שר על אלה השנים גם בידו נפש כל חי
כי הוא חי עולמים וכל לשון בריאה בדידיה
עבידא ועליו נאמר שבת וינפש והוא מדת יום
השבת . ועליו נאמר זכור את יום השבת לקדשו
והא ג"כ כתיב שמור ההוא במדה שביעית
עשירית ובשביעית נאמר את שבתותי מדת
שביעית . הוי אומר תשמרו זו מדת שביעית

ומצאם מתביישים לבקש פת אחרת כלומר לא
שמרנו ואחר נבקש גם המלך כעם ולקח אותו
פת המעופש וצוה עליו ליובשו ולתקנו כפי
היכולת . ונשבע לאלה האנשים פת אחרת לא
אתן להם עד שיאכלו כל הפת המעופש הזה .
שלחו להם מהדש מה עשו אמרו לחלוק אותו
חלקוהו ונטל כל אחד הלקן מהם הזריו שם חלקן
באויר לשמרו ואכלו טוב . והאחר נטל ואכל
בתאוה והשאר הניהו ולא שמרו כי נתייאש
ממנו והפסיד יותר ונתעפש ולא יכלו כלל לאכלו
ונשאר רעב עד שמת . נפקד עליו עון גופו
במותו למה הרגת עצמך לא די שהפת קלקלתם
לכם מתחילה והחזרתי אותו לכם מתוקן וקלקלתם
אותו ואתה קלקלת הלקך ונתרשלת מלשמרו .
ולא עוד אלא שהרגת עצמך והוא משיב אדוני
מה היה לי לעשות ועניו אותו היה לך לשומרו
וא"ת לא היה יכולת לך היה לך להשגיח בחביריך
ושכניך שהלקן עמך הפת ותראה מעשיהם
ושמירתם ותשתדל לשמור (לראות) כמותם ועוד
דורשין אותו למה הרגת את עצמך. לא די שקלקלת
את הפת אלא עוד הוספת והרגת חומר גופר
וקצרת ימיך וגרמת ואפשר שהיו בנים טובים
יוצאים ממך והיו מצילין אותך וקלקולך ואחרים
וקלקולם לבן מכל צד ירבו עליך יסורין . נבהל
להשיב והשיב מה הייתי יכול לעשות מאחר
שלא היה לי פת . וממה הייתי יכול להחיות .
אמר ואם היה היית עמל ויגע בתורה לא היית משיב
כסילות ועוות כזאת שמתוך תשובת דבריך ניכר
שלא היית יגיע בתורה כי לא על הלחם לבדו
יהיה האדם כי על כל מוצא פי ה' יחיה האדם
(ומה) היה לך לדרוש ולשאול מה הדבר אשר
יהיה האדם בו ומאי ניהו מוצא פי ה' .
הוי אומר יהיה בתורה דהיינו מוצא פי ה' .
מכאן אמרו ולא עם הארין הסיד אם עליו אינו
גומל הסד איך אפשר להקרא הסיד . ואע"פ
שמתחסד עם הבריות והוא עם הארין לא הסיד
יהיה נקרא

ובמה יתחסד עם קונו (אם אינו גומל
הסד איך אפשר לחקרא הסיד עם קונו) אם לא
בתלמוד תורה . שכל הלומד תורה גומל הסד
לקונו דכתיב רוכב שמים בעזרך . בשאתם

לומדים תורה לשמי אני אתם עוזרים לי ואני
רוכב שמים . ואז ובגאותו שחקים ומאי שחקים
הוי אומר בחדרי חדרים כדמתרגמין מטרי בשמי
שמיא הלכך לא על הלחם לבדו יהיה האדם
וגו' הלכך כתיב ועשיר יענה עזות . שאם
למדת תורה לא תענה כאשר ענית הלכך נינש
ומה ענשו כבר פירשתי .

מאי דכתיב והחכם

יענה דעת רוח מאי דעת רוח אלא שדעתו קרוב
לרוח דכתיב ונחה עליו רוח ה' רוח חכמה ואח"כ
בינה ובבינה עצה וגבורה ודעת ויראת ה'
והאמרת לן עצה וגבורה ודעת ויראת ה'
פי' והאמרת לן עצה זו ג"ח גבורה זו מדת הדין
דעת זו האמת וכן הדעת שבו בוהן האדם את
האמת יראת ה' היא אוצרו של תורה והיינודאמרי
אינשי אלא שוו למעלה מזו דאר"ע כל מה
שברא הקב"ה בעולמו לא בראו אלא לכבודו
שנאמר כל הנקרא בשמי ולכבודי בראתיו יצרתיו
אף עשיתיו וכתיב ה' ימלוך לעולם ועד כמותם
כתיב יראת ה' היא אוצרו לפיכך צריך האדם
להיות ירא שמים ואח"כ ילמוד תורה . משל לאדם
שהלך לקנות דבש של תמרים ולא הוליך עמו
כלים להביאם אמר אביאם בהיקן כבד משאאם עליו
נתפזר הדבש פן יקרעו בגדיו ויתבלבלו וירקבבארןכדרך
נענש שתים א' משום הפסד אוכלים וא' משום
איבוד ממונו .

יראת ה' היא למעלה בכפו של

הקב"ה גם היא עוו ואותו הכף נקראו כף זכות
משום דמטה עולם לכף זכות והיינו דכתיב והייתי
ביראת ה' לא למראה עיניו ישפוט ולא למשמע
אזניו יוכיח אלא מטה כלפי הסד ומטה כל העוליו
לכף זכות ומשם עצה יוצאת ומשם בריאת
יוצאות לעולם וטעם רועה אבן ישראל והוא
המקום שנקרא שם שנאמר ושם הביון עוזו

דכיון שבאה טלתא זו חדדה מאי (חיבור' אימא לך
קנאיינים י' כיון) מילתא הדודא (מאי הידודא)
אימא לך מאי ניהו קרניים מידו לו ומאי ניהו
דקאמר קרנים ואח"כ מידו ידיו טיבעיא ליה ללא

קשיא דהיינו דכתיב ויחר אף משה וישלך
מידיו וגו' . טידו כתיב והיינו דכתיב ויהי ידיו
אמונה עד בא השמש ולא אמונות ר' אנו
מקשינן לך לתריץ ואתה מכסה עינינו למדתנו
רבינו משיבין על ראשון ראשון ועל אחרון אחרון
ומה פי' קרנים מידו לו העבודה כבר פרשתי לכם
עתה בתוך דברים שאמרתי אכסיפו כיון דחזנהו
דאכסיפו התחיל ואמר להם והלא המים הוו ומהם
יצא האש אמרו דברי הכל א"כ המים כוללים
האש ומאי נינהו (ה') קרנים אמר להם ה' קרנים
כנגד ה' חומשי תורה וכנגד ה' אצבעות שביד
ימינו של אדם

189

ור' את הוא דאמרת ליה משמיה
דר' יוחנן דאינו אלא שתי זרועות עולם א"ל ברם
הכא קרנים משמש לשתי קרנים . דשלמטה
הימנו ומאי ניהו אמר להם (למטה) בכעם
ולמעלה מאי אמר להו יראת ה'.

190

ומאי ניהו
יראת ה' . האור הראשון דאמר ר' מ"ד ויאמר
אלהים וגו' ויהי אור ולא אמר ויהי כן אלא
מלמד שהאור ההוא היה גדול מאד ואין כל
בריה יכולה להסתכל בו גנזו הקב"ה לצדיקים
לעתיד לבא והיא מדת כל סחורה שבעולם והיא
כח אבן יקרה שקורין סוחרת ודר (נ"א ודר
וסוחרת) על מה היא מדת דר מלמד שנטל
הקב"ה מזיווה א' מאלפים ובנה ממנה אבן יקרה
נאה ומקושטת וכלל בה כל המצות ובא אברהם
ובקש כח לתת לו ונתנו לו אבן יקרה זו ולא רצה
אותה זכה ולקח מדת החסד דכתיב חסד לאברהם
ובא יצחק ובקש כח ונתנו לו ולא רצה בה זכה
ולקח את מדת הגבורה דהיינו פחד דכתיב וישבע
יעקב בפחד אביו יצחק . בא יעקב ורצה בה ולא
נתנו לו אמר לו הואיל ואברהם למעלה ויצחק
תחתיו אתה תהיה באמצע וטול [נ"א ותכלול]
שלשתן ומאי ניהו אמצע היינו שלום והכתיב
תתן אמת ליעקב היינו שלום והכתיב
[דברי שלום ואמת] שלום ואמת יהיה בימי והיינו
דכתיב והאכלתיך נהלת יעקב אביך דהיינו נחלה
גמורה דלית ליה הסור החס"ד והפח"ד והאמ"ת

והשלו"ם ולפיכך אמר אבן מאסו הבונים היתה
לראש פנה (פירוש) אבן שמאסו אברהם יצחק
ויעקב שבנו העולם היתה לראש פנה .

191

ולמה
מאסו בה והלא נאמר עקב אשר שמע אברהם
בקולי וישמור משמרתי מאי משמרתי כך אמרה
מדת החסד כל ימי היות אברהם בעולם לא
הוצרכתי לעשות מלאכתי שהרי אברהם עמד
שם במקומי וישמור משמרתי כי אני זאת
מלאכתי שאני מזכה העולם ואפילו נתחייבו אני
מזכם . ועוד משיבם ומביא בלבם לעשות רצון
אביהם שבשמים וכל זה עשה אברהם דכתיב
ויטע אשל בבאר שבע [ויקרא שם בשם ה' גו']
סדר להמו ומימיו לכל באי עולם והיה מזכה
ומדבר על לבם למי אתם עובדים עבדו את ה'
אלהי השמים ואלהי הארץ והיה דורש להם עד
שהיו שבים ומנלן שאף החייבים היה מזכה שנא'
המכסה אני מאברהם וגו' ואברהם היו יהיה וגו'
אלא אזכהו שידעתי שיבקש (נ"א שידע ויבקש)
עליהם רחמים ויזכה וכי אפשר לומר שלא ידע
הקב"ה שלא יוכלו להנצל אלא לזכותו קאמר
מכאן אמרו הבא לטהר מסייעין לו . הבא
לטמא פותחין לו (נ"א פתחים לו . מאי פתחים
לו אותן הפתוחים לו) אותן הפתוחים תמיד

192

מצותי חקותי ותורותי אמר הואיל ולא הפצתי
בה אשמור מצותי ומאי תורתי אלא אפילו
הוראות ופלפולים שמורים למעלה הוא ידעם
וקיימם .

193

ומאי משם רועה אבן ישראל שמשם
נזון אבן ישראל ומאי משם הוי אומר צדק עליון
ומאי הוא היינו שכר (נ"א האור) הגדול הצפון
והיינו סוחר' והאבן הדרה למטה נקרא דר ומאי
ניהו קרנים שנאמר קרנים מידו לו היינו ה'
אצבעות [של יד ימין] :

194

אמר רבי רחומאי כך קבלתי כשבקש משה
רבינו עליו השלום לידע ידיעת השם
הנכבד ית' ואמר הראני נא את כבודך בקש
לדעת מפני מה צדיק ורע לו ורשע וטוב לו ולא
הודיעו . ולא הודיעו סלקא דעתך אלא לא הודיעו
מה שבקש . וכי תעלה על דעתך שמשה לא היה
יודע סוד זה אלא בן אמר משה · דרכי הכוחות
אני יודע אבל איני יודע היאך ואיך המחשבה
מתפשטות בה יודע אני שבמחשבה האמת אך
לא ידעתי חלקיו ובכש לדעת ולא הודיעוהו .

195

מפני מה רשע וטוב לו וצדיק ורע לו מפני
שצדיק כבר היה רע לשעבר ועתה נענש . ואם
תאמר וכי מענישין על ידי נערות והאמר רבי
שמעון שאין מענישין בבית דין של מעלה אלא
מבן עשרים שנה ולמעלה · אמר ליה אטו (לא)
בחיי אמרינא אנא דאמרינא שכבר היה לשעבר .
אמרו לו חבריו עד מתי תסתום דבריך · אמר
להם צאו וראו משל לאדם שנטע כרם לעשות
ענבים ועשה באושים ראה שלא הצליח גדרו
ונטע ונקה הגפנים [ונטען אחר] ראה שלא הצליח
[זה] ועקרו ונטען עד כמה . אמרו לו לאלף דור
דכתיב דבר צוה לאלף דור והיינו דאמרו רבותינו
תתקע"ד דורות חסרי ועמד הקב"ה ונטען ושתלן
בכל דור ודור .

196

אמר רבה אי בעי צדיקים ברו
עלמא מי מבדיל עונותיהם דכתיב כי אם
עונותיכם היו מבדילים ביניכם ובין אלהיכם הא
אם לא היו עונותיכם לא היה הפרש ביניכם ובינו
כו' . דהא רבא ברא גברא שדריה לקמיה דרבי
זירא הוי קאי משתעי בהדיה ולא מהדר אמר
להו אלמלא עונותיכם הוה מהדר וממאי הוה
מהדר מנשמתיה ומי הוי ליה נשמה לאינש
למיעל ביה . אמרו ליה יה אין דכתיב ויפח באפיו
נשמת חיים ולאינש הוי ליה נשמת חיים והיינו
ואלמלא עונותיכם שאין הנשמה טהורה והיינו
הפרש שביניכם לבינו דכתיב ותחסרהו מעט
מאלהים מאי מעט דאית ביה (אינו מדבר בכאן

אלא על המדות לבד) . עונות והקב"ה לית ליה
עונות וברוך הוא וברוך שמו לעד ולנצח עונות
הוא דלית ביה האיצ"ה'ר אית ביה בתמיה מיניה
אתיא אתיא סלקא דעתך אלא אימא הוה קאתי
מיניה דהוא בראו עד דאתא דוד והרגו .
הדא הוא דכתיב ולבי חלל בקרבי כך אמר דוד
הואיל (ולא) ויכלתי לו לא יגורך רע ובמה יכול
לו דוד בגרסתו שלא היה שותק לילה ויום והיה
מהזר להקדוש ברוך הוא תורה של מעלה כי כל
שעה שאדם לומד תורה לשמה תורה התורה של
מעלה מתחברת להקדוש ברוך הוא והיינו
דאמרינן לעולם ילמד אדם תורה ואפילו שלא
לשמה שמתוך שלא לשמה בא לשמה ומאי
ניהו תורה דאמרת . היינו כלה שמקושטת
ומעוטרת ומוכללת בכל המצות והיא אוצר
התורה והיא ארוסתו של הקדוש ברוך הוא
דכתיב תורה צוה לנו משה מורשה א"ת מורשה
אלא מאורסה הא כיצד כשישראל עוסקים
בתורה לשמה היא ארוסתו של הקדוש ברוך הוא
והיא מורשה לישראל :

197

ישב רבי רחומאי ודרש מה זכתה תמר
שיצאו ממנה פרץ וזרח מפני שהיה
שמה תמר (והיא) [והיא] תמר אחות אמנין היא
דעבידא לכך . ואמאי אקרי פרץ על שם הלבנה
שהלבנה נפרצת לעתים וזרח אקרי ע"ש ההמה
שהחמה זורחת תמיד כענין וזרח השמש והא
פרץ הוא החבור וחמה גדולה מן הלבנה ל"ק דהא
כתיב ויתן יד וכתיב ואחר יצא אחיו אשר על
ידו השני ויקרא שמו זרח דהוא היה לו להיות
החבור ומפני שידע הקדוש ברוך הוא שעתיד
לצאת ממנו דוד ושלמה שעתיד לומר שיר
השירים החזירו

198

ומ"ט אקרית תמר ולא שאר
שמות מפני שהיא נקבה נקבה סלקא דעתך
אלא אימא מפני שכוללת זכר ונקבה דכל אילני
תמרים כוללים זכר ונקבה והיאך שהלולב הוי
זכר והפרי מבחוץ הוי זכר ומבפנים הוי נקבה
והיאך בגרעיני התמר שהיא סדוקה כעין אשה
כנגדה כה הלבנה למעלה והקדוש ברוך הוא

ברא אותם זכר ונקבה שנאמר זכר ונקבה ברא
אותם אפשר לומר כך והא כתיב ויברא אלהים
את האדם בצלמו ואהר כך אעשה לו עזר כנגדו
ויקה אהת מצלעותיו ויסגור בשר תחתנה אלא
אימא כתיב בהו יצירה וכתיב בהו עשיה וכתיב
בהו בריאה בעת עשיית הנשמות עשיי' זכר
ונקבה היה ושם אותה יצירה בעת שהרכיב
הנשמה על הגוף לכל אחד ואחד נאסף הכל.
ומנלן דהאי יצירה לישנא דאסיפה הוא דכתיב
וייצר ה' אלהים מן האדמה כל חית השדה ואת
כל עוף השמים ויבא אל האדם לראות מה
יקרא לו וגו' והיינו דכתיב זכר ונקבה בראם
וכתיב ויברך אותם אלהים

199

נשמת הנקבות מן
הגו"ן הם הנוטה ליצד צפון ונשמת הזכרים מן
הזי"ן והיינו (דכתיב) דקאזיל הנחש בתרה דהוה
אמר והואיל ונשמתה מן הצפון אסיתנה מהרה
ומאי הסתה היה משום דבא עליה:

200

שאלו תלמידיו אימא לן גופא דעובדא
היכי הוה אמר להם הלך סמאל
הרשע וקשר עם כל צבא מעלה על רבו משום
שאמר הקב"ה גרדו בדגת הים המלאכים ובעוף
השמים אמר האיך נוכל להחטיאו ולגרשהו

מלפניו קיבין כל הילותיו וביקש לו בארץ חבר
כמותו ומצא הנחש היה לו דמות וקומה וזקופה
[ס"א דמות גמל] ורכב עליו והלך לו אל האשה.
אמר לה. אף כי אמר אלהים לא תאכלו מכל עין
הגן. אמר אבקש יותר ואוסיף כדי לגרשם (כך
אמרה הנחש) [שתגרע היא] אמרה לא מנענו
אלא מפרי עין אשר בתוך הגן אמר אלהים לא
תאכלו ממנו ולא תגעו בו פן תמותון והוסיפה
שתי דברים אמרה ומפרי העין אשר בתוך הגן
ולא נאמר אלא ומעין הדעת. ואמרה לא תגעו
בו פן תמיתון. מה עשה סמאל הרשע הלך ונגע
ודהף האשה עליו ונגעה בעין הדעת ולא מתה.
אמר כמו שלא בא מיתה לך על הנגיעה כך לא
יבא לך על האכילה מיד לקחה ואכלה ונתנה גם
לבעלה ונענשו מיתה בשביל שדברי הרב ודברי
התלמיד דברי מי שומעין וגם הנחש נענש על גהונך
תלך ומיעפר תאכל כל ימי חייך. והוא ישופך
ראש ואתה תשופנו עקב. וסמאל נענש שנעשה
שר מעשו הרשע לעתיד כשיעקוד הקב"ה מלכות
אדום במהרה בימינו. ישפילהו תחלה שנאמר
יפקוד ה' על צבא מרום במרום. והאמירה
והמיתה והעונש כל זה על שהוסיפה על ציווי
של הקב"ה ועל זה נאמר כל המוסיף גורע'
והשם יאיר עינינו במאור תורתו. וישים בלבנו
יראתו. ויזכנו לקראתו. אשר הלבבות יאיר.
ולב בינה יאיר. והעינים זוהר יזהיר:

סליק ספר הבהיר

INDEX

Bible Quotes